LANGUAGE AND CULTURAL PRACTICES IN COMMUNITIES AND SCHOOLS

Drawing on sociocultural theories of learning, this book examines how the everyday language practices and cultural funds of knowledge of youth from non-dominant or minoritized groups can be used as centerpoints for classroom learning in ways that help all students both to sustain and expand their cultural and linguistic repertoires while developing skills that are valued in formal schooling.

Bringing together a group of ethnographically grounded scholars working in diverse local contexts, this volume identifies how these language practices and cultural funds of knowledge can be used as generative points of continuity and productively expanded on in schools for successful and inclusive learning. Ideal for students and researchers in teaching, learning, language education, literacy, and multicultural education, as well as teachers at all stages of their career, this book contributes to research on culturally and linguistically sustaining practices by offering original teaching methods and a range of ways of connecting cultural competencies to learning across subject matters and disciplines.

Inmaculada M. García-Sánchez is Associate Professor of Anthropology at Temple University, USA.

Marjorie Faulstich Orellana is Professor of Urban Schooling in the Graduate School of Education and Information Studies at University of California, Los Angeles, USA.

LANGUAGE AND CULTURAL PRACTICES IN COMMUNITIES AND SCHOOLS

Bridging Learning for Students from Non-Dominant Groups

Edited by Inmaculada M. García-Sánchez and Marjorie Faulstich Orellana

Routledge
Taylor & Francis Group

NEW YORK AND LONDON

First published 2019
by Routledge
52 Vanderbilt Avenue, New York, NY 10017

and by Routledge
2 Park Square, Milton Park, Abingdon, Oxon, OX14 4RN

Routledge is an imprint of the Taylor & Francis Group, an informa business

© 2019 Taylor & Francis

Library of Congress Cataloging-in-Publication Data
Names: García-Sánchez, Inmaculada Ma. (Inmaculada María), editor. | Orellana, Marjorie Faulstich, editor.
Title: Language and cultural practices in communities and schools : bridging learning for students from non-dominant groups / edited by Inmaculada M. García-Sánchez and Marjorie Faulstich Orellana.
Description: New York, NY : Routledge, 2019. | Includes bibliographical references.
Identifiers: LCCN 2019009935 (print) | LCCN 2019980332 (ebook) | ISBN 9781138597877 (hbk) | ISBN 9781138597884 (pbk) | ISBN 9780429486708 (ebk)
Subjects: LCSH: Linguistic minorities–Education. | Minorities–Education. | Education, Bilingual | Culturally relevant pedagogy. Classification: LCC LC3715 .L355 2019 (print) | LCC LC3715 (ebook) | DDC 371.829–dc23
LC record available at https://lccn.loc.gov/2019009935
LC ebook record available at https://lccn.loc.gov/2019980332

ISBN: 978-1-138-59787-7 (hbk)
ISBN: 978-1-138-59788-4 (pbk)
ISBN: 978-0-429-48670-8 (ebk)

Typeset in Bembo
by Integra Software Services Pvt. Ltd.

To all the young people in our lives: the children and youth we have worked with in our research studies over the years, our students (past, present, and future), and our own children (Elisa Noemí, Andrés Gabriel, and Jack Douglas) ...

... Who taught us to honor the amazing learning that happens every day beyond the walls of the classroom.

CONTENTS

ILLUSTRATIONS

Figures

Tables

ACKNOWLEDGEMENTS

It has been quite the intellectual journey, since the afternoon in the early summer of 2016, when sitting at Marjorie's kitchen table, we began envisioning this book. We were joined in this journey by the 22 fine scholars, who, very generously, put their time and scholarship at the service of this project and who worked with us through multiple drafts as we crafted and refined the vision and message. So our first thanks go to the chapter contributors. We could not have done any of this without you and we are honored to have your work represented in this edited collection.

Our next thanks go to our families for the big and small ways in which they have helped and endured us throughout this process. Inma's son, Jack, was a baby when this book was begun, and we had many sweet moments of working on it while Jack played with cars and trains on the floor beside us, in Los Angeles or Philadelphia. (To Marjorie, at least, these were sweet moments, but the hard work of juggling career and motherhood fell to Inma at this stage of her life.) Special thanks to Marjorie's daughter, Elisa Noemí, whose creative art work adorns our cover. Her enthusiasm for the project from the moment we approached her meant a lot to us.

When we talk about our families, we cannot forget our kinship ties and debts of gratitude that go to our intellectual ancestors. In particular, we thank Dr. Carol D. Lee, who was extremely supportive of this project from the very beginning and graciously agreed to write an afterword; Carol also served as discussant in a presentation of early versions of this work, helpfully challenging our thinking. Most importantly, her own research was a major inspiration for this volume, as it provided an early and robust model for how to think substantively and critically about the analogies between everyday practices and schools.

Our gratitude also goes to the Spencer Foundation and National Academy of Education (NAEd). This project would not have been possible without their financial support *and* without the vigorous intellectual community that they foster and bring together every year in Washington, DC, for their Fellows Program retreats. Specifically, the research featured in Inma's chapter was carried out with the support of a Spencer/NAEd Postdoctoral Fellowship, and the work reported in Marjorie's chapter began with that same fellowship some 20 years ago. The very idea for this volume was hatched during a Fellows Program retreat, during the course of several conversations among Dr. Carol D. Lee (Inma's faculty mentor during her year as a post-doctoral fellow), Marjorie (who was there as someone else's faculty mentor, and who has been Inma's long-time mentor), and Inma.

We also want to thank the dozens of colleagues who attended the various panels we have organized around this work over the last two years, namely at the 2017 American Education Research Association (AERA), the 2018 American Anthropological Association (AAA), and the 2018 Literacy Research Association (LRA). We greatly benefitted from your serious engagement with these symposia. Thank you for pushing our thinking with your insightful questions and comments, and thank you for sharing your experiences in this area as researchers, practitioners, and/or teacher trainers. We would like to mention, in particular, Betsy Rymes who was our discussant at the 2018 AAA. Thank you for writing comments that were simultaneously gracious and supportive, as well as thought provoking. Many thanks also to Stanton Wortham and Gabrielle Oliveira for their invitation to present and discuss some of these ideas with the faculty and students of the Boston College School of Education in Spring 2018.

Last, but not least, we want to thank Karen Adler, our Routledge editor, her editorial assistant, Will Bateman, and the two anonymous reviewers who provided very helpful feedback on the prospectus of the volume and several sample chapters. Our thanks also go to Janelle Franco, Amanda Quezada, Krissia Martinez, and Sophia Ángeles who, in the final stretch of submission, helped us with the formatting of the manuscript.

AUTHOR BIOGRAPHIES

Maricela Correa-Chávez is an Associate Professor of Developmental Psychology at California State University Long Beach. Her research examines children's learning as cultural practice that develops through participation in activity with others. She has worked in Mexico, Guatemala, and in California with both immigrant and nonimmigrant families.

Leah Durán is an Assistant Professor at the University of Arizona. She is a former teacher who worked in bilingual and ESL classrooms in Texas. Her research focuses on bilingualism and biliteracy in young children, and the design of literacy pedagogies for culturally and linguistically complex classrooms.

Jacqueline D'warte is a Senior Lecturer in English language and literacy curriculum and pedagogy in the School of Education, Western Sydney University, and a Senior Researcher in the Centre for Educational Research. Jacqueline's research explores connections between equity, language, identity, and learning in culturally and linguistically diverse educational settings.

Lucila D. Ek is a Professor in Bicultural-Bilingual Studies at the University of Texas, San Antonio. She received her PhD from UCLA. Her research focuses on the bilingualism, biliteracy, and identities of Latinxes. Her research has been published in *Anthropology & Education Quarterly*, *International Multilingual Research Journal*, and *Bilingual Research Journal*.

Patricia Enciso is a Professor of Literature and Literacy at Ohio State University. Her research focuses on middle-school youth and the ways they produce and interpret their own and others' storyworlds. She is coauthor of *Reframing*

Sociocultural Theory in Literacy Research (2007), coeditor of *The Handbook of Research on Children's and Young Adult Literature* (2010), and coeditor of the *Handbook of Research on Reading: Volume V* (forthcoming).

Sarah Gallo is an Associate Professor of Bilingual and Immigrant Education at the Ohio State University. Sarah teaches courses in bilingualism, biliteracy, and immigrant education. She seeks to understand the intersections of immigration and education policies for children from mixed-status Mexican heritage families residing in Mexico and the United States.

Inmaculada M. García-Sánchez is Associate Professor of Anthropology at Temple University. Her research focuses on language and the immigrant experience of children and youth. She is a past postdoctoral fellow of the National Academy of Education, and author of *Language and Muslim Immigrant Childhoods: The Politics of Belonging* (2014).

Michiko Hikida's scholarship focuses on making classrooms more humane for elementary students and particularly for students of color, bi/multilingual students, and students identified as learning disabled or "struggling" readers. She examines classroom language and literacy practices of and around students located at the intersection of race, language, and ability.

Holly Link is Director of Educational Programming and Research at a non-profit dedicated to the empowerment of the Latinx community through education and the arts. There she is co-developing a participatory research center with young people and adults through which they can promote social transformation and inform public policy.

Angélica López Fraire received her PhD in developmental psychology from UC Santa Cruz. She is currently an Assistant Professor of Psychology at Marymount California University where she teaches courses in human development, intercultural psychology, research methods, and capstone. Her research focuses on children's prosocial development from a sociocultural perspective.

Tia C. Madkins is an Assistant Professor in the STEM Education Program and the Department of Curriculum and Instruction in the College of Education at the University of Texas at Austin. Her work focuses on issues of equity in TK-12 STEM + computing teaching and learning, teacher education, and elementary science education.

Ananda Marin is an Assistant Professor of Qualitative Research Methods in Education and affiliated faculty in American Indian Studies at the University of California-Los Angeles. She explores sociocultural dimensions of development across contexts. The significance of place, the body, and mobility in research and learning are foci of her work.

Danny C. Martinez is Associate Professor of Adolescent Literacy at the University of California, Davis. His research explores the cultural and communicative practices of Black and Latinx youth in secondary literacy classrooms. He was formerly an English language arts teacher in San Francisco and Los Angeles.

Ramón Antonio Martínez is an Assistant Professor in the Graduate School of Education at Stanford University. His research explores the intersections of language, race, and ideology in the public schooling experiences of racialized students, with a particular focus on literacy learning among bi/multilingual Chicana/o/x and Latina/o/x children and youth.

Elizabeth Montaño is a faculty member at the University of California, Davis' School of Education. Her research has explored charter school teacher unions, and secondary literacy learning for linguistically diverse youth in secondary settings. She was formerly a teacher in Oakland and Los Angeles.

P. Zitlali Morales, PhD, is Associate Professor of Curriculum & Instruction at the University of Illinois at Chicago. Her research focuses on the linguistic practices of Latinx bilinguals, the language ideologies of multilingual immigrant communities, and bilingual education. She is a teacher educator preparing pre-service and inservice teachers to work with emergent bilingual students.

Na'ilah Suad Nasir is the sixth president of the Spencer Foundation, which supports research about education. She is also a Professor (on leave) at the University of California, Berkeley, where she has taught since 2008. Her work focuses on issues of race, culture, learning, and identity.

Marjorie Faulstich Orellana is Professor of Urban Schooling in the Graduate School of Education and Information Studies at UCLA. Her work focuses on language, literacy and learning in new immigrant communities, and on ways of linking home and school experiences in creative, dynamic, and heart-centered ways.

Mariana Pacheco's research focuses on meaningful opportunities for bi/multilingual and English learner students to employ their cultural, linguistic, and intellectual resources for learning and self-determination, particularly given their politically and ideologically charged schooling experiences. She employs ethnographic and linguistic anthropological methods to examine language, teaching, learning, and curriculum processes.

Jennifer F. Reynolds is Professor of Anthropology and the graduate program in Linguistics in the College of Arts and Sciences at the University of South Carolina. She studies both the constraining and enabling dimensions of language and discourse practices in the dialectics of family and community life and identity formation.

Javier Rojo is a doctoral student at the University of California, Davis' School of Education in School Organization and Educational Policy. His research explores how parents of English language learners participate and advocate for their children within California schooling contexts. He is a former elementary school teacher.

Enid Rosario-Ramos is an Assistant Professor of Educational Studies at the University of Michigan. She conducts qualitative research in the areas of Latinx education, critical pedagogy, and youth civic engagement. Her work includes ethnographic and community-based participatory research with use of methodologies including participant observation, interview research, and survey research.

Jenny L. Sawada is a doctoral candidate in the Literacy, Language, and Culture program at the University of Michigan. Her work is deeply rooted in her history and family: Amparo, her mother from Guadalajara, Mexico; Toshiaki, her father from Asahikawa, Japan; and her brother, Edgar, who shares her first-gen experience.

Jessica Somerville is a PhD candidate in the Department of Teaching & Learning at The Ohio State University. Jessica has taught courses in bilingualism and biliteracy, language arts methods, and English as an additional language. Her research focuses on asset-based pedagogies and translanguaging in bilingual middle childhood classrooms.

INTRODUCTION

Everyday Learning: Centering in Schools the Language and Cultural Practices of Young People from Non-Dominant Groups

Inmaculada M. García-Sánchez and Marjorie Faulstich Orellana

Playing dominoes, walking in urban forests, fighting for environmental justice in their neighborhoods, reading the Bible, helping with household chores, translating for their parents, telling stories, communicating with family members across national borders via skype, advocating for immigrant rights, playing hopscotch ... these are just a few of the many cultural and linguistic practices that the young people featured in this volume—all members of non-dominant or minoritized cultural groups—participate in with their families and friends when they are not in school. These practices both demand and develop complex social, cultural, cognitive, and linguistic competencies. While the abilities that students from non-dominant groups develop from such everyday experiences are often unrecognized or thought unimportant, many of those competencies map onto the skills schools want students to learn. What's more, young people's everyday proficiencies often *transcend*—in socially relevant and expansive ways—the narrow framing of these skills that they generally encounter in schools. In this volume, we set out to display the skills young people gain from their lived experiences outside of school.

We center and honor the knowledge and experience of youth from non-dominant groups, while also using them as centerpoints for the standards schools seek to cultivate.

The chapters in this volume do this first by showcasing a variety of language practices and cultural funds of knowledge (González, Moll, & Amanti, 2005; Moll, 1992) that youth engage in in their lives outside of school, and carefully analyzing the skills and competencies that these require. Each author then suggests specific ways in which those experiences could be used as linchpins for classroom learning. The aim is to help all students, particularly students from non-dominant groups, both to *sustain* and *expand* their cultural and linguistic repertoires, as they learn to connect their own repertoires to a variety of academic skills, as well as to their peers' everyday lived experiences—while also helping schools achieve truly pluralist and democratic educational outcomes. We identify points of leverage for the acquisition of skills that are valued in formal schooling, and further, suggest ways of "leveling" (Zisselsberger, 2016), or raising the status of, the learning that happens in community contexts by recognizing and valuing everyday practices just as much as school practices. Importantly, the chapters suggest ways of using out-of-school practices to support school practices, but also vice versa: as something useful and desirable for young people's developing ability to navigate their own worlds.

Bringing together a diverse group of ethnographically grounded scholars who work with a broad range of populations that are usually considered *non-dominant* within their local, national and/or global contexts (indigenous, immigrants, and ethnic/racial/linguistic minority communities), across diverse geographical and cultural contexts in United States as well as in Spain and Australia, the authors provide prototypes for how particular cultural practices and local funds of knowledge can be used as generative points of continuity and productively expanded on in schools. We further consider how schools could support the kind of learning that happens in homes and communities, rather than just vice versa, as is usually the case. We ground our work in rich descriptions of how youth from non-dominant backgrounds learn and deploy linguistic repertoires, discursive practices, relational norms and modes of reasoning in communities, households, and peer groups, and then identify analogues and points of continuity in the learning experiences that youth engage in as they move across the contexts of their lives, and that may serve them in many ways in an increasingly intercultural world.

Crucially, the chapters detail *how the skills that youth from non-dominant groups already possess can be used as strengths* that can be critically expanded through sharing in the classroom, and used to connect with a variety of academic skills, rather than treating everyday experiences as obstacles to be overcome, deficits to be remedied, or mere token stepping stones to academic skills. The volume as a whole shows a variety of ways to approach the design of learning environments, and to center peer and community ways of knowing, doing, and speaking. Each chapter provides substantive examples of interventions that go beyond superficial and folkloristic celebrations of cultural and linguistic difference. Collectively, the chapters document a considerable range of youth practices that involve linguistic, literate, cognitive, discursive, physical, social, and artistic skills; ones that take place in a variety of contexts: homes, churches, neighborhood parks, after-school programs, story clubs, community organizations, and other informal learning spaces.

While the book compiles a diverse set of practices, we recognize that the volume does not nearly do justice to the huge array of practices that young people participate in every day. Significantly absent here are online social media, video, gaming, and musical practices that are ubiquitous in global youth culture. That would be material for a second volume, or perhaps an entire encyclopaedia (*The Encyclopaedia of Youth Cultural Knowledge and Skills?*). We can also imagine many other common practices that are not fully represented here: sports of many kinds, transnational family trips to places of origin, the growing variety of digital face-to-face communication and messaging technologies, popular young people's activities as these cycle in and out of fashion (pogs, jacks, marbles, Pokemon cards, and more) as well as more specific canonical cultural practices unique to indigenous, minority, and/or immigrant groups. Our aim is not to represent all possible practices. Rather, we want to show a variety: from longstanding practices that have been handed down across generations to emergent forms in new contexts of hybridity and diversity. We use this sampling to illustrate *ways of seeing* the specific competencies they involve as well as how they might be connected to multiple school tasks: discrete aspects of language and literacy, science, math, social studies, and more.

Seeing—and hearing—the cultural and linguistic skills of minoritized youth is particularly important because schools have a history of not recognizing the knowledge and abilities of such young people. Often, they are treated as remedial cases needing to be fixed, precisely because the linguistic and cultural practices we showcase in these chapters are seen not only as a source of unbridgeable cultural *difference*, but also as defective. This volume models *ways of thinking* about how to bridge home and school in generative ways: ways that elevate the significance of minoritized youths' multilingual and multicultural knowledge and experiences, decenter the monolingual and limited cultural ways of learning around which schools have historically organized their practices, help schools transform sociolinguistic inequities, and support teachers in designing learning environments that center multiple ways of knowing, of doing, and of taking from the world.

A Few Words about Terminology

At this point, perhaps some readers are wondering about some of the terminology we have used in this introduction, and that we and the volume contributors will use throughout the book. There are a number of terms that we have purposefully selected for use, even as we recognize that all labels have limitations and that all can be inherently problematic in one way or another. These include all words used to name categories of people, whether based on age, race/ethnicity, gender, national origin, immigration status, or socioeconomic status relevant to other people. We recognize that labels matter, insofar as they can signify ways of thinking about these categories of people: either reinforcing essentialized stereotypes or opening up new understandings. We also recognize that members of these groups—and others who work with them—may have different preferences for the labels they choose. As much as possible, we strive to strike a balance between honoring the names the people who are represented in these chapters would choose for themselves and using labels that reflect contemporary thinking about the most inclusive and culturally appropriate labels, as well as ones that may promote new ways of thinking. But we know it is difficult to get the words just right, especially as preferences, and the logics for choosing them, are sensitive to particular historic and socio-political contexts, and thus change over time and across contexts. Sometimes, using various terms rather than a single one can help us all to hold the meanings of these labels a little more contingent, and more fully see their socially constructed nature.

In this volume, we mostly refer to the young people who are at the heart of our work as just that—*young people*, or *children and youth*. The fact that they are young, relative to teachers and the authors of this book, seems important, because age-based categories are alive and well in school. We try to avoid reducing young people *only* to their institutional label as "students," as this flattens their full identities and limits them to the category they occupy in school, rather than across the diverse contexts of their lives; at the same time, when we talk about their positioning in schools, we recognize that they *are* students, and thus the label marks their positionality in that setting. While young people may refer to themselves as "kids"—see Thorne's 1993 argument for researchers to use that term as well—some older youth may eschew the notion of their being "kids." Further, we hope that K-12 teachers will all find something of use in this book; we do not want to limit the possibilities for application to work with either just "children" or "adolescents."

And why do we speak of "minoritized youth," and "youth from non-dominant communities?" This term places the non-dominance on relations of power vis à vis the larger society, not on the youth themselves. We are trying to dissuade readers from making assumptions of cultural homogeneity based on essentialized notions of culture. We are not trying to prescribe practices that link to specific cultural groups as much as to the experiences of youth whose lives and experiences are so often devalued, dismissed, ignored, or erased in school. The specific practices that particular populations engage in vary, and change over time and across contexts—but all of the practices that we highlight in this book are ones that are engaged in by youth whose families and communities exist outside of the mainstream of any given social context.

For more specific labels for particular populations, we defer to chapter authors' choices. We recognize that these may or may not be labels that participants would choose for themselves, or that some others might choose for them. Some, like the term "Latinx," are part of a larger move to push for gender neutral and inclusive labels. The issues developed in these chapters may or may not be particular to youth who fit the population label that we and the volume contributors utilize in this book. We hope that readers will look for things that can be applied to other, similar populations, however those people might label themselves.

Why This Book Now?

As foreshadowed above, one of the most persistent and recurrent socio-educational discourses in the last half century is that which links the lack of educational and socioeconomic success of youth from non-dominant communities either to their supposed sociolinguistic deficits or to ideologically exaggerated discontinuities between home and school cultural practices, even to the point that this discourse still continues to frame a considerable amount of educational research on these diverse group of young people, both in and outside the US. Indeed, in the years leading up to the conceptualization and production of this volume, we, along with others (Miller & Sperry, 2012) have witnessed in dismay the virulent return of many of the deficit perspectives about the linguistic, cultural, and cognitive assets of young people from economically disadvantaged and minoritized communities—deficit perspectives that sociolinguists, linguistic anthropologists, and educational ethnographers since the 1970s have dispelled with extensive, detailed and compelling evidence (e.g., Alim, 2004; Citrón, 1997; García-Sánchez, 2010; González, 2001; Labov, 1972; Miller, 1982; Orellana, 2009; Paris, 2011; Philips, 1983; Villenas & Deyhle, 1999; Zentella, 1997). Thanks to these studies and other critical sociocultural and ethnographic work that we review below, the field has made important theoretical advances to reframe much research beyond and away from the deficit perspectives that have historically predominated. But many practitioners and policymakers (and some researchers) are still trying to "fix" students from non-dominant backgrounds who are seen as deficient and lacking in some way, linguistically, culturally, and/or cognitively. And schools are the key place where students are sent to be "fixed."

One prominent example of how these pernicious ideologies have kept a strong grip in the imagination of politicians, policymakers, and educators is the powerful resurfacing of the so-called *language gap* discourse. Based on an almost 40-year-old, unreplicated study with a small and unrepresentative sample conducted by Hart and Risley (1995), its adherents posit that young people living in poverty (very often youth of color) have supposedly heard 30 million fewer words by age three than their economically better off (very often white) peers!; an "early catastrophe," to echo the words used by Hart and Risley, that irremediably detracts from their chances of educational success and socioeconomic mobility. While the notion that specific communicative styles—those deployed by poor parents—or the hearing of a particular number of words is somehow responsible for poverty and truncated educational trajectories would seem absurd on the face of it, the language gap discourse has not only profoundly resonated, but has also shown incredible staying power as evidenced by its recirculation in academic, media, teaching, and parenting circles. Moreover, despite the many cogent critiques that have been leveled at the original study and its biased premises (among the most notable of these, see Avineri et al., 2015; Baugh, 2017; Blum, 2017; García & Otheguy, 2017; Miller & Sperry, 2012), this discourse has become the inspiration for a new wave of neuroscience scholars (e.g., Hutton et al., 2015; Noble et al., 2015) whose research reproduces many of the same built-in racial and class biases as the original study. The proponents of this deficit ideology have even coopted the now decades-long body of research documenting and recognizing the differential knowledge and skills that minoritized students bring to classrooms (e.g., Ballenger, 1992; Delpit, 1986; Heath, 1983, 1986; Pease-Alvarez & Vasquez, 1994; Philips, 1983) to "show" how poor children fail to arrive to classrooms "school ready" because of the linguistic practices of their parents and communities. These studies actually made the much more complex and nuanced argument that schools, by privileging quintessentially white, middle-class, monolingual practices, fail youth from non-dominant backgrounds with their hegemonic "one size fits all" institutional and educational practices, which do not allow space for these youth to build on the rich bodies of sociocultural and linguistic knowledge that they already possess and that are more common in their communities.

The language gap discourse is but one example of the many harmful orientations that still abound in the world of educational practice and policy. So, in this politically charged atmosphere, when deficit discourses have come back in full force, often authoritatively dressed in "scientific" modes of representation, we want to take stock of the important progress that ethnographic and socioculturally based theories of pedagogy, learning, and human development have made in moving away from these blaming-the-victim discourses. Our hope is that we can inspire practitioners to embrace more fully these critical theoretical developments, providing models to build diverse and heterogeneous pathways of educational achievement that are based on the positive and central presence of minoritized students' cultural and linguistic repertoires of practice in the classroom. In other words, we believe that there are many committed educators who want to adopt the theoretical developments in culturally responsive teaching that since the early 1990s have become the gold standard in the field for socially just and progressive pedagogy. Yet, there are still relatively few examples of how educators can substantively level, sustain, and expand the cultural and linguistic knowledge that students from non-dominant groups bring to the classroom. One of the main objectives of this volume is to bridge this gap between theory and educational practice by showing a few models and identifying ways of approaching how to make these connections.

So, where are we now in terms of ethnographic and socioculturally based theories of pedagogy and learning? And how did we get here? Undoubtedly, one of the most powerful interventions that has recently taken hold in our field and that seeks not "to fix" minoritized students, but rather to change schooling for positive social transformation is Paris and Alim's (2017) Culturally Sustaining Pedagogy paradigm (henceforth CSP). It is safe to say that many of the chapters in this volume have been explicitly inspired by CSP, which calls for researchers and educators to reimagine schools as sites where the heterogenous linguistic and cultural practices of non-dominant youth are not only positively acknowledged or used as starting points, but critically and continually sustained as part of the learning process. The CSP paradigm transcends previous approaches to culturally sensitive and responsive teaching by urging educators to take young people's knowledge and experience outside of school not just as resources to be used in students' acquisition of academic knowledge, but as worthy targets of learning in their own right. This paradigm further argues that schools, rather than *erasing* that knowledge and those skills, as they have done historically, could be reshaped in ways that deliberately support and *sustain* them. With this important corrective, CSP has also recovered the progressive legacy of earlier culturally responsive teaching from assimilationist cooptions and problematic interpretations that have occurred in the 30 or so years since the publication of the groundbreaking work of Luis Moll, Norma González, and others on *Funds of Knowledge* (henceforth FoK) (González et al., 2005; Moll, 1992; Moll et al., 1992). Indeed, FoK work established a strong precedent for the ethnographic approach that the authors of this volume took to identifying cultural resources in households and neighborhoods and pointing to ways of sustaining them in schools.

Some of the cooptions that many of the authors of this volume have, in CSP fashion, continually returned to or struggled with in their chapters involve the worry that the cultural and linguistic practices of youth from non-dominant backgrounds may be treated as discardable *assets*, only used insofar as they can aid in the acquisition of those skills and practices valued in schools, but without any commitment to the continuing presence of these practices in students' repertoires, particularly in the case of minority language varieties (e.g., D'warte, Chapter 12; García-Sánchez, Chapter 8; Madkins & Nasir, Chapter 3; Martínez, Durán, & Hikida, Chapter 10; Reynolds & Orellana, Chapter 11). There is also the concern that schools may use community practices in ways that are experienced as culturally inappropriate and/or epistemologically harmful, particularly in communities with long histories of cultural and linguistic erasure, disenfranchisement, and even genocide (e.g., Marin, Chapter 2; Rosario-Ramos & Sawada, Chapter 4). While we further unpack these and other tensions below, we believe that it is helpful and important in this section to re-evaluate the potentialities of the FoK approach and other earlier precursors of the CSP paradigm. After all, for the last few decades this knowledge has been one of the primary approaches used, for instance in teacher education programs, to call for greater institutional acknowledgement of home language practices and diverse cultural funds of knowledge that youth in non-dominant communities are exposed to in their everyday lives, as well as for greater alignment between the latter practices and those of educational institutions. Beyond the pitfalls and correctives already mentioned, however, there are several issues to consider in relation to how this research has been used to inform pedagogical practice:

First, and perhaps most crucially for the purposes of the volume: too often these calls to acknowledge and build on minoritized students' cultural and linguistic FoK have consisted of general appeals without substantive examples that demonstrate just how to do this (beyond the excellent examples provided by the original FoK research team, such as those presented in González et al., 1995). Moreover, the cultural practices that are discussed in teacher preparation programs are often based on superficial knowledge about non-dominant communities and on static, unchanging, and essentialized notions of culture that sometimes border on stereotyping and that may have little actual bearing on the contemporary experiences of youth from diverse backgrounds. This trend has continued despite repeated calls by researchers from the FoK approach to anchor discussions about membership in cultural communities in actual ethnographic research that can address the emergent, ever-evolving, and changing nature of cultural practices in communities of practice. This is particularly important in new immigrant and diasporic communities, where contact with other groups and syncretism can sometimes accelerate the rate of intergenerational cultural shift.

Second, these superficial, general appeals are often compounded by the fact that the cultural practices that tend to be highlighted are those of adults in a community, while emergent and dynamic new practices of young people themselves are ignored, dismissed, or rendered invisible (cf. Alim & Paris, 2017, p. 4). Despite the significant theorization that has occurred in anthropology and sociology during the last 25 years about the robustness of young people's peer groups and cultures, as well as the learning, social competence, and forms of social organization that occur therein (e.g., Cekaite et al., 2014; Corsaro, 2000; de León Pasquel, 2007; García-Sánchez, 2017; Goodwin, 1997; Kyratzis, 2004; Ochs, 2002), the practices and learning environments that young people create for themselves and their peers in their everyday lives are not often considered as legitimate cultural resources for schools to build on—or even seen at all as "cultural" practices in their own right. This is perhaps not surprising, given that a fairly widespread ideology of childhood, even in some academic circles, still tends to interpret any form of children's social behavior as inherently or developmentally "natural" rather than the product of sociocultural processes (the extensive and growing body of research cited above notwithstanding). In this volume, while we certainly pay attention to "adult" and longstanding community practices (e.g., Correa-Chávez & López-Fraire, Chapter 1; Ek, Chapter 6; Marin, Chapter 2; Madkins & Nasir, Chapter 3; Pacheco & Morales, Chapter 7), as well as to emergent new forms of intergenerational cultural practices and relationships (e.g., Enciso, Chapter 9; Gallo, Link, & Somerville, Chapter 5; Rosario-Ramos & Sawada, Chapter 4), we have also made sure to include examples of linguistic and cultural practices from young people's peer cultures that happen independently of adults' socialization efforts and that are experienced outside of primary socialization contexts (e.g., García-Sánchez, Chapter 8; Reynolds & Orellana, Chapter 11).

Third, until recently, much of the work calling for greater acknowledgment of diverse FoK in schools has collectively tended to emphasize discontinuities between everyday community and school practices, rather than seeing schools as sites of possibility for connecting those differences and discovering similarities. An increasing number of researchers, however, have been calling for a shift in frame to identify, instead, generative points of continuity across contexts (Rogers, 2004). They have also shone a light on some of the unintended consequences of such a heavy and intense focus on home–school dichotomies: namely the reification of differences between in- and out-of-school practices that are, then, ideologically constructed as unbridgeable, particularly those of youth from non-dominant groups, and often considered incommensurable with disciplinary knowledge and modes of reasoning (cf. Rosa & Flores, 2017). The Cultural Modeling paradigm (henceforth CM), in contrast, argued for the importance of finding robust points of continuity between the skills that youth from non-dominant communities themselves use and develop in their lives in and out of the classroom (Lee, 1995, 1997). In this spirit, CM-inspired research has suggested specific ways for these everyday abilities to become a base for the generation of hybrid spaces in the classroom that allow students to tap into their full linguistic repertoires (Lee, 2000, 2007; Gutierrez, Baquedano-López, & Tejeda, 1999; Orellana & Reynolds 2008). The CM paradigm, like the FoK literature, which powerfully combines ethnographic and sociolinguistic methods, deeply informs the work in this volume. CM has been a key source of inspiration for this edited collection as a whole, as we have all focused our efforts on identifying similarities and generative points of continuity between everyday and school practices in order to develop a responsive approach to classroom practices that centers linguistic and cultural diversity as the bedrock of educational achievement and expands possibilities for all.

Big Take-Aways from This Volume

In the processes of thinking about ways to center in the classroom the everyday linguistic repertoires and cultural practices of young people from non-dominant backgrounds, we—all of the chapter authors—had to struggle through important theoretical, epistemological, and political tensions. We have already mentioned and acknowledged some of these above. We were not surprised to encounter these issues; our own ongoing work had already led us to anticipate that we would have to work through many of these hurdles. And yet, it is fair to say that we were at times surprised by the recalcitrant nature of some of these tensions and of the institutional limitations that many practitioners encounter. So, as we prepare to tell you what are, in our view, the key contributions of this volume, we feel that it is also important to recognize that moments of great hope and optimism about this work were tempered by moments of deep pessimism and frustration, not just for us, but also for many of the contributors of this volume who reached out to us throughout this process. Looking back on this journey, we now realize that some of the most important ideas we would like researchers and practitioners to take away from this edited collection are ones that we had to think about and wrestle with a great deal. Our aim in this section is to briefly summarize what we consider to be some of the most important take-home messages of this book—recapitulating many points we have already alluded to above—as well as to indicate where they arise in the various chapters and throughout the book. We hope this serves as an introduction to the chapters as well to point to ways of reading the book with these big issues in mind.

Take-Away # 1: Interrogating Traditional Approaches to "Cultural Practices" in Education

One noteworthy contribution that this volume makes, both as a whole and at the level of individual chapters, is to offer a more nuanced orientation to what constitute *cultural practices*, particularly for educational practitioners. Rather than reify a limited number of dimensions (e.g., food, music, clothing, religious festivals ... etc.) that are considered "cultural" and that tend to be overemphasized in school celebrations of diversity, the authors of this volume examine practices that derive their sociocultural significance from their centrality in defining everyday life, participation, and belonging in a community. In other words, young people's quotidian, sustained, and meaningful engagement and participation in practices (rather than historical and folkloristic criteria) should guide how teachers approach learning about their students' social lives in communities of practices outside of school, and then the more difficult task of deciding what to center and sustain and how to do so (cf. Lee, 2017). This orientation allows for the recognition of the varied set of practices (from the more local to the more general; from the more traditional to the more emergent ... etc.) that may be relevant in young people's life.

In this spirit, the practices featured in this volume include longstanding practices that have been handed down across generations (e.g., playing dominos in African-American communities, Madkins and Nasir, Chapter 3), practices of enduring significance in children's peer cultures worldwide (e.g., playing hopscotch, García-Sánchez, Chapter 8), and more emergent practices that are a response to changing contexts and new needs (e.g., immigrant child language brokering, Reynolds & Orellana, Chapter 11). Some authors studied a very specific practice (e.g., reading the land in forest walks among Native American families, Marin, Chapter 2), whereas others focus on a more general epistemological orientation to learning in a community (e.g., the Learning by Observation and Pitching In (LOPI) ethos in indigenous communities, Correa-Chávez & López Fraire, Chapter 1). Some practices rely on canonical forms of religious language and literacy (e.g., Bible reading, Ek, Chapter 6), while others examine the hybrid and shifting linguistic practices that materialize in contexts of mobility where young people have to bridge across geographical and symbolic borders (e.g., the translanguaging practices described in Martínez et al., Chapter 10, and D'warte, Chapter 12, among others). Some authors highlight practices that are part of formal and stable rituals (such as those of Evangelical Christianity described in Pacheco and Morales, Chapter 7); yet others emphasize the significance that fleeting daily family interactions can have in how children and youth learn about the multiple meanings and limits of citizenship (Gallo et al., Chapter 5). A couple of the chapters even show the power of thoughtful adults (community organizers, researchers, teachers) in creating safe spaces—or preparing to create them (as in the work done by Martinez et al., Chapter 13, with teachers)—where young people of diverse backgrounds can bring in their divergent cultural and linguistic knowledge and practices and work together either to solve a problem that affects the whole community (e.g., youth fighting for environmental justice in Detroit, Rosario-Ramos & Sawada, Chapter 4) or for the purposes of self-expression and literary exploration (such as the story club described in Enciso, Chapter 9).

Take-Away # 2: Interrogating Academic Literacy

Academic literacy is often apolitically thought of as a range of skills (in reading, writing, listening, speaking, using technology … etc.) and modes of reasoning (critical thinking, cognitive skills in interpretation, analysis, and application of knowledge … etc.) that young people develop first and foremost in schools, and in the context of traditional disciplinary content areas. Yet decades of sociocultural literacy research and educational ethnography belie this innocuous understanding of academic literacy by showing that learning orientations and linguistic varieties that are considered "academic" (or institutionally sanctioned) are deeply intertwined with relations of power in society; so that practices and experiences that have traditionally been sustained and expanded in schools are those centered around (white) middle-/upper-class monolingual and monocultural practices and cultural funds of knowledge. A second important contribution of this volume is to question directly this neutral understanding of academic literacy, illuminating instead the contextual dimensions of academic and disciplinary literacy, and its ideological, and thus contested, nature. The individual chapters do this in two ways.

First, the chapter authors demonstrate that the literacy processes and competencies that people often assume can only be found and developed in the classroom (particularly when it comes to youth from non-dominant backgrounds) are indeed occurring in these youth's communities and peer groups on an everyday basis. This is important because, while the belief that "academic" linguistic varieties and "critical" thinking skills are prerequisites for educational success is widespread, young people from non-dominant groups are believed not to possess them or not to have access to them. Some of the complex forms of everyday language use and modes of reasoning that the authors documented in these communities include: forms of perspective taking during forest walks to understand ecosystemic relations (Marin, Chapter 2); mathematical reasoning in domino games (Madkins & Nasir, Chapter 3); analyzing relevant texts and data to craft compelling messages about social change for different community audiences (Rosario-Ramos & Sawada, Chapter 4); regular engagement with archaic, figurative, and metaphorical linguistic registers in religious texts, often in more than one language (Ek, Chapter 6; Pacheco & Morales, Chapter 7); forms of storytelling that blend literary and popular genres, as well as various cultural traditions (Enciso, Chapter 9); combining literacy strategies (such as explaining, enacting, and demonstrating) to make abstract game rules visible and concrete (García-Sánchez, Chapter 8); and sophisticated approaches to translation tasks that strive to balance the poetics and semantics of texts (Reynolds & Orellana, Chapter 11).

Second, the chapter authors also take direct issue with the ideological trappings of what counts as academic literacy in schools. In exposing the power-laden ideological bases of literacy, we imagine alternatives that would not only disrupt educational and sociolinguistic inequalities, but also provide more meaningful literacy experiences for all students. In other words, we challenge what academic literacy is, but also discuss what it could and should be. Gallo et al. (Chapter 5), for example, show what truly critical class discussions about civic engagement can look like when teachers seriously incorporate the perspectives of those students whose families are disenfranchised from the citizenship process. Martínez et al. (Chapter 10) pointedly ask: why is the epitome of *good* academic writing a monolingual writer who can write effectively for different monolingual audiences? They then go on to show that the audience awareness of bilingual student-writers (who write for both monolingual and bilingual audiences in authentic situations) is more sophisticated than what they are asked to do in schools under Common Core. This idea that, ironically, schools may be the context in which many students from non-dominant backgrounds experience the least diverse and most narrowly defined forms of literacy, is one that is also discussed explicitly in many of the other chapters (see also, Rosario-Ramos & Sawada, Chapter 4; Ek, Chapter 6; Pacheco & Morales, Chapter 7; Reynolds & Orellana, Chapter 11).

Chapter 13 (Martinez et al.) allows us to ponder how our definition of academic literacy would begin to change if teachers were given the opportunity, during their training or professional development, to conceptualize how to teach language arts in ways that capture the communicative richness and usefulness of students' varied linguistic registers, and not just standard varieties. Other authors openly interrogate other ideologies surrounding bilingualism and linguistic diversity in schools. García-Sánchez's work (Chapter 8) questions whose political (not educational) interests are being served when we teach "national" languages that have a long and close history of contact as completely different and separate, even to the point of preventing youth who speak both from using them as a mutual support system for their bilingual language development. Reynolds and Orellana (Chapter 11) suggest what can happen when the more *narrow* definitions of literacy are taken up by students and brought back into their home literacy brokering experiences, effectively *constraining* what they do with words. D'warte (Chapter 12) poses the ultimate challenge by asking what if, instead of starting from the ideological assumption that linguistic diversity is unmanageable for educational systems, we center linguistic flexibility and start by asking our students who live in multilingual communities how they themselves navigate, conceptualize, and represent this diversity.

Take-Away # 3: Rethinking Discontinuities in Literacy Socialization

While this third take-away is a corollary of the second we have just discussed, we have decided to discuss it separately for heuristic purposes and for clarity of exposition. Indeed, one of the most under-interrogated and taken-for-granted assumptions of many of the educational sociolinguistic ethnographies mentioned above and throughout this introduction is the idea of discontinuities between school and out-of-school literacy practices. This is again particularly the case for young people from non-dominant backgrounds (since literacy practices in what were viewed as "mainstream," middle-class communities were always thought of as being more aligned with school practices). One of the unintended consequences of how this assumption has been perpetuated in subsequent research is that school and out-of-school literacy and linguistic practices of children and youth from non-dominant communities have been ideologically constructed as more different than they really are in many cases. The scholarly popularity and generativity of the "discontinuities" framework itself may have inadvertently biased a whole generation of researchers to look for differences, which are often the most salient, while overlooking many similarities. Ironically, this unwitting bias may have played right into the deficit discourses these researchers were working to undermine, by reinscribing the idea that language and literacy practices valued in formal schooling and thought necessary for educational success are not found in non-dominant communities.

One of the most important theoretical interventions of this volume is to rethink literacy socialization across social and community settings in ways that explicitly challenge the ideologically constructed assumption that school and out-of-school literacy and linguistic practices, particularly in non-dominant communities, are very different and "discontinuous." Before we demonstrate how the chapters in this volume challenge this assumption, we want to make an important clarification. We are not saying that there are no differences; in fact, when discussing the fourth take-away below, we write about the challenges of bridging practices across learning contexts because, of course, differences *do* exist. What we are saying is that these differences often do not reside in the nature of the linguistics practices and modes of reasoning themselves, or on whether certain practices can be found or not in certain communities, which is what became overemphasized and ideologically reified in the "discontinuities" framework. What we actually find in the following chapters is that most of the time these differences emerge from *differences in the social organization* of the classroom and activities, goals, and practices outside of school; issues that we will return to directly below (overtly discussed in many of the chapters, e.g., Correa-Chávez & López Fraire, Chapter 1; Marin, Chapter 2; Rosario-Ramos & Sawada, Chapter 4; Gallo et al., Chapter 5; García-Sánchez, Chapter 8, among others).

In terms of the nature of the literacy practices themselves, most of the chapters in the volume emphasize, in Cultural Modeling-inspired fashion, commonalities in the types of literacy strategies found across formal (classrooms) and informal (community, familial, peer) learning contexts. For specific examples of some of these commonalities across contexts, we refer readers to the summary of chapters in the previous section. All of the everyday language practices and modes of reasoning highlighted there (e.g., perspective taking; civic orientations; audience awareness; mathematical reasoning, analysis of texts ... etc.) will be easily and immediately recognizable as also being competencies highly valued in content areas in schools, from STEM to social studies and language arts.

Take-Away # 4: Exploring Possibilities and Challenges of Centering the Cultural and Linguistic Practices of Youth from Non-dominant Communities in the Classroom

While the dual goals of helping youth sustain and expand their cultural and linguistic repertoires and supporting them to develop skills valued in formal schooling, are not and do not have to be mutually exclusive, the truth is that, given current educational and structural inequalities, these goals often coexist in a state of tension with one another. In the fourth and final take-away, we want to tell you what we, along with the chapter authors, have learned from our efforts to explore these tensions inherent in trying to bridge what happens outside of schools and what happens in classrooms. How do we point to concrete orientations and pathways for schools and classrooms to build on and center rich community practices while at the same time being critically aware that what is currently valued in schools is not objective and neutral, but very much symbolically, structurally, and materially predicated in relations of power? How do we engage in these bridging exercises in the service of creating more democratically and socially just educational spaces for all our children, and not in unwitting collusion with a deeply unfair status quo (a status quo that welcomes leveraging exercises undertaken without a critical awareness, especially when what happens outside the classroom is valued insofar as it can be "useful" in schools for the acquisition of ideologically constructed "appropriate" academic language and literacy)?

These questions are at the heart of the tensions that we, and the rest of the authors, have been inhabiting. And, by showing the richness and robustness of out-of-school practices among youth from non-dominant groups, one of the prime goals of the volume as a whole is to challenge (and, if we may be so bold, inspire people to change) precisely what is (is not) currently valued in schools. But to do all this critically, while at the same time acknowledging the institutional constraints and political realities of contemporary schooling has been a challenging task for all of us.

Chapter authors grappled with the challenges in a variety of ways, and point to different ways through these tensions. Some offered suggestions in the form of specific ideas that teachers could take up. Others proposed more general orientations to ways of thinking for teachers. Some make fairly explicit connections between everyday practices and disciplinary modes of reasoning/discursive practices in the spirit of Cultural Modeling, featuring a wide array of traditional content areas: civic education, Gallo et al., Chapter 5; natural sciences, Marin, Chapter 2; STEM, Madkins and Nasir, Chapter 3; or literature and language arts, e.g., Ek, Chapter 6; Enciso, Chapter 9; Pacheco and Morales, Chapter 7. Other authors offered suggestions for more generalized academic practices in schools and across content areas (e.g., Correa-Chávez & López Fraire, Chapter 1; D'warte, Chapter 12; Martínez et al., Chapter 10; Reynolds & Orellana, Chapter 11). While most authors attempted to be encouraging about the possibilities, none of us was blind to the limits and constraints facing practitioners who do, or want to do, this kind of work in increasingly assessment-driven, neoliberal educational systems.

For example, Correa-Chávez and López Fraire (Chapter 1) wrestle with how a focus on individual achievement in schools can limit the kind of learning that is possible with community-based indigenous ways of knowing, such as LOPI. Marin (Chapter 2) reflects on the static nature of learning in schools in relation to the peripatetic ways of learning about nature found in Native American families. Ek (Chapter 6) and Pacheco and Morales (Chapter 7) grapple with the issue of how we can respectfully build on our students' religious knowledge and experiences in secular educational institutions. García-Sánchez (Chapter 8) describes the significant differences in the social organization of the classrooms, including forms of participation and goals of activities, that make it difficult to capture in schools what young people are doing with their friends outside the classroom. Martínez et al. (Chapter 10) and Martinez et al. (Chapter 13) in different ways confront the limits of the interventions they offer, if monolingual literacy or forms of standard language are the only ones accepted in the classroom. Similarly, D'warte (Chapter 12) comes up against language ideologies that position multilingualism and linguistic/cultural hybridity as problematic in educational spaces. (See also Enciso, Chapter 9; García-Sánchez, Chapter 8.) Others land even more on the side of sounding cautionary notes to schools and teachers, such as Rosario-Ramos and Sawada (Chapter 4) who explicitly discuss issues of cooption or distortion of everyday community practices in schools. (See also Marin, Chapter 2.) We hope that this explicit attention to the tensions involved in doing this work will make the volume useful to many of our readers who will surely face similar institutional constraints, and others that we have not considered here.

A Note to Our Readers

This book was written with two primary audiences in mind: educational researchers, especially those who are oriented to ethnography, and who want to connect their ethnographic work to pedagogical practice in schools; and practitioners, both inservice and preservice teachers. We speak to each of these two audiences in turn, although we hope that many readers will see themselves as both researchers *and* practitioners.

For Educational Researchers

For educational researchers, especially ethnographers, this book offers models for connecting theory and ethnographic knowledge production to everyday educational practice, an enterprise that, as we have discovered once more in the process of putting together this volume, is not for the faint of heart. Connecting theory to pedagogical practice, especially when those connections involve bridging what happens outside of schools (home, neighborhoods, places of worship … etc.) with what happens inside the classroom, is difficult both because it is epistemologically messy and full of uncertainties, and because it is politically risky and full of potential pitfalls. Indeed, the difficulties inherent in making these connections, without (1) further contributing to the ideological reification of "home/community language(s)/practices" versus "school/academic language/practices," (2) falling into the trap of valuing community-based practices and knowledge only as disposable scaffolding to more "prestigious" academic practices and knowledge, or (3) helping to mask the socioeconomic and sociolinguistic inequalities that shape educational systems, were clearly in our minds as we conceptualized this volume and wrote this introduction. All the contributors to this volume also recognized the challenges of making these connections.

Despite such challenges, however, we feel that it is more important than ever for educational researchers who work with non-dominant communities to engage in theory–practice debates and dialogues across contexts and audiences, especially as interventions in culturally responsive and culturally sustaining teaching have become more prominent and central in education (Ladson-Billings, 2009; Lee, 2007; Moll et al., 2005; Paris & Alim, 2017). These positive developments in pedagogy have meant that there is an increasing number of practitioners who would like to honor and center their students' linguistic and cultural practices, but who find very little clear guidance on how to do that. We believe that ethnographers, especially anthropologists of education, are particularly well positioned to have an important voice in this discussion, since it has been a disciplinary hallmark of anthropology as a whole to explore how local epistemologies, as actually practiced, shape and are shaped by local forms of social organization. Or, in other words, historically what precisely has distinguished anthropology from other forms of ethnographic work is our attention to how the ways in which people produce and circulate knowledge is deeply intertwined with the ways people relate to one another in a community.

Given this focus and a longstanding, vibrant ethnographic tradition in the anthropology (and sociology) of education, it is surprising that these academic traditions have not been used more to inform the design of learning environments and instructional classroom practices, even when they have direct relevance for the social and instructional organizations of classrooms. Who can forget, for example Susan Philips's classic research on participant structures in reservation classrooms? Yet, many education scholars and practitioners alike tend to view research based on experimental and/or statistical designs as the most valid and reliable sources of data informing meaningful educational intervention in classroom praxis, with anthropological and sociological-inspired ethnography often utilized only for its value in explaining the structural conditions of the social contexts of education. To be fair, many ethnographers have not gone out of their way to write for practitioners or to engage with questions of how their work could inform pedagogical practice in classrooms, often preferring to remain in theoretical and analytical "safer" zones. While we fully understand the many reasons for this caution (including the difficulties mentioned above, the little professional value given to publishing in practitioners' journals, the fear of the unintended consequences that sometimes happen when intervening in a complex system ... etc.), it is our hope that this volume will inspire more educational ethnographers to step out of their comfort zones and add their voices to this important conversation. We are well positioned to imagine curricular approaches that respond constructively to the increasingly diverse cultural and linguistic contexts surrounding young people's learning and to finding continuities and connections that can help schools imagine alternative developmental paths to academic success that truly honor and center the everyday linguistic repertoires and cultural practices of young people from non-dominant backgrounds. Therefore, we have a moral and political imperative to speak about how classrooms can and should be organized around diverse epistemologies and forms of social organization.

For Practitioners

Taking seriously the audience of practitioners presented the authors of these chapters with significant challenges. We all came to see that drawing specific, feasible, and useful connections between everyday practices and school-valued ways of doing and learning is not easy. First, there is the challenge of how teachers can learn about what their students do when they are not in school, rather than presuming they know based on surface understandings of students' lives, or essentialized, static notions of culture and stereotypes about racial, ethnic, and religious non-dominant groups. This is particularly hard in the rapidly changing social, cultural, and technological world of young people today. We know that teachers do not have time for full-on immersion or for deep and focused analyses of particular cultural practices, as ethnographers are expected to do (and have the time and supports for so doing). The practices that youth engage in vary across households, peer groups, activity settings and communities; teachers can never become experts in the varied cultural and linguistic practices that their students may participate in. (Neither, of course, can ethnographers, who tend to focus on a narrow set of such practices.) But there are ways of integrating learning about students' lives into instructional practice. The chapter by D'warte (Chapter 12) models how ethnography can be built into the fabric of instruction and how teachers can learn along with students, about both traditional and emergent community practices, as lived experiences become objects of study and material for the learning of math, language, and literacy. Teachers might further consider other ways of learning about their students as part of their ongoing curriculum: through quick writes, journal entries, share arounds, informal conversations, drawings, photos, sharing of items from home, listening to their "small stories" (Enciso, Chapter 9), and more.

The important thing we want to emphasize to teachers is that we must move beyond superficial investigations of home/family/community "cultures." We need to go beyond the basic questions that typically get asked, such as what kids' favorite foods are, what they did over summer vacation, or the makeup of their families. We need to go deeper than making essentialized assumptions about their cultural practices—beyond piñatas, food and fiestas. We can find out more substantively what kids do when they are not in school: who they talk with; where they go; what games they play; what they read, write, listen and view. Do they go to church, synagogue, a mosque? Do they read the Bible, recite the Koran, sing in the church choir? Do they play hopscotch, tetherball, hand games, dominoes, double dutch jump rope, chess, basketball, soccer, video or other games? Do they trade Pokemon cards? How about imaginary games, based on longstanding tropes like "playing house" or other kinds of world building, or reenactments of popular culture? Do they translate, interpret, or "language broker" for others—and where, for whom, with what texts, in what ways? Are they living in new immigrant communities where families may talk about migration status, adopt practices to protect themselves from deportation, navigate complex legal and institutional circumstances, and find ways to "do family" across borders?

Some of the specific examples that this book offers (e.g., Bible reading, playing dominoes, reading the land during hikes or nature walks, translating for family members) may be things your students engage in; the suggestions in these chapters may have direct relevance for your classrooms. We suggest ways of looking at those practices, understanding how they are organized, and contemplating what may be learned from participating in them that may be adapted to the experiences of your students with relatively small adjustments and in ways that are not felt as epistemologically harmful or violent (e.g., essentialized tokenization, decontextualized/unrecognized cultural appropriation, superficial celebrations of "culture" or "diversity," using everyday practices as mere starting points or stepping stones … etc.) by the minoritized students in your classroom. But even if your students do not engage in these exact kinds of practice, we hope you can take inspiration from the book as ways of *orienting* to everyday activities. We hope that our modeling will encourage you to learn about the practices your own students engage in, recognizing that language and cultural practices in communities are diverse, dynamic, and shifting even as they may also be decades or centuries old, handed down across generations, and symbols of resistance against dominant structures of power.

We recognize that the connections between what youth do every day and what schools want youth to learn are not always transparent, neither for teachers nor for students, who at least initially will need your leadership and guidance in helping them see the richness and the value of even the practices they themselves engage in, let alone those of others. The difficulty in perceiving these connections is magnified by two longstanding ideological processes in education that we have already discussed in this introduction, but that bear repeating: On the one hand, we have decades of educational research and discourses that have tended to overemphasize the discontinuities between "home" and "school," as if these were two completely separate and inconmensurable domains, rather than sometimes overlapping spheres of teaching, learning, and educational experience (in the Deweyan sense of the word); and on the other hand, we have powerful deficit discourses that have consistently positioned "home" language and cultural practices, particularly those of students from non-dominant groups, as inferior to those of "school," if not downright obstacles to students' academic and educational success. We suggest as a starting point a change in orientation that is illustrated across the chapters in this book: simply to recognize that youth do engage in rich and complex practices every day. They play, read, write, talk and work with their peers and families, using language (often multiple linguistic varieties) to do a wide range of things including to entertain, argue, compare, contrast, and take action in the world. They observe and participate in a wide range of relationships, activities, and tasks. They learn from that engagement. Starting with the assumption that learning happens everywhere, every day—not just in school—can go a long way toward countering "deficit" ideas about non-dominant communities. Indeed, when we find ourselves noticing what students *don't* know or *can't* do, we can ask ourselves: What *do* they know? What *can* they do? And how might this be visible in contexts other than school?

We recognize that there is still a double challenge here: that of seeing the connections across community and school domains, and that of how to make those connections to classroom practice in meaningful, feasible, and appropriate ways. The authors of this volume did not always find it easy to make those connections, but across the book we model both small and large ways for doing just this. Some of the suggestions involve relatively small adjustments to the ways schools typically do things. Some require shifts in our orientation as teachers, so that we can better recognize culturally divergent ways with words, or ways of organizing for learning. Other connections are more direct, because some out-of-school practices, such as translating story books, or reading the Bible, map rather directly onto what schools value. Yet the ways these practices are organized in home and school contexts may be quite different, informed by different values, beliefs, norms and relationships, as García-Sánchez unpacks in her chapter (Chapter 8). So the challenge for teachers is to grapple with the different logics in the organization of learning in home and in school, and see how school practices might be reshaped. There is much that can be gained from understanding *how* learning happens in everyday contexts, because often that learning is powerful, influential, and longlasting.

Writing with these different audiences in mind presented us with challenges that are not unlike those faced by the children of immigrants when they broker language for people who bring different experiences and interests to the conversation. As one young man said in a conversation with Marjorie years ago: "It's hard, not to seem, or to swing, either way" when translating between people who speak in very different ways and face different constraints. We hope that our words resonate with the concerns and interests of both scholars and practitioners, and that this book can contribute to breaking down false binaries: between theory and practice, scholarship and service, everyday ways and academic competencies, home and school language practices.

References

Alim, H. S. (2004). *You know my steez: An ethnographic and sociolinguistic study of style shifting in a black American speech community*. Durham, NC: Duke University Press.

Alim, H. S. & Paris, D. (2017). What is culturally sustaining pedagogy and why does it matter? In D. Paris and H. S. Alim (Eds.) *Culturally sustaining pedagogies: Teaching and learning for justice in a changing world* (1–21). New York: Columbia University Teachers College Press.

Avineri, N., Johnson, E., Brice-Heath, S., McCarty, T., Ochs, E., Kremer-Sadlik, T., Paris, D. (2015). Invited forum: Bridging the "language gap." *Journal of Linguistic Anthropology, 25*(1), 66–86.

Ballenger, C. (1992). Because you like us: The language of control. *Harvard Educational Review, 62*, 199–208.

Baugh, J. (2017). Meaning-less differences: Exposing fallacies and flaws in "the word gap" hypothesis that conceal a dangerous "language trap" for low-income American families and their children. *International Multilingual Research Journal, 11*(1), 39–51.

Blum, S. D. (2017). Unseen WEIRD assumptions: The so-called language gap discourse and ideologies of language, childhood, and learning. *International Multilingual Research Journal, 11*(1), 23–38.

Cekaite, A., Blum-Kulka, S., Grøver, V., & Teubal, E. (Eds.) (2014). *Children's peer talk: Learning from each other*. Cambridge: Cambridge University Press.

Citrón, R. (1997). Angels' town: Chero ways, gang life, and rhetorics of the everyday. Boston, MA: Beacon Press.

Corsaro, W. A. (2000). Early childhood education, children's peer cultures, and the future of childhood. *European Early Childhood Education Research Journal, 8*(2), 89–102.

De León Pasquel, L. (2007). Parallelism, metalinguistic play, and the interactive emergence of Tzotzil (Mayan) siblings' culture. *Research on Language and Social Interaction, 40*(4), 405–436.

Delpit, L. D. (1986). Skills and other dilemmas of a progressive black educator. *Harvard Educational Review, 56*, 379–385.

García, O. & Otheguy, R. (2017). Interrogating the language gap of young bilingual and bidialectal students. *International Multilingual Research Journal, 11*(1), 52–65.

García-Sánchez, I. M. (2017). Friendship, participation, and multimodality in Moroccan immigrant girls' peer groups. In M. Theobald (Ed.) *Friendship and peer culture in multilingual settings* (1–33). Bingley: Emerald Books.

García-Sánchez, I. M. (2010). Serious games: Code-switching and identity in Moroccan immigrant girls' pretend play. *Pragmatics, 20*(4), 523–555.

González, N. (2001). *I am my language: Discourses of women and children in the borderlands*. Tucson: University of Arizona Press.

González, N., Moll, L. C., & Amanti, C. (Eds.) (2005). Funds of knowledge: Theorizing practices in households, communities, and classrooms. Mahwah, NJ: Lawrence Erlbaum Associates.

González, N. E., Moll, L. C., Tenery, M. F., Rivera, A., Rendon, P., Gonzales, R., et al. (1995). Funds of knowledge for teaching in latino households. *Urban Education, 29*(4), 443–470.

Goodwin, M. H. (1997). Children's linguistic and social worlds. *Anthropology Newsletter, 38*(4).

Gutiérrez, K. D., Baquedano-López, P., & Tejeda, C. (1999). Rethinking diversity: Hybridity and hybrid language practices in the third space. *Mind, Culture, and Activity*, 6(4), 286–303.

Hart, B. & Risley, T. R. (1995). *Meaningful differences in the everyday life of America's children*. Baltimore, MD: Paul Brookes.

Heath, S. B. (1986). What no bedstory means: Narrative skills at home and school. In B. B. Schieffelin and E. Ochs (Eds.) *Language socialization across cultures* (97–124). Cambridge: Cambridge University Press.

Heath, S. B. (1983) *Ways with words: language, life, and work in communities and classrooms*. Cambridge: Cambridge University Press.

Hutton, J. S., Horowitz-Kraus, T., Mendelsohn, A. L., DeWitt, T., Holland, S. K., & C-MIND Authorship Consortium (2015). Home reading environment and brain activation in preschool children listening to stories. *Pediatrics*, 136(3), 466–478.

Kyratzis, A. (2004). Talk and interaction among children and the co-construction of peer groups and peer culture. *Annual Review of Anthropology*, 33, 625–649.

Labov, W. (1972). *Language in the inner city: Studies in the Black Vernacular*. Philadelphia: University of Pennsylvania Press.

Ladson-Billings, G. (2009). *The dreamkeepers: Successful teachers of African American children*, 2nd edn. San Francisco: Wiley & Sons.

Lee, C. D. (2017). An ecological framework for enacting culturally sustaining pedagogy. In D. Paris and H. S. Alim (Eds.) *Culturally sustaining pedagogies: Teaching and learning for justice in a changing world* (261–273). New York: Columbia University Teachers College Press.

Lee, C. D. (2007). *Culture, literacy, and learning: Taking bloom in the midst of whirlwind*. New York: Teachers College Press.

Lee, C. D. (2000). Signifying in the zone of proximal development. In C. D. Lee & P. Smagorinsky (Eds.) *Vygotskian perspectives on literacy research: Constructing meaning through collaborative inquiry* (191–225). Cambridge: Cambridge University Press.

Lee, C. D. (1997). Bridging home and school literacies: Models for culturally responsive teaching, a case for African American English. In J. Flood, S. B. Heath, & D. Lapp (Eds.) *Handbook of research on teaching literacy through the communicative and visual arts* (334–345). New York: Macmillan.

Lee, C. D. (1995). Signifying as a scaffold for literary interpretation. *Journal of Black Psychology*, 21(4), 357–381.

Miller, P. J. (1982). *Amy, Wendy, and Beth: Learning language in South Baltimore*. Austin: University of Texas Press.

Miller, P. J. & Sperry, D. E. (2012). Déjà vu: The continuing misrecognition of low-income children's verbal abilities. In S. T. Fiske & H. R. Markus (Eds.) *Facing social class: How societal rank influences interaction* (109–130). New York: Russell Sage.

Moll, L. C. (1992). Funds of knowledge for teaching: Using a qualitative approach to connect homes and classrooms. *Theory into Practice*, 31(2), 132–141.

Moll, L. C., Amanti, C., Neff, D., & Gonzalez, N. E. (2005). Funds of knowledge for teaching: Using a qualitative approach to connect homes and classrooms. In *Funds of Knowledge: Theorizing Practices in Households, Communities, and Classrooms* (71–88). Mahwah, NJ: Lawrence Erlbaum Associates.

Moll, L. C., Amanti, C., Neff, D., & Gonzalez, N. (1992). Funds of knowledge for teaching: Using a qualitative approach to connect homes and classrooms. *Theory into Practice*, 31(2), 132–141.

Noble, K. G., Houston, S. M., Brito, N. H., Bartsch, H., Kan, E., Kuperman, J. M. et al. (2015). Family income, parental education and brain structure in children and adolescents. *Nature Neuroscience, 18*(5), 773.

Ochs, E. (2002). Becoming a speaker of culture. In C. Kramsch (Ed.) *Language acquisition and language socialization: Ecological perspectives* (99–120). London: Continuum.

Orellana, M. F. (2009). *Translating childhoods: Immigrant youth, language and culture.* New Brunswick, NJ: Rutgers University Press.

Orellana, M. F. & Reynolds, J. F. (2008). Cultural modeling: Leveraging bilingual skills for school paraphrasing tasks. *Reading Research Quarterly, 43*(1), 48–65.

Paris, D. (2011). *Language across difference: Ethnicity, communication, and youth identities in changing urban schools.* Cambridge: Cambridge University Press.

Paris, D. & Alim, H. S. (Eds.) (2017). *Culturally sustaining pedagogies: Teaching and learning for justice in a changing world.* New York: Columbia University Teachers College Press.

Pease-Alvarez, C. & Vasquez, O. (1994). Language socialization in ethnic minority communities. In F. Genesee (Ed.) *Educating second language children: The whole child; the whole curriculum; the whole community* (82–102.) New York: Cambridge University Press.

Philips, S. (1983). *The invisible culture: Communication in classroom and community on the Warm Spring Indian Reservation.* Prospect Heights, IL: Waveland Press.

Rogers, R. (2004). Discursive alignment and conflict in social transformation. In R. Rogers (Ed.) *New Directions in Critical Discourse Analysis* (51–78). Mahwah: NJ: Lawrence Erlbaum Associates.

Rosa, J. D. & Flores, N. (2017). Do you hear what I hear?: Raciolinguistic ideologies and culturally sustaining pedagogies. In D. Paris & H. S. Alim (Eds.) *Culturally sustaining pedagogies: Teaching and learning for justice in a changing world* (175–206). New York: Columbia University Teachers College Press.

Thorne, B. (1993). *Gender play: Girls and boys in school.* New Brunswick, NJ: Rutgers University Press.

Villenas, S. & Deyhle, D. (1999). Critical race theory and ethnographies challenging stereotypes: Latino families, schooling, and resilience, and resistance. *Curriculum Inquiry, 29*(4), 413–445.

Zentella, A. C. (1997). *Growing up bilingual: Puerto Rican children in New York.* Oxford: Blackwell.

Zisselsberger, M. (2016). Toward a humanizing pedagogy: Leveling the cultural and linguistic capital in a fifth-grade writing classroom. *Bilingual Research Journal, 39*(2), 121–137.

1

LEARNING BY OBSERVING AND PITCHING IN: IMPLICATIONS FOR THE CLASSROOM

Maricela Correa-Chávez and Angélica López-Fraire

In this chapter, we outline some of the ways that learning in classrooms can more closely mirror what we see when children engage in Learning by Observing and Pitching In (LOPI) to family and community activity. LOPI is more than one particular behavior or practice, it is an approach to organizing learning that includes children having the opportunity to routinely observe and listen in on mature activities to which they are expected to contribute. This form of organizing children's lives and learning is especially common in communities that have historical Indigenous roots in the Americas (Correa-Chávez, Mejía-Arauz, & Rogoff, 2015). Luis Urrieta (2013) described a particularly illustrative example of LOPI from the P'uhérpecha community of Nocutzepu in Michoacán, México:

> Daniela (pseudonym), age five, was regularly observed making small, awkwardly shaped tortillas that her mother Isaura cooked on a *comal* (clay griddle) over a fiery *parangua* (hearth). Isaura, usually very busy, seemed not to pay too much attention to Daniela as she usually struggled with the dough. Isaura would, however, once in a while say "*fíjate*" (look with fixation) to Daniela, as she turned half of her upper torso toward Daniela while shaping a tortilla with her hands. Daniela would respond by looking at and imitating her mother's movements, until Isaura resumed her position facing the *metate* (grinding stone), and placed the finished tortilla on the *comal*. Every attempt Daniela made at shaping a tortilla ended up cooked on the *comal*, and Isaura would quickly offer Daniela more dough. On occasion when Daniela started to head out of the kitchen, Isaura would quickly say "*toma*" (take this) and would again hand her more dough. Even when Daniela's dough ended up on the dirt floor, Isaura cooked it and fed it to the dog

and advised Daniela by saying *"cuidado* Dani" (careful Dani). Daniela's better tortillas were always placed at the top of the pile, and were the first to be eaten as Daniela watched smiling silently, thus rewarding Daniela for her effort and contribution and encouraging her to continue to pitch in to tortilla making.

(Urrieta, 2013, p. 325)

We begin by reviewing some of the research findings that have explored different aspects of LOPI. We do not describe all facets of LOPI (see Rogoff, Mejía-Arauz, & Correa-Chávez, 2015), but rather focus on the community organization of LOPI, the means of learning in LOPI, the social organization of endeavors in LOPI, the means of communication and coordination in LOPI, autonomy in LOPI, and motivation in LOPI. Following each research section there is a brief classroom tip that relates the research to the classroom context. At the end of the chapter, we consolidate the findings to provide larger suggestions that can be implemented in schools. We outline steps individual teachers can take in their classrooms, and suggest changes that would be beneficial at the institutional level to change our paradigms of learning and incorporate some strengths of LOPI.

Throughout this chapter we contrast LOPI with traditional ways of structuring school learning with teachers as transmitters of information that children soak up as they sit at their desks, in what Rogoff and her colleagues have called Assembly-Line Instruction (ALI) (Rogoff et al., 2003). Decades of research have shown that ALI is not the ideal way to structure learning (Bransford, Brown, & Cocking, 1999), but it is still common in many schools. When Texas first-graders from Latino immigrant families (who attended a school organized by ALI) were shown videos of first-graders at a nearby school taking agency in learning by moving from their desks to help one another and seek answers, the interviewed students characterized the children in the video as "bad" for not following the rules and sitting quietly at their desks (Adair, 2015). LOPI starts from a different place. In this way of learning, children are not receptacles of information, or even necessarily co-constructers of knowledge; rather they are valued participants in important ongoing activity. Because of this, we see different patterns of interaction when we compare children's behaviors in communities where LOPI is common to the behaviors of children in communities where ALI is common. This contrast is one we turn to next, outlining some of the results of studies where this comparison has been central to examining learning.

Community Organization of Learning in LOPI

At the heart of LOPI is children's inclusion in ongoing family and community activity in meaningful ways. Children are not "being prepared" for future participation in community activity (sometimes referred to as adult activity), rather their participation is ongoing and already valued, even if not at an expert level. The example of Daniela making tortillas at the beginning of this chapter clearly illustrates this idea. Although Daniela's end results still needed work, she was nevertheless able to see that her contribution was important because the tortillas served to feed the family and occasionally its animals.

In this example, Daniela was not "playing" at making tortillas, neither was she taking part in a "tortilla-making exercise" where the only purpose was to teach her. Rather, Daniela was involved in the actual activity alongside her mother, observing her mother's work, and engaging to the best of her abilities even though she was not participating at a competent or expert level. Nonetheless, she was part of the real activity and her contribution was seen as legitimate and important. This inclusion in central and productive ongoing activity is not incidental, but rather fundamental to the organization of LOPI, and has been for centuries (Chamoux 2015; Flores et al., 2015).

Accounts such as Daniela's have been seen in the historical record dating back to the Mesoamerican codices outlining family life prior to the European invasion and colonization of the Americas. What is common in both the historical record and in the ethnographic accounts and interviews of the present day is the idea that children learn through co-presence in activity, through facilitation by more knowledgeable others, and through observation (Chamoux, 2015). Another important theme present in both historical records as well as in current day interviews (Cardoso, 2015; Garcia, 2015) is that children are learning not only one important skill or practice through their participation (for example "just" learning how to make tortillas or how to care for crops), but rather they are also learning how to be members of the community, with all that this entails. Learning to be everyday participants of a community involves being aware of others, attentive to the needs of others, and respecting others' initiative, topics we will discuss in more detail.

Brief tip: Include children in the meaningful work of the community (in schools, the community could be the classroom), and not only in exercises that prepare for later inclusion in the larger community or labor market. Children can, for example, take the initiative in helping peers with their work, can help teach or demonstrate a subject or topic of interest, or can plan an event or activity around an academic topic.

Means of Learning in LOPI

In LOPI, because young children are regularly included in the wide range of social and productive activities of their community, they are often in positions to observe and listen to ongoing events, and are expected to pay attention in order to be able to contribute to them in the future. Psychological research shows that young children are especially interested in adults and pay close attention to what they are doing (Coppens & Rogoff, 2017a); thus co-presence and collaboration with others is likely rewarding to most young children. Nevertheless, in most middle-class communities, children are often largely segregated from adults in early childhood and instead encouraged to engage in developmentally appropriate child-focused activities (Morelli, Rogoff, & Angelillo, 2003). However, when children are included in the work of family and community, as they are in many Indigenous heritage communities of the Americas, they are not only generally interested in the activities, but can also see how their contributions help their families and communities. Adults in communities where LOPI is common urge children to be attentive to what is taking place around them and seek out moments when their help or contribution is needed (Chavajay, 1993). Interviews with parents and other adults have shown that observation of others and of ongoing activity is one of the principal means through which learning takes place in LOPI (Chamoux, 1992; Mejía-Arauz, Rogoff, & Paradise, 2005; Rogoff, et al., 2003). For example, parents in a Mazahua community in central Mexico reported that observation as a form of learning is a more direct and effective way of transmitting knowledge compared to lessons or giving directions (de Haan, 1999).

Sentiments such as the one expressed by the Mazahua parents are common in many Indigenous communities of the Americas and research has shown that children from communities where LOPI is common often managed their attention differently compared to children from middle-class communities where ALI is more common. A series of studies examining what children attended to when they had the opportunity to observe a nearby activity, but were not expected or required to attend to it, showed that children from Mexican immigrant and Guatemalan Maya families (where LOPI is common), were more likely to pay attention to the actions of the others compared to children from families who were more familiar with schooling and middle-class practices. The children whose families had more experience with school practices, in contrast, were more likely to attend to a distractor toy, pay attention to the room itself, or seem to "space out." Additionally, these studies focusing on third party attention also consistently showed that children who observed the ongoing task could remember and use that information a week or more later when they were given the opportunity to engage in the same activity. In fact, all children who had paid attention to the activity learned something about the task (regardless of cultural background); unsurprisingly, the children who did not pay attention to the activity of others, did not learn (Correa-Chávez & Rogoff, 2009; López, Correa-Chávez, Rogoff, & Gutiérrez, 2010; Silva, Correa-Chávez & Rogoff, 2010).

Other studies examining cultural differences in children's attention and LOPI found that toddlers, children, and adults from Guatemalan Maya and Mexican immigrant communities (where LOPI is common) were skilled at attending to multiple ongoing activities in their environment in a smooth uninterrupted manner compared to people who were more familiar with school ways of organizing learning (Chavajay & Rogoff, 1999; Correa-Chávez,

Rogoff, & Mejía-Arauz, 2005; Rogoff et al., 1993). Whether attending to the activities of others or skillfully attending to two activities, the attentional skills demonstrated by children whose families had Indigenous history and familiarity with LOPI were often different than the way attention in school is typically displayed (Paradise et al., 2014). School actively discourages attending to the work of others in one's environment by labeling it as cheating and asks that attention to learning be demonstrated by undividedly focusing on either the teacher or one's own work. Yet expecting only these school-like forms of attention from children may also prevent children from using some of the tools they have commonly used in their families and communities for learning.

Brief tip: Attention to others' activities is an important and valued means of learning in communities that have Indigenous heritage. This can be incorporated in classrooms by encouraging children to learn from one another's work throughout the day—rather than talking about cheating or copying, talk about how children can become productively informed by others. There are likely many activities where children can be encouraged to observe and learn from peers.

Social Organization of Endeavors in LOPI

In LOPI, the expectation to observe ongoing activity is usually accompanied by an expectation of help, or participating in the activity itself. The following quote was an answer given by a P'urhépecha (Mexican) mother with eight years of schooling to researchers when asked how her children helped at home:

> Sometimes when they see that I am washing, the older one (10 years old) will tell the younger one (8 years old), "start hanging the clothes to dry or clean up." I'll see my older daughter sweeping and the younger one washing dishes in the kitchen … she'll clean up and they'll tell me, "mom we already cleaned the kitchen while you were washing" or something like that [and I tell them] "that's good, thank you."
>
> (Mejía-Arauz et al., 2015)

Later in the interview this same mother went on to say that the children help her because they wanted to, not because they were given rewards for helping or punishment for not helping. Collaboration in family and community work from early ages has been found to be common in Indigenous heritage communities of the Americas including in: household chores, childcare, animal care, participation in celebrations and festivals, and translation for adults (Gaskins, 2000; González, Moll & Amantí, 2005; Orellana, 2001; see also the chapters by García-Sánchez and Reynolds and Orellana in this volume).

Several studies have also found collaboration and helping as common among Indigenous heritage and Mexican heritage communities in peer inter-actions. For example, compared to children whose families were familiar with middle-class ways, Mexican heritage siblings (from immigrant families familiar with LOPI) were more likely to work together and build off one another's actions on a joint activity (Correa-Chávez, 2016). When asked to work together on a planning task, Mexican heritage sibling pairs from immigrant families with basic experience with western schooling showed sophisticated patterns of blending their agendas by collaborating fluidly, anticipating each other's actions and sharing leadership and exchanging roles in order to accom-plish the task (Alcalá, Rogoff, & López Fraire, 2018). This contrasts with sib-ling pairs of highly schooled European American families who often divided the task, collaborated half as much, and instead of sharing ideas, took turns while sometimes excluding a sibling. In Mexico, P'urhepecha children were more likely to work together as a team when playing a board game against another team than were middle-class children from a Mexican cosmopolitan city (Correa-Chávez, Mangione, & Mejía-Arauz, 2016).

Brief tip: In LOPI, collaboration is a built-in expectation and may be a taken for granted way to demonstrate learning as well as a way to continue to engage in learning. If we create classroom cultures where learning from others is encouraged then we will likely also see children taking the initiative to work together and collaborate.

Communication and Coordination in LOPI

Although many schools and educational researchers have called for increased collaboration in schools, the model of collaboration presented is often one that is particular to schools and different from the LOPI model. For example, in one study, children from a traditionally organized classroom who were asked to collaborate mostly used tests and quizzes instead of interacting in ways that built off others' efforts (Matusov, Bell, & Rogoff, 2002). Additionally, among people who are familiar with schools, collaboration is usually accomplished and organized through extensive use of talk with assigned and divided roles (Dixon et al., 1984; Kim, 2002). However, the participation patterns for collaboration often look different in communities where LOPI is common, perhaps because of the assumption that participants are already paying attention to what others around them are doing. (See the chapter by Marin in this volume for further exploration of joint attention to local environments between parents and chil-dren in urban forest walks.)

In teaching interactions between Zinacantec Mayan siblings, children with only a few years of schooling used more talk when teaching a younger sibling compared to children who had not been to school, who tended to use more bodily closeness and bodily guidance as teaching tools (Maynard, 2004). When children were placed in groups of three with an adult who was teaching them a new task, European American children were more likely to communicate with one another using talk, whereas U.S. Mexican heritage children whose families had few years of schooling (and whose families had immigrated from rural Mexico) were more likely to engage in multiple nonverbal turns at communication (Mejía-Arauz et al., 2007). Similarly, when Mexican heritage sibling pairs in California were working together to construct a three-dimensional puzzle, pairs whose parents had few years of schooling and more familiarity with LOPI collaborated more but also did so in a way where talk was used in conjunction with ongoing activity to advance the task. Contrariwise, pairs whose families had more school experience more commonly used talk to organize the activity overall and figure out what to do next (Correa-Chávez, 2016).

From an early age, talk may be just one of many tools that children use in their interactions with others in communities where LOPI is common. For example, when asking for help from their mothers who were busy with something else, Mayan toddlers relied on gaze, touch, and body posture in their requests more often than European American toddlers who rarely used these (Rogoff, et al., 1993). Similarly, school aged Mexican heritage children in the U.S. were ten times more likely to patiently wait, checking that an adult was not busy before asking for help compared to European American children who loudly and frequently interrupted ongoing activity (Ruvalcaba et al., 2015). The idea of blending agendas in collaboration where participants build on other's actions as they work together and may not necessarily need extensive verbal explanations of ongoing activity appears to be more common in Indigenous heritages communities familiar with LOPI than in middle-class communities. When programming a computer game together, pairs from Indigenous heritage U.S. Mexican families collaborated twice as much compared to European American pairs and when they did so engaged in a form of shared thinking that did not require stopping for proposals. The European American pairs rarely engaged in this form of collaboration (Ruvalcaba & Rogoff, 2016). However, traditionally organized schools tend not to promote these forms of collaboration (Matusov et al., 2002), focusing instead on individual accomplishments and narrowly defined verbal competency (Hart & Risley, 1995).

Brief tip: In LOPI, collaboration may involve blending of agendas between participants and talk may be used in ways that are different than how it is used in school. Paying attention to what children are doing while they are working together, and not only what they are saying (or the end product) may help make these forms of collaboration more visible.

Autonomy in LOPI

Ethnographic research indicates that collaboration and helping are expected and often voluntarily offered among Indigenous heritage and Mexican heritage children (de Haan, 2001; Coppens et al., 2014; Orellana, 2001). For example,

Mexican and Central American heritage children in California serve as active agents in supporting their families and schools, and these everyday work and contributions to their home and school provide avenues for learning and linguistic and cultural brokering between their home and the outside world (Orellana, 2001; see also Reynolds and Orellana, this volume). This has also been shown with Moroccan children living in Spain; see García-Sánchez, this volume, for further elaboration on differences in the ways children's work is valued in out-of-school contexts and in schools. But what is often most striking to middle-class audiences regarding collaboration in LOPI, especially in the home context, are the assertions by parents that they do not have to make children participate, but rather that children either "want to help" or simply engage in help without being asked.

Ramírez Sánchez (2007) describes childhood in a system of reciprocity and exchange among the Nahuas of Tlaxcala, Mexico where everyone helps members of their family, especially those in the same household. The Nahua children claim not to be working even when heavily involved in family work. It is described as just "helping as a matter of being part of the family". "Working" in the community is defined as paid work. Similarly, children from the Yucatan peninsula seemed surprised by the question when they were asked why they help. The answer seemed obvious to them and they viewed helping as a part of living in that home or being part of the family (Alcalá & Cervera, 2019). Both Indigenous heritage mothers and children in California and Mexico also indicated the importance of helping with initiative because it comes from the heart and without parental control. The children themselves also described wanting to help because they are a part of the family (Coppens et al., 2014).

Studies conducted with families of toddlers showed that three-year-old children were often eager to participate in chores; however, this desire disappeared as children were not allowed to participate or not deemed competent enough to participate. Interviews with European American and Mexican heritage mothers of two- to three-year-old children in California showed that the Mexican heritage mothers incorporated their toddlers in ongoing work, whereas European American mothers tried to avoid having their children involved in ongoing work. In the interviews, over half of the European American mothers said they avoided including their toddler in joint work, often because they wanted to spend the time engaging with their child in a more meaningful or cognitively enriching way. Sometimes, this was also done in the name of efficiency (Coppens & Rogoff, 2017b). Mexican heritage mothers, in contrast, emphasized the joint nature of the activity and the idea that helping developed the desire to help even more within their children.

Similarly, a sociolinguistic study examining ongoing interaction as toddlers attempted to engage in activity in a Chamula Maya community in Chiapas, Mexico illustrates how toddlers' initiative is respected even when adults would rather not have children's help in the moment. For example, in one analysis a three-year-old insisted multiple times on washing her clothes even though adults tried to distract her from the activity. However, the child's insistence and desires were respected in the end and her activity was allowed to proceed (Martinez, 2015). This respect for others' wishes, even the desires of a three-year-old, are also part of learning to value an individual's autonomy in addition to valuing responsibility to a group (Mosier & Rogoff, 2003).

The cultural value of being *acomedido/a* (helping with initiative without being asked) might also be related to this respect for a toddler's or child's desire to help (López et al., 2012). Based on the studies described in earlier sections, children in these Indigenous communities may be more prepared to recognize such cues at earlier ages because of access to everyday mature activities and because of a community expectation to become involved. Studies have shown that children showed more prosocial behavior or agency where such behavior was encouraged, required, or expected (Adair, 2015; Mejía-Arauz et al., 2015).

These examples illustrate the intersection of autonomy and interdependence. In order to help others, children need to have a sense of interdependence, but also a sense of autonomy to act as agents. This respect for autonomy is something schools often fail to do in small and large ways. For example, some schools require all classrooms of the same grade to engage in the exact same schedule, leaving no room for individual children to engage in something of interest not on the schedule (Adair, 2015). Presumably this schedule is followed to ensure all children in a school are learning similar things. However, a close look at the example presented in Martinez' analysis of the toddler wanting to wash clothes shows that in LOPI children do not have an infinity of choices presented to them. Rather, it is when children express an interest in something that is already taking place or something that might be possible in that particular context that an individual's autonomy is respected. In schools, this autonomy is often punished. It is therefore not surprising that six- to seven-year-old Mexican heritage children in California were contributing help to their families more often out of their own initiative compared to European American middle-class children (Coppens & Rogoff, 2017b).

Yet even in some classroom-like activity, we can see spontaneous help from children who come from communities where LOPI is common. When learning how to make origami figures, triads of Mexican heritage children from families that likely had experience with Indigenous practices more often offered spontaneous help than triads of European American children and Mexican heritage children whose families had extensive experience with western schooling (López et al., 2012). In a classroom-like activity, U.S. Mexican heritage sibling pairs from families with limited experience in western schooling showed more helping towards an adult during 15 scripted opportunities to help when compared to sibling pairs of European American families

(López Fraire, Rogoff, & Alcalá, 2016). Mothers were then interviewed about their initiative with household work and it was found that U.S. Mexican heritage children also helped more at home under their own initiative than European heritage children who helped more via contingent rewards and adult control (Alcalá et al., 2018). Interestingly, a group of U.S. Mexican heritage children from families with extensive experience in western school were similar to the other U.S. Mexican heritage children with initiative in household work by helping with initiative but like the European American group in not offering help during the classroom-like activity (Alcalá et al., 2018; López Fraire et al., 2018).

Brief tip: If we desire to see spontaneous help from children both in and out of school, we should respect their autonomy when they attempt to become involved in ongoing community activity. Allow children some leeway in activities to explore related issues, and allow children to take the lead in some activities.

Motivation in LOPI

The accounts of child autonomy in helping in Indigenous heritage communities where LOPI is common contrast with the narrative from middle-class parents about having to be "on top" of children to get them to help or participate in household work (Klein & Goodwin, 2013). Often the solutions middle-class parents reported resorting to in order to get children to participate mimicked school, and, in fact, many of the helping tasks that children in middle-class families were expected to do were similar to the exercise and drill work of school in important ways. Children's help at home in middle-class families was often relegated to small solitary tasks that did not seem central or important to children, such as washing one's dishes alone, making one's own bed alone, or putting away one's own clothes alone. Mejía-Arauz and colleagues (2015) argue that it is this separateness from others in household work that may lead to lower levels of initiative on the part of children, and that the communal aspect of work may be one of the most attractive things to children whose families practice LOPI.

Another important observation is that many of the helping tasks middle-class children were asked to do seemed to contribute very little to the well-being of the family or of others in the family. Parents in these families rarely talked about how their children knew that they (the parents) needed help, and thus children offered it freely. Instead parents often discussed how they turned to tools often used in school, such as calendars and chore charts, to motivate children into participating. The rewards used (stickers, happy faces, and gold stars) were also rewards frequently used by schools. There are therefore parallels between the solitary chores children were often asked to do at home and the solitary exercises they engaged in at school.

Additionally, just as small chores like putting away one's clothes are not central to the "work" of family and home, many of the exercises and drills children engage in at school are not central to the larger lessons and activities that we think children should learn on their way to full participation in community. Just as a child may not be able to see how making her bed is helping the family as a whole, she may not grasp the relationship that a geometry worksheet has to the task of building a doghouse, or the relationship that a grammar quiz has to writing a letter to an elected official. Leaving aside the question of whether exercises and worksheets are satisfying for children, it is the case that these are solitary activities, and much of the time in schools children are expected to engage in these activities on their own, neither receiving nor providing help that is similar to how children often engage in chores in middle-class families.

Brief tip: Rewarding children with small awards for simple practices or exercises does not seem to be related to continued involvement or investment in the activity. However, being involved in productive and legitimate community work with others *does* seem to be rewarding to children. By allowing children to build collaborative classrooms, we may see more cohesion in the classroom and investment in the activities they help design and to which they contribute.

Ideas for LOPI in Schools

We've reviewed research showing how children from families where LOPI was common were included in productive community work and how, as a result, studies found different patterns in the use of observation, attention, collaboration, talk, and in help with initiative compared to children whose middle-class families were more familiar with ALI. However, school in and of itself does not need to be based on an Assembly-Line model (Brown & Campione, 1990; Rogoff, Turkanis, & Bartlett, 2001). There are many ways, big and small, that practices congruent with LOPI can be incorporated into classrooms. Here we would like to suggest a few, although undoubtedly there are many others that teachers and administrators might suggest.

Our argument in this chapter has been that children are motivated to participate in what they see as meaningful activity and that engaging children in small exercises is not as motivating or rewarding. This is likely one of the biggest challenges in classrooms where instruction is often focused on small pieces of information that will build up to a bigger task, or to the bigger picture. However, it is also likely the case that bigger concepts and ideas are the ones that are more interesting to learners.

We think it is possible to keep an eye on bigger ideas and concepts and start from there, even if those ideas have to be adapted somewhat for the intended audience. However, by keeping things interesting in the classroom and allowing learners to see the big picture, they will likely be more motivated to participate. And as students engage in a larger task, or with a larger idea, they will learn the constituent parts. In Urrieta's (2013) example of Daniela making tortillas at the beginning of the chapter, Daniela was not necessarily interested in learning how to estimate the amount of dough needed to make a tortilla—she likely just wanted to learn to make a tortilla! She also was likely not interested in learning how hot the *comal* (griddle) needed to be, or in how long to leave the tortilla on the *comal* before turning it. But in the process, she very likely learned how to estimate the proper amount of dough, how to gauge the *comal*'s heat, and how to estimate how long to leave the tortilla—of course with some guidance. The same thing can be done in school. When people are involved in something they think is interesting or important, the details of the activity then become meaningful. In this way, children are still learning the constituent parts, but can also see the reason for learning the smaller details. Incorporating projects and portfolios that are evaluated in conjunction with student interviews is one way many educators have incorporated "the bigger picture" or larger themes into their classrooms (Rogoff et al., 2001). (See the chapter by Rosario-Ramos and Sawada for suggestions for having students take on meaningful real-world social issues as part of their classroom work.)

Of course, in order to engage in activities that children think are meaningful, we have to respect children's autonomy in learning. This is also a challenge in many schools, especially ones where the idea of standardization for all children is central. However, we think that within most lesson plans and curricula, it is possible to allow time and space for children to expand from the original plan to explore related themes and ideas that might be of interest to them. This can also be incorporated in a more formal way into the classroom by checking in with children and finding out their interests and how these could be incorporated into the planned instruction. (Of course the children would also need to be a part of these discussions and planning.) Just as the previous example with the toddlers participating in community work, respecting children's autonomy in the classroom does not mean that everything under the sun is fair game, rather that children's related, but not planned for, interests are respected.

Some nontraditional schools already evaluate children's efforts and contributions to ongoing tasks and to the setup of the task (as opposed to evaluating only end products) through dynamic assessment (Campione & Brown, 1987) and proximal formative assessment (Erickson, 2007). Rogoff and colleagues suggest that assessment of initiative would be a valuable addition to some of these other assessment practices, for example, by taking note of when children become fascinated by a new bit of information and take steps to investigate and find out more about it (Rogoff et al., 2015). The research on children's participation and helping at home in communities where LOPI is common suggest that acknowledging and allowing children to take the initiative in learning may lead to increased participation in learning overall. Although we have not studied this empirically we believe that children who might otherwise not be motivated to participate in traditional school might be more engaged as they see their contributions as valid and appreciated in the classroom.

Similarly, acknowledging children's initiative also means allowing them to observe one another and collaborate while they are engaged in work in the classroom even if that activity were intended to be individual work (which can still be graded as individual work if needed). Although this suggestion sounds modest, it may be difficult to incorporate due to the fact that collaboration may not be recognized as such in cases where children are working without using the kinds of verbal marker that are common to traditional classroom activity. However, we believe that making teachers and administrators aware of the cultural variability in collaboration may lead to increased recognition in schools and classrooms. Recognizing the forms of communication present in interaction when children are working together and building off one another's work and ideas is an important first step, but an equally important step is acknowledging how important this interaction with others is to learning over-all. This interaction and collaboration not only motivates many children to learn, but is also an important way that many children learn in community. Additionally, this interaction with others means being accepting of the variability that is inevitably present in any community of learners.

The idea of allowing children to participate is one that we have mentioned multiple times and is the one that we would like to emphasize as we end this chapter. In LOPI, children are allowed to participate even if their skill level would not be deemed to be "sufficiently competent" in certain areas. We would note that children become more competent in activity if they are allowed to par-ticipate in it; however, age-graded schooling is built on the assumption that there are skills that are only available to children once they have reached the appropri-ate level of maturity, the right age, or the right level of competence (Rogoff et al., 2005). This is counter to the idea that everyone can contribute, which is often seen in family and community activity where LOPI is common.

Perhaps one of the reasons for schools' persistent use of age gradation is due to its insistence on evaluating only end products to sort students rather than using evaluation as a way of providing feedback to move towards the comple-tion of a goal or activity (Rogoff et al., 2003). However returning again to the example of Daniela and the tortillas, assessment was present in the fact that her best tortillas were always placed on top and eaten first, which is different than being placed in a "lower" or remedial group due to skill level. This is a way of excluding learners who are not deemed competent enough. Assessment of efforts in LOPI is not done to exclude or restrict participation in the ongoing activity, but rather to provide guidance so the learner can continue to partici-pate and improve. In our current school system, we do not use assessment to encourage and improve participation. That does not mean that we cannot, but more work is needed in this area. One important step in this regard is acknowledging the variability present in all communities, and seeing it not as a hindrance but as an asset that can be useful as children work together. We believe that incorporating what we know from LOPI into classroom learning can help teachers and students work with one another to reach their goals and build a community of learners in the classroom.

References

Adair, J. K. (2015). "My teacher is going to think they're crazy": Responses to LOPI practices in U.S. first grade classrooms. *Advances in Child Development and Behavior, 49*, 341–379.

Alcalá, L., & Cervera, M. D. (2019) Yucatec Maya parental ethnotheories: Learning requires will and initiative. Manuscript submitted for publication.

Alcalá, L., Rogoff, B., & Fraire, A. L. (2018). Sophisticated collaboration is common among Mexican-heritage US children. *Proceedings of the National Academy of Sciences, 115*(45), 11377–11384.

Bransford, J., Brown, A., & Cocking, R. (1999). *How people learn: Brain, mind, experience and school*. Washington, DC: National Academies Press.

Brown, A. & Campione, J. (1990). Communities of learning and thinking, or a context by any other name. *Human Development, 21*, 108–126.

Campione, J. C. & Brown, A. L. (1987). Linking dynamic assessment with school achievement. In C. S. Lidz (Ed.) *Dynamic assessment* (82–115). New York: Guilford.

Cardoso, R. (2015). Learning and human dignity are built through observation and participation in work. *Advances in Child Development and Behavior, 49*, 289–302.

Chamoux, M. N. (2015). Conceptions of educational practices among the Nahuas of Mexico: Past and present. *Advances in Child Development and Behavior, 49*, 253–271.

Chamoux, M.-N. (1992). Aprendiendo de otro modo [Learning in another way]. In M.-N. Chamoux, *Trabajo, técnicas y aprendizaje en el México indígena* (73–93). Mexico City: Centro de Investigaciones y Estudios Superiores en Antropología Social, Ediciones de la Casa Chata.

Chavajay, P. (1993). Afterword: Independent analysis of cultural variations and similarities in San Pedro and Salt Lake. *Monographs of the Society for Research in Child Development, 58*(8, Serial no. 236), 162–165.

Chavajay, P. & Rogoff, B. (1999). Cultural variation in management of attention by children and their caregivers. *Developmental Psychology, 35*(4), 1079.

Coppens, A. D., Alcalá, L., Mejía-Arauz, R., & Rogoff, B. (2014). Children's initiative in family household work in Mexico. *Human Development, 57*(2–3), 116–130.

Coppens, A. D. & Rogoff, B. (2017a, April). Divergent trajectories of children's prosocial helping across cultural communities. Society for Research in Child Development Biennial Meeting. Austin, TX.

Coppens, A. D. & Rogoff, B. (2017b, April). Socialization practices and cultural values guide divergent trajectories of prosocial helping. Society for Research in Child Development Biennial Meeting. Austin, TX.

Correa-Chávez, M. (2016). Patterns of collaboration and communication while working together among U.S. Mexican heritage sibling pairs. *Journal of Learning, Culture, and Social Interaction, 11*, 130–141.

Correa-Chávez, M., Mangione, H. F., & Mejia-Arauz, R. (2016). Collaboration patterns among Mexican children in an Indigenous town and Mexican City. *Journal of Applied Developmental Psychology, 44*, 105–113.

Correa-Chávez, M., Mejía-Arauz, R., and Rogoff, B. (Eds.) (2015). Children learn by observing and contributing to family and community endeavors. *Advances in Child Development and Behavior, 49*, 303–313.

Correa-Chávez, M. & Rogoff, B. (2009). Children's attention to interactions directed to others: Guatemalan Mayan and European-American patterns. *Developmental Psychology, 45*, 630–641.

Correa-Chávez, M., Rogoff, B., & Mejía-Arauz, R. (2005). Cultural patterns in attending to two events at once. *Child Development, 76*, 664–678.

de Haan, M. (2001). Intersubjectivity in models of learning and teaching: Reflections from a study of teaching and learning in a Mexican Mazahua community. In S. Chaiklin (Ed.) *The theory and practice of cultural-historical psychology* (174–199). Aarhus: Aarhus University Press.

de Haan, M. (1999). *Learning as cultural practice: How children learn in a Mexican Mazahua community.* Amsterdam: Thela Thesis.

Dixon S. D., LeVine R. A., Richman A., & Brazelton T. B. (1984). Mother–child interaction around a teaching task: An African-American comparison. *Child Development, 55*, 1252–1264.

Erickson, F. (2007). Some thoughts on "proximal" formative assessment of student learning. In P. Moss (Ed.) *Evidence and decision-making in education* (186–216). Chicago, IL: National Society for the Study of Education.

Flores, R., Urrieta, L., Chamoux, M. N., Lorente Fernandez, D., & López, A. (2015). Using history to analyze the Learning by Observing and Pitching In (LOPI) practices of contemporary Mesoamerican societies. *Advances in Child Development and Behavior, 49*, 314–340.

Garcia, F. A. (2015). Respect and autonomy in children's observation and participation in adults' activities. *Advances in Child Development and Behavior, 49*, 137–153.

Gaskins, S. (2000). Children's daily activities in a Mayan village. *Cross-Cultural Research, 34*, 375–389.

González, N., Moll, L., & Amantí, C. (2005). *Funds of knowledge: Theorizing practices in households, communities, and classrooms.* Mahwah, NJ: Lawrence Erlbaum.

Hart, B. & Risley, T. (1995). *Meaningful differences in the everyday experience of young American children.* Baltimore, MA: P.H. Brookes.

Kim, H. S. (2002). We talk therefore we think? A cultural analysis of the effect of talking on thinking. *Journal of Personality and Social Psychology, 83*(4), 828–842.

Klein, W. & Goodwin, M. (2013). Chores. In E. Ochs and T. Kremer-Sadlik, *Fast forward family* (11–129). Berkeley: University of California Press.

López, A., Correa-Chávez, M., Rogoff, B., & Gutiérrez, K. (2010). Attention to instruction directed to another by U.S. Mexican-heritage children of varying cultural backgrounds. *Developmental Psychology, 46*(3), 593–601.

López, A., Najafi, B., Rogoff, B., & Mejía-Arauz, R. (2012). Collaboration and helpfulness as cultural practices. In J. Valsiner (Ed.) *The Oxford handbook of culture and psychology* (869–884). New York: Oxford University Press.

López, A. & Rogoff, B. (2016, April). Attentive helping as a cultural practice. Presented at the Western Psychological Association Meeting, Long Beach, CA.

López, A., Rogoff, B., & Alcalá, L. (2016, April). Attentive helping as a cultural practice. Presented at the Western Psychological Association Meeting, Long Beach, CA.

Martínez-Pérez, M. (2015). Adults' orientation of children – and children's initiative to pitch in – to everyday adult activities in a Tsotsil Maya Community. *Advances in Child Development and Behavior, 49,* 113–135.

Maynard, A. E. (2004). Cultures of teaching in childhood: Formal schooling and Maya sibling teaching at home. *Cognitive Development, 19,* 517–535.

Matusov, E., Bell, N., & Rogoff, B. (2002). Schooling as cultural process: Shared thinking and guidance by children from schools differing in collaborative practices. *Advances in Child Development and Behavior, 29,* 129–160.

Mejía-Arauz, R. Correa-Chávez, M. Keyser-Ohrt, U., & Aceves-Azuara, I. (2015). Collaborative work or individual chores: The role of family social organization in children's learning to collaborate and develop initiative. *Advances in Child Development and Behavior, 49,* 25–51.

Mejía-Arauz, R., Rogoff, B., Dexter, A., & Najafi, B. (2007). Cultural variation in children's social organization. *Child Development, 78*(3), 1001–1014.

Mejía-Arauz, R., Rogoff, B., & Paradise, R. (2005). Cultural variation in children's observation during a demonstration. *International Journal of Behavioral Development,29,* 282–291.

Morelli, G., Rogoff, B., & Angelillo, C. (2003). Cultural variation in children's access to work or involvement in specialized child-focused activities. *International Journal of Behavioral Development, 27,* 264–274.

Mosier, C. E., & Rogoff, B. (2003). Privileged treatment of toddlers: cultural aspects of individual choice and responsibility. *Developmental Psychology, 39*(6), 1047.

Orellana, M. F. (2001). The work kids do: Mexican and Central American immigrant children's contributions to households and schools in California. *Harvard Educational Review, 71*(3), 366–389.

Paradise, R., Mejía-Arauz, R., Silva, K. G., Dexter, A. L., & Rogoff, B. (2014). One, two, three, eyes on me! Adults attempting control versus guiding in support of initiative. *Human Development, 57*(2–3), 131–149.

Ramírez Sánchez, M. A. (2007). "Helping at home": The concept of childhood and work among the Nahuas of Tlaxcala, Mexico. In B. Hungerland, M. Liebel, B. Milne, & A. Wihstutz, *Working to be someone: Child focused research and practice with working children* (87–95). London: Jessica Kingsley Publishers.

Rogoff, B., Correa-Chávez, M., & Navichoc-Cotuc, M. (2005). A cultural-historical view of schooling in human development. In D. Pillemer & S. H. White (Eds.) *Developmental psychology and social change* (225–263). New York: Cambridge University Press

Rogoff, B., Mejía-Arauz, R., & Correa-Chávez, M. (2015). A cultural paradigm – Leaning by Observing and Pitching In. *Advances in Child Development and Behavior, 49,* 1–18.

Rogoff, B., Mistry, J., Göncü, A., & Mosier, C. (1993). Guided participation in cultural activity by toddlers and caregivers. *Monographs for the Society for Research and Child Development, 58* (Serial No. 236).

Rogoff, B., Paradise, R., Mejía-Arauz, R., Correa-Chávez, M., & Angelillo, C. (2003). Firsthand learning through intent participation. *Annual Review of Psychology, 54,* 175–203.

Rogoff, B., Turkanis, C.G., & Bartlett, L. (2001). *Learning together: Children and adults in a school community.* Oxford: Oxford University Press.

Ruvalcaba, O. & Rogoff, B. (2016, April). Cultural differences in children's pair collaboration: Engaging fluidly versus managing individual agendas in a computer programming activity. Presented at the Western Psychological Association Meeting, Long Beach, CA.

Ruvalcaba, O., Rogoff, B., López, A., Correa-Chávez, M., & Gutierrez, K. (2015). Children's avoidance of interrupting others' activities in requesting help: Cultural aspects of considerateness. *Advances in Child Development and Behavior, 49*, 187–206.

Silva, K., Correa-Chávez, M., & Rogoff, B. (2010). Cultural variation in children's attention and learning in events not directed at them: Patterns in a U.S. Mexican community. *Child Development, 81*(3), 898–921.

Urrieta, L. (2013). Familia and comunidad-based saberes: Learning in an Indigenous heritage community. *Anthropology & Education Quarterly, 44*(3), 320–335.

2

SEEING TOGETHER: THE ECOLOGICAL KNOWLEDGE OF INDIGENOUS FAMILIES IN CHICAGO URBAN FOREST WALKS

Ananda M. Marin

Education researchers interested in improving science teaching and learning have increasingly focused their inquiries on understanding learning in informal or everyday contexts and potential relationships with scientific knowledge (e.g., Bang et al., 2015; Bell et al., 2012; Brayboy & Castagno, 2008; Marin & Bang, 2018; Medin & Bang, 2014; Warren et al., 2001). Along with others, I have argued that learning about/with the natural world is a cultural process embedded within everyday human activity (e.g., Cajete, 2000; Deloria & Wildcat, 2001) and that it is central to scientific endeavors, as well as science education (NRC 2007, 2012). Basic research on orientations to the natural world and associated knowledge building practices can support the design of teaching practices and learning environments for science education, particularly place- and field-based science education.

In 2005, I was invited to participate in a community-university research project that came to be named Living in Relationships (LiR). This ten-plus year collaborative research program began as a partnership between the American Indian Center of Chicago (AIC), Menominee Tribe of Wisconsin, and Northwestern University; later the University of Washington joined. Understanding nature–culture relations across learning contexts was a goal of the project. We also considered how science, a discipline with a fraught history among Indigenous and other minoritized communities, might be used to support community well-being and sustainable futures grounded in Indigenous ways of knowing and being (e.g., Bang et al., 2013).

In pursuit of the goals outlined above, the LiR team engaged in three lines of research: (a) studies of culture and cognition, (b) studies of everyday practices, and (c) community-based design research. For example, children and parents were asked to participate in a variety of research-based activities including card sorting tasks, diorama play, and picture book reading. To study everyday practices, adults and families were interviewed about their experiences with a range of outdoor activities (fishing, hunting, berry picking, etc.). These activities were designed to explore cross-cultural variation in the development of beliefs about biological concepts and we intentionally invited a diverse group of children and parents to participate, including Native American parents. In addition, Menominee tribal members and community members at the American Indian Center of Chicago were invited to participate in community-based design research (CBDR) projects that were place based and unique to the local context and history of each site. At its heart, CBDR locates community members as decision makers in the design of teaching and learning environments (Marin & Bang, 2015). In addition, CBDR is driven by iterative stages of curriculum design, enactment, and refinement, with the aim of building theory. Broadening who participates in research is not trivial and, as many scholars have noted, the success of such efforts is connected to community-based accountability and a commitment to the 4 Rs—relationality, responsibility, respect, and reciprocity (Brayboy et al., 2012; McCarty & Lee, 2014). Moreover, increasing diversity in research endeavors can deepen our understanding of human potential and foster new forms of teaching and learning relationships that are emancipatory (Medin et al., 2017). I see LiR as one project where those involved actively worked toward this larger research agenda.

I first joined the project in the role of community designer, working with other members of the American Indian Center to develop a science curriculum that bridged Native and western scientific ways of knowing. I later took on the role of teacher, researcher, and coach. Over a ten-year period, we designed and implemented an out-of-school, community-based science education program, which came to be known as Urban Explorers. Throughout this process, we continually asked questions about pervasive discourses of settler colonialism—past, present, and future—that produce stories of urban Indigenous peoples as culturally deficient and without ties to land. As a team, we consciously named urban places as the homelands of Indigenous peoples with histories before colonialism (Bang et al., 2014). We also re-membered Chicago, present day and throughout history, as a gathering place for tribes, and as a part of the ancestral homelands of many tribes including the Pottawatomi, Ojibwe, Odawa, Miami, Ho-Chunk, Menominee, and Illinois (Yousef, 2012).

The curricular content of the Urban Explorers program focused on local Chicago ecosystems including tallgrass prairies and wetlands as well as savanna and woodland communities. Teachers and designers in the program regularly talked about Chicago as an urban forest. In addition to the trees and plant communities in Chicago neighborhoods, there are forests throughout the city. These forests, now known as forest preserves, are unceded Pottawatomi territory. The forest preserve system in Chicago was our classroom and lessons were organized around the big idea of living in relationships.

Walking-based activities (e.g., neighborhood walks, forest walks, scavenger hunts) became a foundational component of the program and, over the course of the project, community designers developed what my colleagues and I call a *pedagogy of walking*. For example, mini-lessons on plant biology and food webs were delivered on neighborhood walks. Family Science Days, in which families learned how to identify plants while on guided walks in a local forest preserve, became a regular activity. Topics such as erosion, soil quality, and animal habitats were also explored. The design of the family days was informed by our basic research on orientations to the natural world, as well as our engagements with iterative cycles of curriculum design. During curricular design cycles, we recorded both planning sessions and program implementation. We then reviewed these records to progressively refine and develop pedagogical practices and models.

My desire to better understand the role of attention, observation, and walking in learning about/with the natural world motivated the design of a video-ethnographic study that more closely examined the embodied and discursive resources families used in urban forest walks. Analysis of videos from families' forest walks provided a grounding to expand on accounts of walking, reading, and storying land as a practice for learning about/with the natural world. In this chapter, I describe the practice of walking, reading, and storying land and contribute to ongoing discussions that recognize and demonstrate the cultural nature of scientific practices. In addition, I share examples that may be useful to developing teaching and learning models for field-based science education in schools. I begin by briefly discussing research on nature–culture relations and the methods used in the video-ethnographic study shared in this chapter. I then describe practices associated with walking, reading, and storying land and use transcript from one family's walk as illustrative examples, considering the role of temporality, place, and movement for learning about/with the natural world. Although I am authoring this piece, the work reflects a collective effort and the ideas in this chapter grew out of long-term relationships and ongoing conversations.

Researching Nature–Culture Relations

Making and defining relationships between the natural world and cultural worlds (typically meaning human worlds), or nature–culture relations for short, grounds much of human activity as well as practices in social and scientific domains. How we as humans perceive our place and role in relation to more-than-human beings, or the degree to which we see ourselves as being a part of or apart from the natural world, varies by participation in cultural communities and influences the moment to moment unfolding of everyday and scientific activity. For example, cross-cultural research in psychology and the learning sciences has demonstrated a tendency in Indigenous communities to organize knowledge in ecological frameworks where lifecycles and seasonal cycles are privileged over taxonomies (Medin et al., 2010). Variation also exists in the degree to which cultural communities view entities such as plants, rocks, and water as agentic in their own right (ojalehto, Medin, & García, 2017). Importantly, ways of knowing and being in relation to the natural world have consequences for the decisions we make regarding ecological and social environments. Moreover, core beliefs about nature–culture relations are firmly embedded in most learning environments and structure how children and teachers are to imagine, know, study, and make meaning of relations between the natural world (e.g., organisms and phenomena of all kinds as well as their interrelationships) and cultural forms of life (e.g., ways of thinking and acting that organize human communities).

What can video ethnographic studies of family interactions in everyday, outdoor learning contexts (berry picking, fishing, forest walks, etc.) tell us about the multitude of ways that people go about making relations, or teaching and learning, about/with the natural world? What insights can we gain about learning by focusing on the organization of talk, action, and embodied movement in these learning environments? These questions have motivated what I research and how I go about research. I have intentionally designed research tasks and established research partnerships to better understand questions about nature–culture relations in out-of-school settings. American Indian youth attending schools in urban areas are often the only Native student in their classroom. Out-of-school settings, including community centers, are a place where Native youth are able to gather and create collaborative and intergenerational learning spaces (an arrangement common in many Indigenous communities) (Rogoff, 2014; see also Correa-Chávez and Fraire-López, this volume). Studying teaching and learning in these spaces is especially important given the assimilative nature of schooling within Indigenous communities. At the same time, working with teachers to create meaningful relationships with Native students, families, and communities is important for transforming power dynamics and structural inequities. Along with my colleagues, I have also partnered with teachers in community and school settings to design learning environments that cultivate forms of nature–culture relations that ground relationality as a principal way of being, knowing, and doing. The degree to which school practices and community practices are incommensurable is a question that we continually return to, as well as the worry that schools may unintentionally adopt community-based instructional practices in ways that are experienced and felt as epistemologically violent.

In this chapter, I work to make visible the micro-interactional practices that Indigenous families, living in urban contexts, use to collaboratively learn about and make relations with the natural world. I asked three Native American mothers and their sons (aged four to eight) to go on a series of summer-fall walks in forest preserves within the city of Chicago (Marin, 2013). The majority of walks were dyadic (focal child and caregiver), however, other family members sometimes went along. A corresponding number of non-Native families also went on walks.

Each walk lasted from 30 minutes to one hour and children were given digital cameras and asked to photograph whatever interested them. Participants also recorded themselves using small wearable cameras, capturing their experiences while walking. This method aligns with ethnomethodological approaches (Stevens, 2010) and what Lahlou (2011) calls subjective evidence-based ethnography (SEBE). SEBE affords opportunities to understand how participants orient their "sensory systems to the environment" (p. 617). This method is just one way of presencing how Indigenous families, living in urban contexts, collaboratively learn about and make relations with the natural world. I have found video-ethnography helpful in producing "viable images" of the everyday experiences of Indigenous families (Brayboy, 2005). For me, this has been especially important, given that research practices habitually erase current day teaching and learning experiences among Indigenous peoples.

A Note about Data Collection Procedures

Since I am interested in how people use their whole bodies to coordinate attention in order to collaboratively build knowledge, it is important to note that the cameras, which were worn on a shoulder mount, did not capture what participants saw at eye level, but rather what they bodily oriented to; capturing the scene and what, specifically, the shoulder and torso were turned towards. This camera position foregrounded the movement of the whole body, allowing me to better understand the multi-modal resources families used and the role of bodily positioning in the coordination of activity.

The parent and child video from each walk was merged and stacked horizontally to create a single video file with a side-by-side view of the child's and parent's perspectives. This view allowed me to think about how children and parents were physically orienting to one another as well as the environment. (See Marin, 2013 for further discussion.) Both the use of wearable cameras and the syncing of video provided a view of the dynamic interaction between peoples and places and an opportunity to examine nature–culture relations in action. In other words, these procedures linked human–nature interactions and human–culture interactions and afforded exploration of the role of place in learning (Tuck & McKenzie, 2015) and how learning in and with the natural world takes shape in cultural ecologies (Gutiérrez & Rogoff, 2003; Lee, 2008; Medin & Bang, 2014). As a research team, we repeatedly viewed video from forest walks and reviewed transcript. We also drew on Indigenous and socio-cultural theory as a lens through which to view video. We identified routine micro-interactional practices (e.g., asking questions, using directives, shifting one's bodily position and movements) that youth and adults engaged to build action while walking, reading, and storying land (WRSL).

Walking, Reading, and Storying Land

WRSL is a methodology for learning about the natural world that has been embedded within Indigenous ways of knowing for generations (Cajete, 2000; Kawagley, 2006) and continues to shape lived human–nature relations. At that same time, I recognize that this is a methodology that has evolved over socio-historic time and varies in importance and influence on action across cultural communities. For example, Magntorn and Helldén (2005) proposed the concept of reading nature or the "ability to go out into an ecosystem and recognize organisms, understand processes taking place and to see the human impact in the particular ecosystem is complex" (p. 1230) as way of developing knowledge about the environment. Although aligned with this view WRSL reflects different substrates about the capacities of more-than-human life as well as beliefs about how to be in relations with land and the more-than-human world. Borrowing from the work of Chuck Goodwin (2018), I take substrate to be those publicly available resources that people use to build action together. These resources may be ideas, material items, or fleeting movements (gestures, bodily turns) that are constructed in the moment or those things that have been constructed over time by our predecessors. For example, in many Native communities, relational frameworks are privileged. Such frameworks take into account multiple perspectives, ecocentric prototypes for agency (i.e., extend agency to more-than-humans), and interdependencies (ojalehto, Waxman, & Medin, 2013). As the cases I will share demonstrate, these orientations impact how practices of walking, reading, and storying land unfold. For example, perspective taking and relationships with more-than-human beings can be a kind of substrate that opens up new lines of investigations and possible explanations for what is observed in the perceptual field.

At its core, WRSL is an ambulatory, place-based, and temporal practice: guided by the experience of our feet, and thus our bodies, meeting and being in motion with the ground over time. Elsewhere, I have described walking, reading, and storying land as being comprised of at least three dimensions: coordinating attention and observing, generating explanations, and finding evidence (Marin & Bang, 2018). The dimensions of WRSL – attending and observing, creating explanations, and finding evidence – are situated within particular contexts and locations. The explanations or stories that are formulated are specific to particular ecosystems and landscapes. The work of WRSL is distributed across people, more-than-humans (MTHs), place, and time. In other words, the knowledge that people build is dependent upon interactions with place and MTHs. These kinds of interactions are organized by our theories of the agency and capabilities of MTH. In addition, the activity of WRSL is structured by sedimented resources including: material tools that have been passed down across generations (compasses, field guides, trail markers); artifacts created by MTHs (deer trails, dens, etc.); and discursive tools (ways of asking questions, storying, and conversing). In addition, WRSL, as a practice that works toward socioecological justice, involves an element of historicity—knowing the histories of land and peoples that have resulted in current systems of powered relations.

Micro-practices that Support Walking, Reading, and Storying the Land

Repeatedly viewing video of forest walks foregrounded the role of land in coordinating attention and observation. The structure of family's walks, including ways that parents and children moved and aligned their bodies in order to organize their interactions, was influenced by the environment. The very contours of the land played a role in how families coordinated attention (the orientation of bodies to one another, land, and other MTH), what families attended to and observed, and where they looked for evidence to support their explanations. In addition, the MTHs that were present shaped the content of talk and joint inquiries. For example, the sound of rustling leaves led families to look for chipmunks and develop stories about the chipmunks' movement throughout the forest.

Families used discursive and embodied micro-practices (question asking, issuing directives, pointing gestures, and shifts in movement) to coordinate attention and observation, develop explanations about observations of the natural world, and find evidence for those explanations. Parents and children wove together multiple forms of questions, directives, and shifts in movement to:

- Make entities, phenomena, beliefs, and thought processes visible. This supported the coordination of attention by highlighting what was available for observation in the perceptual field (auditory, visual, kinesthetic) and what might be observable on the horizon. Making thought processes and observations visible to another also created opportunities for carrying out investigations, analyzing and interpreting data, generating explanations and finding evidence—all important science practices identified by NGSS.
- Establish oneself as a leader or knower, capable of making meaningful contributions. These positionings created an ecology for collaborative learning and supported science-related identities.
- Mark and remember places of importance, thus shaping possibilities for future joint inquiries. As families returned to the locations, memories of place served as guideposts for their inquiries and the routes they took. From viewing recordings of families' second and third walks, it became obvious that the recall of memories, at least in this context, was both an embodied and an emplaced activity.

- Engage in imaginative perspective taking to hypothesize about the lives of MTHs and relations with MTHs. This was often supported by the telling of micro-stories or small stories (Georgakopoulou, 2006; see also Enciso, this volume). Micro-stories were no more than four to five sentences in length and reported ongoing observations of phenomena or hypotheses around possible future observations.

In the next sections, I present transcript excerpts and snapshots from one family's video of their second and third walks. The selected excerpts show how parents and children use questions (e.g., "You see the chipmunk?" "How do you know?") and directives (e.g., lookit, come here, move closer, etc.) to make an entity in the environment observable for another and then create explanations or stories of observed phenomena. In addition, they illustrate how inquiry about particular MTH kinds extends across walks to include new participants and additional explanations about biological properties and physical processes. Importantly, the son and mom disagree about explanations on more than one occasion. Disagreements gave rise to questions about what is known and how one knows something. These kinds of questions supported the coordination of attention between people and place. In addition, at least in this case, questions about knowing helped to position both mom and child as contributors.

The Meadows Family

The Meadows family went on five walks between the end of July and the end of October. The focal participants include the mother, Jackie and her son Jason (six and a half years old). Jason's father went on two walks and his younger brother (four years old) went on three. The family has some experience with forest walks, however, they had little prior experience with this particular location. I share excerpts from transcripts of the second and third walks. In the second walk, I focus on two key exchanges 1) retracing the steps of a deer and 2) simultaneously observing chipmunks and a fallen over tree. The third walk illustrates how families' everyday science investigations span time and place. The transcript highlights families' talk and action as they revisit a fallen tree.

The Second Walk

In mid-September the family went on their second walk. On their first walk, the river that runs through the forest preserve had overflowed the bank and a large portion of land under the forest canopy was covered by water. By their second walk, the river had receded, and Jason and Jackie collaboratively made sense of their changing perceptions of the landscape, commenting on the difference in the temperature, and land that was no longer under water.

Retracing the Steps of a Deer

About nine minutes into their walk, Jason came upon what he believed was a deer trail. The trail ran along the river and Jason, who was in the lead position, followed this path. The decision to follow the deer trail and resultant actions were made possible and sustained by a series of questions, imaginative perspective taking, and directives. When Jason suggested that they make their way by following a deer trail, his mom requested that he explain how he knew that what they were seeing were deer trails. As they followed the deer trails, Jason first engaged in imaginative perspective taking ("walk like a deer"), then narrated a micro-story about his observations, and called his mom into this MTH interaction by using a directive to make his thinking visible to her. Transcript from Jason's and Jackie's cameras are shared below.

Turn	Speaker	Utterance	Micro-practice
1	Jackie:	("laughs") I don't think there's any more trail left (0.02)	Mom makes her own thinking visible
2	Jason:	no there's a deer trail right here	Son disagrees and puts a counter claim on the table
3	Jackie:	That's a deer trail?	Mom questions the son's claim
4	Jason:	[yea, I can]	
5	Jackie:	[but] how do you know?	Follow-up question, requesting that the son make his thinking visible
6	Jason:	because!	
7	Jackie:	ouch	
8	Jason:	because, I know what Tyler does retracing the steps (.) of a deer trail (.) deer, deers take dis, walk like a deer (0.02) they make trails by wa, walking	Draws on prior experience in the Urban Explorers program
10	Jackie:	O: (0.02)	
11	Jason:	They mu, the deer mu (0.02) The deer musta crossed here	Tells as micro-story to create an explanation for observations
12	Jackie:	m:h:?(0.03)	
13	Jason:	but then they got stuck (0.03) this a, this musta been, like a long time ago when it's flooded, because lookit, there's a deer trail in the river	Micro-story Son uses a directive, making his thinking visible
14	Jackie:	heh heh (0.01)	

(Continued)

(Cont.)

Turn	Speaker	Utterance	Micro-practice
		ya think those are deer trails in there?	Mom asks a question, requesting the son make his thinking visible
15	Jason:	Yahh	
16	Jackie:	m:. I think it just might be ss like, uh:m:, like holes Holes in the (0.1) the riverbed. (0.02) (11 min and 36 seconds into the walk)	

The path that Jason and Jackie had been walking along took them right up to the river. Jason believed that the holes he could see at the bottom of the riverbed had been made by deer who have crossed the river. Jackie suggests that they might just be holes. Following this discussion, Jason suggested that they continue on. Jackie responded by saying: "If this was like a little tiny stream we could try to cross it but this is too big right now." Jason was eager to cross the body of water and suggested that the river could turn into a stream further up. His mom once again used epistemic language and said: "You don't know, it may or it may just stay a river." At this point, Jason turned back to look at his mother saying: "Well, there's only one way to find out." Jackie agreed to keep going and Jason again took on the perspective of the deer saying, "a deer would gone this way ... well this a trail ... the deer musta walked through here." On this new path, the family looked once again for tracks. Jackie, in tune with Jason's interests, used a directive to point at a track for Jason to look at: "Comear I wanna show you something. Look at these ones." Excited by this discovery, Jason exclaimed, "O, those are deer ... that's deer," and bent down to take a picture. Jason suggested that these tracks looked like the same tracks he found earlier. Jackie again asked an epistemic question: "How come we di, we didn't notice this going down there?" and then suggested that maybe they had "went a different way." Jason offered an alternative explanation—that what they were noticing were not tracks they had missed before but fresh tracks. In response Jason, like his mother, used an epistemic question ("Because ya know how you can tell?"), creating a conversational space for evidential reasoning. As Jason asked this question, he stopped walking. His mom responded by asking "How?" This created an opportunity for Jason to provide evidence for his claim. ("Yea they're fresh because the dirt's still wet.")

This exchange highlights two important aspects of micro-practices used to engage walking, reading, and storying the land that offer lessons for classrooms.

First, it shows how questions might be used to support collaborative meaning making. Mom, as the teacher, supported Jason as knower and contributor by meeting his question with a question. I see this as an instance of epistemic navigation and openness where both mom and son were able to make their thinking visible to another and explore multiple explanations (Marin & Bang, 2018; Vossoughi, 2014). Second, the excerpt foregrounds the role of the body in learning. I would suggest that Jason's shift in movement acted like a pause, giving extra emphasis to his question, and indicating that this was a line of thought he would like to collectively pursue. Jackie and Jason used their whole bodies as communicative tools (Ma, 2017) as they engaged in field-based science practices (question asking, model development, etc.) and learned together while on the move (Taylor & Hall, 2013). In many classrooms, learning activities to promote scientific reasoning occur in arrangements where students are seated, usually at desks, and in configurations where the focus is at the front of the classroom on the teacher. In this example, Jason's freedom to use his whole body, rather than just his eyes, to guide his attention supports joint meaning making in the moment and over time. The use of movement and the whole body to direct and coordinate attention is also evident in the next example.

Hunting for Chipmunks and the "Humongous Tree that Fell out of the Ground"

Further down the trail, Jason observed and then followed chipmunks. Soon he noticed that a "big tree" had fallen down. He paused, and moved closer, exclaiming "that humongous tree fell out of the ground. You have to see this mom. Lookit, it's like a coyote den." Again, Jason used discursive resources in the form of directives (lookit) and embodied resources (shifts in movement) to request his mom's attention. His excitement about the possibility of animals living in the tree was clear. As he squatted down, presumably to get a better look, he declared: "I think things are living in there. I see eyes!" At this point, Jackie used a question and directives to direct Jason's attention to a chipmunk that was nearby. ("You see the chipmunk? (0.03) There see, stay still. Lookit he's got something in his mouth.") Jackie and Jason alternated their attention between the chipmunk and the tree. In this back and forth exchange, Jackie made a subtle move and elevated a MTH frame (she said: "he's waiting for ya not to pay attention (laughs)"). Their attention then shifted to jointly focus on the tree. Jason remained focused on the tree, reiterating that his mom should not go near it. Jackie responded to Jason by asking what he thought happened to the tree. This request of Jason to make his thinking visible opened an opportunity to develop an explanation. Jason suggested that lightning hit the tree, causing it to fall over. Jackie agreed and then immediately offered an alternative explanation "yea, sometimes, trees though, they fall over like that."

Jason continued to develop an explanation that was centered around lightning. In response Jackie again repeated her alternative explanation, offering additional supporting information: "No, but I mean, when a tree gets diseased, or when a tree dies, then it'll just fall over like that." In this, Jackie disagreed with Jason ("No") and simultaneously clarified her own thinking ("but I mean"), building on her earlier explanation. With this clarification, Jason accepted his mom's explanation saying, "Ah, so it must have just died." Jackie extended the conversation and introduced new information about the lifecycle of the tree:

JACKIE: No but I mean, when a tree gets diseased, or when a tree dies, then it'll just fall over like that
JASON: Ah, so it must've just died
JACKIE: Then it'll get turned to compost and fertilize new trees
JASON: yea, that's the life cycle

With this, Jason moved on to talk about the path they were on.

In this interaction, there are several notable exchanges. We again see Jason using his whole body to direct the activity and investigate his observations. When he squatted down to look at the tree, he effectively paused their movement. The space between Jason, his mom, and the tree became a place to investigate relationships with MTHs. Jackie indexed the chipmunk as a co-observer, effectively recognizing the chipmunk's agency. She also used epistemic language to make her thinking visible and to support joint hypothesizing about what happened to the tree. The two disagreed with each other at least once. In this case, voicing disagreement was generative and created an opportunity to explore multiple explanations. I understand this disagreement as a form of epistemic openness.

The Family's Third Walk: Revisiting the "Humongous Tree that Fell out of the Ground"

After six days, the family went on a third walk, this time joined by Jason's younger brother Andrew. Talk about animals living in the humongous tree that fell over continued. Remembering the path, Jason stated: "we had walked this way. We're kinda, we're retracing our steps Mom." Shortly after this, Andrew screamed "monster" as he pointed at the tree with a stick—the very tree that Jackie and Jason discussed on their previous walk. Jason explained that the tree was not a monster, but cautioned Andrew not get too close because there were glowing eyes inside.

JASON: Ah, that's not a monster.
ANDREW: What is it?
JASON: It's a dead tree.

ANDREW: It's a dead tree?

JASON: Yes.

ANDREW: I never saw a dead tree.

JASON: Yeah don't go too close. I see like, the- there like glowing eyes in there sometimes Or it might just be the sun.

At this point, Jackie entered the conversation asking Jason if he knew what erosion means. Jason responded with a question "What is erosion mean?" This move, rather than simply saying "I don't know," seemed to allow Jason to maintain his position as knower and gain useful information. In response, Jackie defined the term erosion and provided an explanation for their shared observation. The transcript follows.

Turn	Speaker	Utterance	Micro-Practice
1	Jackie:	Jason, do you know what erosion means?	Question to make thinking visible
2	Jason:	What is erosion mean?	Question to elicit information and maintain position as a knower
3	Jackie:	Erosion? It's like when ah, things wash away	Defining a science term
4	Andrew:	Batter up	
5	Jackie:	you know like when you're at the beach	
6	Jason:	Yeah	
7	Jackie:	and stand by the edge and the sand kinda washes away	
8	Jason:	Yeah	
9	Jackie:	Well this tree probably fell over because the soil, er ah, the [soil erosion. And maybe like the roots came up and it was too heavy and a big wind came and blew it over]	Micro-story providing an explanation for their shared observation
10	Andrew:	[((hitting a can with a stick))]	
11	Jackie:	Leave it alone ↑	
12	Andrew:	another soda can	
13	Jackie:	and then it just toppled over!	
14	Andrew:	I don't see anything (inaudible)	
15	Jason:	We should first check with the stick. Something, came out, maybe. Don't get to, that close	
16	Andrew:	Hello? Hello?	

(Continued)

(Cont.)

Turn	Speaker	Utterance	Micro-Practice
17	Jackie:	When you say that, do you think some-thing's going to answer you? ((laughter))	
18	Jason:	Nothing's in there, guess I was wrong. Maybe, it just a illusion, that I was seeing	
19	Jackie:	Some people say that like animals, they a, they'll understand, like um, if you speak in Annishnabe, so maybe you should be saying "bozhoo"	
20	Jason:	Bozhoo?	
21	Jackie:	Mm hm	

Here, we again see the question-question form. Jason responds to Jackie's question with a question. As in the second walk, this form of talk-in-interaction allowed Jason to gain information while simultaneously maintaining his position as knower and contributor. We also see Jackie telling a micro-story, or reporting on her developing explanation of past events. Jackie explicitly named and mobilized Anishinabe language as a resource, both for sensemaking, and as an identity frame (Nasir, 2011). Further, the temporality marked by the introduction of Indigenous language functioned to presence Indigenous identities. Mom did not historicize Indigenous ways of knowing; for example, she did not say "some people used to say …" and she used the word speak instead of spoke. Moreover, she oriented to the future (e.g., "you should be saying"). This shift signaled that there may be a different mode, or in this case, language for inquiry.

Studies of Walking, Reading, and Storying and Possibilities for Schools

The analyses made possible by the use of wearable cameras can support praxis-based approaches to the design of teaching and learning contexts. LiR community designers and teachers regularly held planning meetings where conversations focused on the kinds of analysis shared in this chapter. These meetings supported our joint reflection on the unfolding of action as teachers and youth collectively built knowledge about/with the natural world. For example, we delved into the role of stories in STEM education (Marin & Bang, 2015) and explored how we might ask questions in new ways to better support the coordination of attention and observation. We regularly shared findings at a locally organized community research conference and at academic conferences. As we reported on findings and used video cases in spaces outside of the community center we became increasingly sensitive to the various kinds of lenses researchers might bring to bear as they make sense of how youth of color, particularly Native American youth, are engaging in activities. Although this work is powerful, from an equity perspective, it is imperative to be cognizant of what political and social relations are captured and perhaps reinscribed within the frame, what is left out of the frame, and the differing perspectives that may develop as a result. (See Vossoughi & Escudé, 2016.)

In this chapter, I have identified particular aspects of walking, reading, and storying land within the larger practice of forest walks. Specifically, my analysis examined how micro-interactional resources in the moment-to-moment unfolding of action supported collaborative knowledge building about/with the natural world. I showed how parents and children use questions, directives, embodied moves and micro-stories to: 1) make their thinking visible and support the coordination of attention and observation; 2) establish themselves as knowers, capable of meaningful contributions; 3) mark and remember places of importance, and 4) engage in imaginative perspective taking to develop hypothesis, explanations, and additional questions about observed phenomena.

My analysis highlighted three big ideas that may be fruitful to consider when planning classroom lessons. First, I noted how both mother and son used questions to develop, support, and sustain *epistemic navigation and openness*. Jackie continually made her thinking visible in a way that left space for alternative possibilities and explanations. We also saw her foregrounding multiple ·forms of knowing—taking on the perspective of more-than-humans and narrating micro-stories to explain observations. Second, I pointed at the *productive nature of small disagreements*. Mother and son used disagreements to expand explanations and open up new lines of inquiry. Finally, I worked to make visible how *whole body movements were a resource for learning about/with the natural world*. Both mom and son shifted from movement to non-movement, positioned their bodies in relation to land, and used gestures as attentional markers for meaning making. Importantly, meaning making occurred in movement across time and place. Inquiry about observed phenomena was sustained across walks and developing questions and explanations were refined over time. These embodied place–time relations deepened possibilities for collaboration and learning.

Walking, reading, and storying land is a developmental activity that is supported by an assemblage of micro-practices (questioning, directing, narrating) that are verbal, embodied, and ambulatory. It is by assembling and layering resources that readings, as well as stories of land, come to life. This process is relational in nature and structured by interactions with other people and MTH life, including land itself. I intentionally foregrounded walking as a method for learning about the natural world and prioritized the role of time in learning. I hope that walking, reading, and storying land can provide a pedagogical frame to assist with the design of learning activities that support place–time relations. In conclusion, I offer that walking, reading, and storying the natural world has real consequences for what we know and how we might design science education in ways that continue to sustain life.

Acknowledgments

I am grateful to all of the community members and families who participated in this work and deeply influenced my own thinking and development as a scholar. Thank you to the reviewers, whose insightful comments helped me to craft a stronger manuscript.

Funding

Institute of Education Sciences [R305B080027]; National Science Foundation [1109210,1205758]; Northwestern University [Dissertation Year] Fellowship, Graduate Research Grant. The opinions expressed are those of the authors and do not represent IES or NSF.

References

Bang, M., Curley, L., Kessel, A., Marin, A., Suzukovich, E., & Strack, G. (2014). Muskrat theories, tobacco in the streets and living Chicago as indigenous land. *Environmental Education Research, 20*(1), 37–55.

Bang, M. & Marin, A. (2015). Nature-culture constructs in science learning: Human-non-human agency and intentionality. *Journal of Research in Science Teaching, 52*, 530–544.

Bang, M., Marin, A., Faber, L., & Suzukovich, E. (2013). Repatriating Indigenous technologies in an urban Indian community. *Urban Education, 48*(5), 705–733.

Bang, M., Marin, A., Medin, D., & Washinawatok, K. (2015). Learning by observing, pitching in and being in relations in the natural world. In R. Mejía-Arauz, M. Correa-Chávez, & B. Rogoff (Eds.) *Advances in child development behavior: Research on how children learn by observing and contributing in their families and communities* (303–313). Burlington: Academic Press.

Bell, P., Tzou, C., Bricker, L. A., & Baines, A. D. (2012). Learning in diversities of structures of social practice: Accounting for how, why and where people learn science. *Human Development, 55*, 269–284.

Brayboy, B. (2005). Toward a tribal critical race theory in education. *Urban Review, 37*, 425–446.

Brayboy, B. M. & Castagno, A. E. (2008). How might Native science inform "informal science learning"? *Cultural Studies of Science Education, 3*(3), 731–750.

Brayboy, B. M. J., Gough, H. R., Leonard, B., Roehl II, R. F., & Solyom, J. A. (2012). Reclaiming scholarship: Critical Indigenous research methodologies. In S. D. Lapan, M. T. Quartaroli, & F. J. Reimer (Eds.) *Qualitative research: An introduction to methods and design* (423–450). San Francisco: John Wiley.

Cajete, G. (2000). *Native science: Natural laws of interdependence.* Santa Fe, NM: Clear Light.

Deloria, V. & Wildcat, D. (2001). *Power and place: Indian education in America.* Golden, CO: Fulcrum Publishing.

Georgakopoulou, A. (2006). Thinking big with small stories in narrative and identity analysis. *Narrative Inquiry, 16*(1), 122–130.

Goodwin, C. (2018). *Co-operative action.* New York: Cambridge University Press.

Gutiérrez, K. D. & Rogoff, B. (2003). Cultural ways of learning: Individual traits or repertoires of practice. *Educational Researcher, 32*(5), 19–25.

Kawagley, A. O. (2006). *A Yupiaq worldview: A pathway to ecology and spirit,* 2nd edn. Long Grove, IL: Waveland Press.

Lahlou, S. (2011). How can we capture the subject's perspective? An evidence-based approach for the social scientist. *Social Science Information, 50,* 607–655.

Lee, C. D. (2008). The centrality of culture to the scientific study of learning and development: How an ecological framework in education research facilitates civic responsibility. *Educational Researcher, 37*(5), 267–279.

Ma, J. Y. (2017). Multi-party, whole-body interactions in mathematical activity. *Cognition and Instruction, 35,* 141–164.

Magntorn, O. & Helldén, G. (2005). Student-teachers' ability to read nature: Reflections on their own learning in ecology. *International Journal of Science Education, 27,* 1229–1254.

Marin, A. M. (2013). *Learning to attend and observe: Parent-child meaning making in the natural world.* Doctoral dissertation. Retrieved from Proquest. (3605744).

Marin, A. & Bang, M. (2018). "Look It, This is how You Know": Family forest walks as a context for knowledge-building about the natural world. *Cognition and Instruction, 36* (2), 89–118.

Marin, A. & Bang, M. (2015). Designing pedagogies for Indigenous science education: Finding our way to storywork. *Journal of American Indian Education, 54*(2), 29–51.

McCarty, T. & Lee, T. (2014). Critical culturally sustaining/revitalizing pedagogy and Indigenous education sovereignty. *Harvard Educational Review, 84*(1), 101–124.

Medin, D. L. & Bang, M. (2014). Who's asking?: Native science, western science, and science education. Cambridge, MA: MIT Press.

Medin, D., ojalehto, B., Marin, A., & Bang, M. (2017). Systems of (non-)diversity. *Nature Human Behavior, 1,* 0088.

Medin, D., Waxman, S., Woodring, J., & Washinawatok, K. (2010). Human-centeredness is not a universal feature of young children's reasoning: Culture and experience matter when reasoning about biological entities. *Cognitive Development, 25,* 197–207.

Nasir, N. (2011). *Racialized identities: Race and achievement for African-American youth.* Stanford, CA: Stanford University Press.

National Research Council. (2012). *A Framework for K-12 Science Education: Practices, Crosscutting Concepts, and Core Ideas.* Committee on a Conceptual Framework for New K-12 Science Education Standards. Board on Science Education, Division of Behavioral and Social Sciences and Education. Washington, DC: National Academies Press.

National Research Council. (2007). *Taking Science to School: Learning and Teaching Science in Grades K-8.* Committee on Science Learning, Kindergarten Through Eighth Grade. Richard A. Duschl, Heidi A. Schweingruber, and Andrew W. Shouse, Editors. Board on Science Education, Center for Education. Division of Behavioral and Social Sciences and Education. Washington, DC: National Academies Press.

ojalehto, b., Medin, D., & García, S. (2017). Grounding principles for inferring agency: Two cultural perspectives. *Cognitive Psychology*, *95*, 50–78.

ojalehto, b., Waxman, S., & Medin, D. (2013). Teleological reasoning about nature: intentional design or relational perspectives? *Trends in Cognitive Sciences*, *17*(4): 166–171.

Rogoff, B. (2014). Learning by observing and pitching in to family and community endeavors: An orientation. *Human Development*, *57*(2–3), 69–81.

Stevens, R. (2010). Learning as a members' phenomenon: Toward an ethnographically adequate science of learning. *NSSE Yearbook*, *109*(1), 82–97.

Taylor, K. H. & Hall, R. (2013). Counter-mapping the neighborhood on bicycles: Mobilizing youth to reimagine the city. *Technology, Knowledge and Learning*, *18*(1–2), 65–93.

Tuck, E. and McKenzie, M. (2015). *Place in research: Theory, methodology, and methods.* New York: Routledge.

Vossoughi, S. (2014). Social analytic artifacts made concrete: A study of learning and political education. *Mind, Culture, and Activity*, *21*(4), 353–373.

Vossoughi, S. & Escudé, M. (2016). What does the camera communicate? An inquiry into the politics and possibilities of video research on learning. *Anthropology & Education Quarterly*, *47*(1), 42–58.

Warren, B., Ballenger, C., Ogonowski, M., Rosebery, A. S., & Hudicourt-Barnes, J. (2001). Rethinking diversity in learning science: The logic of everyday sense-making. *Journal of Research in Science Teaching*, *38*(5), 529–552.

Yousef, O (2012). "Do descendants of Chicago's Native American tribes live in the city today?" *Curious City WBEZ91.5 Chicago*, July 11. https://www.wbez.org/shows/curious-city/do-descendants-of-chicagos-native-american-tribes-live-in-the-city-today/42633cd1-325e-4ee2-a254-ecf36c555cc0

3

BUILDING ON STUDENTS' CULTURAL PRACTICES IN STEM

Tia Madkins and Na'ilah Nasir

In this chapter, we present two examples of possibilities for leveraging the cultural practices of students from non-dominant communities in STEM classrooms. In so doing, we provide tools to support teachers' understandings of how to recognize, interpret, and leverage students' repertoires of practice to promote equity in STEM learning contexts (Gutiérrez & Rogoff, 2003; Nasir et al., 2006; Windschitl & Calabrese Barton, 2016). The first example builds on a study of domino play among African Americans[1] ranging in age from fourth graders to adults. Playing dominoes is a common tradition in many African American communities where players utilize a variety of complex game strategies involving mathematics. This case highlights how teachers can facilitate learning that honors students' mathematical reasoning and problem-solving skills and builds on the principles of teaching and learning embedded within the game. The second example builds upon the first and focuses on a case study of a middle school teacher who fluidly incorporated students' everyday communication patterns into a science lesson. This case illustrates what it looks like when classroom teachers engage students in STEM learning activities that recognize and build upon students' lived experiences. Taken together, these examples demonstrate how leveraging[2] students'

---

1 We use the terms, African American and Black interchangeably; in each case, the term utilized represents terms used preferentially by the communities we worked with and/or in the research literature.

2 Similar to other authors in this volume, we use the phrase *leveraging cultural practices* to indicate the importance of 1) centering students' experience in the classroom; 2) incorporating students' experience and literacies developed in out-of-school contexts into classroom learning; and 3) the reciprocal relationship of providing culturally sustaining learning experiences (Paris & Alim, 2017; see also García-Sánchez & Orellana, this volume). Additionally, phrases such as *out-of-school* or *everyday practices* are used interchangeably with *repertoires of practice* throughout this chapter.

cultural practices can improve student learning outcomes and the transformation of STEM learning environments.

Why this Work Matters

Sociocultural theories of learning and critical perspectives on STEM education focus on the social, cultural, and political influences on learning, such as race, ethnicity, and gender, as key factors in young people's lived experiences. Research emphasizes asset-based approaches to learning that decrease opportunity gaps for students from non-dominant communities (e.g., Nasir et al., 2014). We focus on how learning grounded in everyday cultural practices and culturally sustaining learning settings in school fosters students' relationships with teachers and peers, deepens students' identification with and interest in learning, and provides opportunities for students to take up learning identities, STEM identities, and racialized identities.

Historically, race has been a key determinant of who has access to high-quality STEM instruction. The sociohistorical marginalization of non-dominant communities, particularly in STEM, makes it imperative for educators to (re)imagine the identity possibilities for students and to better support student learning (Gutiérrez & Calabrese Barton, 2015; Nasir, 2012). One example of how sociohistorical marginalization plays out in classrooms is *racial storylines*, the stereotypical narratives prevalent in schools and society related to ability or disparities in math achievement across racial and/or ethnic groups (Nasir et al., 2012). Racial storylines can dissuade students from enrolling and engaging in rigorous math courses or learning; position students as less competent in their math classrooms; and prevent optimal academic identity development.

In addition to stereotypes, the broader, sociohistorical marginalization of non-dominant communities has also influenced some students' engagement with STEM. For example, teachers' beliefs about student abilities and/or tracking practices in schools has led to some students' exclusion from rigorous K-20 STEM learning opportunities (Bryan & Atwater, 2002; Oakes et al., 2005). Thus, STEM teachers must explicitly and implicitly address these stereotypes and sociohistorical realities in their classrooms to promote equity and improve student learning outcomes (Madkins, 2017; Nasir, 2016).

Rather than employing schooling practices that can be "discontinuous with the ways of knowing and doing" of students from non-dominant communities (Windschitl & Calabrese Barton, 2016, p. 1106), critical perspectives on STEM education value students' out-of-school practices (Gutiérrez & Johnson, 2017). Research suggests that when STEM learning experiences are grounded in students' cultural practices (Bang et al., 2014; Rosebery, Warren, & Tucker-Raymond, 2016; Warren et al., 2001; see also Marin, this volume), they have the power to transform learning environments and promote equity by:

1   fostering meaningful and positive teacher–student *and* student–student rela-
     tionships (e.g., Nasir et al., 2014; Vakil, 2014)
2   centering student engagement and interest (Esmonde & Caswell, 2010;
     Mejia & Wilson-Lopez, 2017)
3   supporting students' identity development, including academic, socioemotional,
     racialized, and ethnoracial identities (Nasir et al., 2014; Shin et al., 2017).

Teachers who employ equity-focused strategies and engage students in robust
learning are missing links for STEM learning environments (Gutiérrez &
Calabrese Barton, 2015) and can have a strong influence on student learning
(Darling-Hammond, 2010). Thus, to facilitate understandings of how teacher
educators and practitioners might leverage students' cultural practices (García-
Sánchez & Orellana, Introduction to this volume) and the lessons learned from
studying these practices, and to create more culturally sustaining learning experiences (Lee, 2017; Paris & Alim, 2017), we offer examples of lessons learned
through two ethnographies in the following sections. The first is focused on
teaching and learning in the game of dominoes, illustrating the rich nature of
teaching and learning that occurs outside school, and the second shows what it
looks like when a classroom teacher takes students' cultural lives and out of school
understandings seriously in a middle school science and engineering classroom.

How we Conducted the Ethnographies

Dominoes Study

The study on learning and thinking in the game of dominoes took place in
southern California across learning settings, and involved approximately 20
dominoes players at three age groups: elementary school students (grades four–
six), high school students (grades nine–12), and adult dominoes players. The
adult players were a group of university staff members who played at
a university campus on their lunch break. At the elementary and high school
levels students played as a part of a school or classroom-wide tournament. Play
was observed and documented using fieldnotes and (less frequently) videorecording. All players were African American.

Dominoes play at all sites was carefully observed and fieldnotes and sometimes video captured the turn-by-turn plays, as well as the expressive talk that
occurred during game play. Approximately 75 games were observed (approximately 25 at each site), and approximately five games were videotaped per site.
Additionally, dominoes tasks that evaluated game strategy were administered to
20 students each at the elementary and high school levels. Analysis involved
both iterative reading and coding of fieldnotes and video, attending to the
strategies (mathematical and strategic) in game situations. We focus on data
from the elementary and high school players in this chapter.

North Pineville Middle School

We observed classrooms at North Pineville Middle School (hereafter, Pineville) for four weeks as part of a larger two-year ethnography of a large, urban school district in the San Francisco Bay Area. Located in an area of the district that historically was underserved, Pineville served slightly more than 200 learners (see Table 3.1 for demographics) and became one of the district's STEM corridor of schools—an effort to increase STEM teaching and learning and the number of non-dominant youth entering the STEM pipeline as undergraduates.

Mr. Coles was the assistant principal at Pineville and substitute teacher of the introductory engineering courses for approximately 25 students in seventh grade.[3] Mr. Coles was a Black man in his late 30s and an area native who attended a district high school with many parents of his current students. He was the focal teacher for the project. Researchers observed his classroom three to four times per week for a total of 12 sets of ethnographic fieldnotes, and the first author conducted a semi-structured interview with Mr. Coles to learn more about his experience working with Black students in the district.

What we Learned from the Ethnographies

In this section, we detail findings from the two studies. The first study highlights the rich learning that happens in informal spaces outside of school, showing how one practice (domino playing) took shape in different groups; from it we draw implications for the transformation of learning in STEM education. The second offers an illustration of how one teacher worked toward such transformation in his classroom. Taken together, the cases suggest a variety of ways in which STEM education could better respond to, sustain and expand science and math learning and identity formation for students from non-dominant groups. As we detail the teaching and learning processes at each site, we pay particular attention to how these learning settings (1) *fostered meaningful relationships*, (2) *centered student interest and engagement*, and (3) *provided opportunities for identity development*.

TABLE 3.1 North Pineville Middle School Demographics

81% Black/African American	54% female
10% Latinx	46% male
8% Southeast Asian	(most classes observed
1% biracial	were gender-balanced)

---

3 During the science and engineering teacher's personal leave time, Mr. Coles became the course's substitute teacher.

Becoming Learners in the Game of Dominoes

Dominoes is a game with many variations that is played all over the world. A common version is one where players work in teams of two and seek to earn points by placing domino tiles on the board such that the sum of all of the ends of the board equal a multiple of five. When that occurs, the team scores that number of points. Typically, games go until a team reaches a predetermined number of points, often 150 or 200 points. In the course of play, then, players are concerned with multiple goals: scoring, blocking opponents from scoring, supporting one's partner in scoring, and having a play each turn (and not pass). It is a game where plays undertake both mathematical goals and strategic goals, utilizing applied mathematics to determine one's score, counting dominoes to make prediction on likely next plays of opponents and teammates, and calculating the probability that a certain domino sits in a certain player's hand, and when it will be deployed.

Importantly, the game is played not only with mathematical and strategic acumen, but also with humor, verbal agility, and wit. Players take pride in using double entendre and engaging in *signifying* (Mitchell-Kernan, 1999; Smitherman, 1995, 2012), thus keeping the game lively and entertaining. Signifying is a form of linguistic practice that involves the use of multiple meanings, often in a joking or teasing fashion (Mitchell-Kernan, 1999; Smitherman, 1995, 2012). Talk during play varies from very focused discussion of the game (a post-hoc analysis after a hand is over is quite common), to discussion of politics and social issues, to personal discussions among players about life and family. This combination of the strategic, and the social and personal created a unique learning space during game play for youth and adults.

Development of Meaningful Relationships

As a learning setting, the game of dominoes had several norms of interaction and structures that fostered the development of meaningful relationships between participants. One key characteristic is the *fluidity of roles* that players could take on during the game (Nasir, 2002, 2005, 2012). This included informal roles such as jokester, teaser, or rule enforcer as well as roles, such as teacher or learner, or co-constructor of strategic meaning.

Players moved fluidly between roles, fostering multidimensional relationships between players. In one example from elementary school play, a novice player, Joel, takes up a learner role in relation to his first dominoes partner, who is quite a bit more knowledgeable than he is, but then takes up an equal competitor role with his next partner, whose skill level is closer to his own. With the first partner, Joel issues instructions about how to play, while with the second partner, both players provide mutual support and talk through prior game play choices with one another. In the first partnership, Joel is in a learner role, while in the second, he is in an equal partner role.

Another way that dominoes sets the tone for meaningful relationships between partners is by the norm of maintaining *playful, humorous interactions* between players and between players and spectators. One example of the way that social interaction in the game fostered connection and humor between players comes from high school play. Lakida is playing with her partner against Zach and his partner. On one play in the game, Zach makes a play that fails to score points, when the expectation was that he might produce a score. Lakida jokingly uses a metaphor from popular culture (the DL, or the "down-low," which is a term that refers to people keeping something secret). Lakida uses the term DL to describe Zach's play, insinuating that he is purposefully not scoring as a strategy. It's a joke because, of course, if he were able to score, he would have done so.

This example highlights the value on humorous, boastful, and witty talk, with a special value on double entendre or signifying. We argue that this playful talk deepened social relationships, in that it created opportunities for discussion and reflection beyond the game itself—talk about family relationships, sports, and social issues.

A third way that dominoes fostered the development of meaningful relationships was through the structure of playing collaboratively with a partner and scoring points as a team. This structure meant that players learned about the game and became better players through playing with a partner (as it was in the best interest of the more skilled partner to teach the less skilled partner), and they learned *about* becoming a better partner as well. In the following interaction, we see how the partner structure incentivized players to learn to play together and to make more sophisticated plays. In the excerpt that follows, David is playing with his partner, Timothy. Timothy is the more skilled player and he is providing play-by-play instruction and feedback to David.

DAVID: (Hesitantly takes out a domino and makes a play.)
TIMOTHY: Call your money. (David moves the domino to the right spot on the board to score points).
DAVID: Four, five ... (pointing to the various ends on the board, unsure).
TIMOTHY: That's it! Call it!
DAVID: Five!
TIMOTHY: Finally! Got your money!

In this sequence, Timothy encourages David to call his points, and to recognize that he has made a score. In doing so, he socializes David into the goal of scoring by using specialized dominoes language, referring to points as "money" and directing him to be mindful to attend to his score. Interactions like these illustrate that the structure of playing in collaboration with a partner created a connection between players; one that incentivized the development of player skill, but also oriented players to build relationships with other players in order to understand one another's playing styles, and thus to support one another.

Centering Engagement and Interest

The game of dominoes was also structured in a way that centered players' engagement and interests. Play itself is an inherently engaging activity, in that it provides an opportunity for people to find enjoyment and to engage in a challenging task together. In addition, dominoes is a game of strategy, such that players learn new and more sophisticated ways to accomplish their in-game goals over time (Nasir, 2005). As new players, young people would often approach the game with the goal of simply matching the tiles (placing a six on a six, for instance), but as their game play develops they would take up additional goals—to score points, to prevent opponents from scoring points, to support their partner in scoring, or to control the game board to facilitate future play. And as the goals for game play shift, players learn new strategies to achieve these goals. Recall the young player, David, learning to score in the previous example. Later in the game, he develops this scoring goal and the strategies to achieve it, moving from putting down a domino tile, then counting to see if he has achieved a score, to deciding which domino tile to play by determining whether or not it would result in a score ahead of time.

The multi-layered strategic nature of the game allows for the sustaining of engagement and interest, even as players master certain levels of the game. Further, the game can be effectively and meaningfully be played from a range of different skill and sophistication levels, thus allowing people with different skill levels to be able to play with one another, and for the game itself to be a teaching context, where one can learn new forms of play through inter-action. For example, in one instance a very novice player learned the point of the game through interaction. He does not know that you play by matching a domino with a certain number of tiles onto a domino with the same number of tiles. Thus, when it is his turn to play, he takes out a domino and pretends that he can't reach down to the other end of the board to play it. Another player takes the domino and places it for him, until the player learns from watching this that the goal is to find a matching tile and play it on that end of the board. Thus, the game itself is structured in ways that not only provides players to become more numerically literate, but also allows them to learn through game interactions the very rules of the game itself.

Supporting Students' Identity Development

There are several components of dominoes play that provide opportunities for players to establish and maintain an identity as domino players and as learners in the game. The first is that the structure of play allows one to be a novice, but still to engage with experts and to learn as you go, without your lack of competence needing to be called out. We saw this in the example of David pretending to not be able to reach across the board in order to elicit help with making a play when he wasn't sure exactly how to do so. Since seeing oneself as competent (or potentially competent) is a key aspect of development and maintaining an identity in a learning setting, the fact that David can gain competence without admitting not knowing and that he can gain access to the teaching he needs to learn the game is a key aspect of the space for providing identity development. (See the chapter by Correa-Chávez and López-Fraire for a related discussion on expert–novice relationships within a model of learning by observation.)

Importantly, the game of dominoes also provides opportunity for players to express themselves in ways that align with longstanding communication practices in the Black community. One example of this is the witty, humorous talk and signifying that is embedded throughout the game. We saw an example of this above, when Lakida teased an opponent about not scoring, but did so in a playful way that utilized double entendre.

As we noted above, the talk surrounding the game included teasing, joking, debriefing game play, and discussing local and national events. In adult play, that meant discussing politics and campus events, in addition to discussing moral/ethical issues, like a discussion one day about what is the best course of action when a woman calls the work line for a married man. In high school play, that included discussion of local school events and a debrief of play styles and personalities. And at all levels of play, there was space for teasing and boasting—as long as it was done in a colorful, expressive, entertaining way—that is in line with community-preferred, accepted, and expected ways of interacting. In some ways, then, the space became a place for political socialization (see the chapter by Gallo et al. in this volume, for discussion of everyday politics learning).

Thus, we can see multiple ways that the game of dominoes provided opportunities for young people to develop meaningful relationships, have their interest and engagement centered, and form identities in relation to the game. We learn a lot about the nuances of how these processes are supported in a learning context outside school. What would it mean to learn from this and bridge this into classroom contexts? We now turn to look at a classroom where one teacher, Mr. Coles, did just this—made connections to learners' cultural and socioeconomic lives in order to support their learning.

Becoming Scientists and Engineers at North Pineville Middle School

Here, we offer examples of how Mr. Coles worked to transform his science and engineering classroom by leveraging learners' cultural practices and communication patterns. Prior to the study, Pineville had been led by a charismatic and effective principal who focused on hiring well-qualified and culturally competent teachers and building a sense of family and community within the school. Pineville was also a part of the district's STEM Corridor—a set of schools focused on STEM teaching and learning as a way to boost educational quality overall, especially in underserved neighborhoods. Thus, the school community had invested a lot of energy in improving STEM teaching and learning and establishing an annual science fair where community members and parents served as judges. Relatedly, Mr. Coles saw as his mission creating STEM courses that connected with youth and allowed them to see themselves as STEM learners. Similar to the dominoes example, we focus our analysis on how the teacher fostered meaningful relationships, centered engagement and interest, and supported identity development.

Fostering Meaningful Relationships

To foster positive teacher–learner (T–L) relationships, Mr. Coles engaged learners in explicit conversations about his role as teacher and their role as learners. In doing so, he draws on a tradition in many African American communities of identifying himself as a respected authority who cares deeply about their learning and well-being. Mr. Coles reminds learners he is there to facilitate student learning, but sets a boundary by stating: "We are cool, but we are not friends" (Fieldnotes May 29, 2014). With this explicit reminder that he is an authority figure they must respect in the classroom, he invokes the cultural referent of educating the village and displays characteristics of a warm demander (Foster, 1994; Ware, 2006). This example highlights the importance of educators expressing deep, empathetic care and setting boundaries and behavioral expectations with learners (Ware, 2006), but also the tension created by implementing strict authority structures in classrooms where adults are inherently in positions of power. We point out that while setting boundaries or expectations are important, we do not use this as an example of—neither do we advocate for—tough-love approaches. This misinterpretation is common and often cited as an effective strategy for working with non-dominant youth (Barrett, 2010; Valencia, 2010).

Similar to expert–novice relationships in the dominoes study, Mr. Coles sets up systems and processes that provide learners with opportunities to work as intellectual partners and where peers or near-peers provide feedback. One example of this was having a panel of eighth graders share their lessons learned from engaging in the annual science fair and STEM courses with sixth and seventh graders (Fieldnotes, May 29, 2014). The eighth graders offered advice, such as how to create an engaging PowerPoint presentation or the importance of making eye contact while talking to judges. In so doing, Mr. Coles not only fosters the development of positive peer–peer relationships, but also positions the eighth graders as capable and knowledgeable individuals the sixth and seventh graders can learn from and highlights the eighth graders' academic experience as valuable.

Centering Student Engagement and Interest

We point out that highlighting learners' experience as valuable can also support student engagement and interest; Mr. Coles also worked hard to accomplish this by drawing connections between the work of science classrooms and learners' home lives. In the following example, he explained the grading rubric that will be used later that evening at the annual science fair, an event that included dinner for families, step team performances (a form of dance) by Pineville and one of the feeder elementary schools, and raffle prizes (Field-notes, May 28, 2014). Mr. Coles invited any adults in students' lives (extended family members, caregivers, after-school program staff), local STEM profes-sionals, and Pineville teachers to serve as judges. To explain the rubric criteria, Mr. Coles mentions "Big Mama," a matriarchal figure in many Black extended families who often cares for young children (Martin & Martin, 1978), along with repeated use of cultural referents to traditional, Black Protestant churches:

> [he] spends a considerable amount of time discussing the science fair (~10 minutes), from modeling what students should do during the judging portion of the fair, what they are expected to wear, and logistical informa-tion. During this time, *he makes several connections to students' lives to help them better understand the meaning and significance of each aspect of the rubric.* For example, for "expertise" and "verbal articulation," he makes the analogy of a student not knowing how to answer a question posed by an adult [at the science fair] to a young child not knowing her Easter speech at church. "When you 12 [sic], you can't get kid credit like that. You had the 'At Least I Disease.' It's contagious, especially in the hood." … Mr. Coles reiterates the importance of parents or family members completing the rubric for each student at the fair. "Only adults' judging sheets matter." "Not, my partna hooked me up." He also reminds students to have their parents sign in, using "no nicknames [to prevent any mix-ups]—no Big Mama, NuNu—We all got a Big Mama!"
>
> *(Fieldnotes, May 28, 2014)*

Mr. Coles mentions the "Easter speech," a rich tradition in Black Protestant churches where school-aged children take center stage to recite poems on Easter Sunday. Whether the child recites the poem perfectly or forgets it entirely for any reason, she still receives applause and support (i.e., "credit") from the audience, commensurate with sociohistorical traditions to value, care deeply for, and educate children in Black churches (Barrett, 2010; Lincoln & Mamiya, 1990; Peele-Eady, 2011). This analogy emphasizes that students will not receive "credit" for "at least" (i.e., the "At Least I Disease") having aesthetically pleasing display boards. Unlike receiving "credit" just for trying in the Easter speech analogy, students with little or no written or verbal evidence of the NRC (2012) scientific practice, *obtain, evaluate, and communicate information*, will *not* meet the rubric expectation. Finally, Mr. Coles acknowledges the range of adults in young people's lives who will appreciate and provide feedback on their projects, which serves as a way to build relationships with youth and families. This also renders their scientific ideas and critiques as valuable and valid—a rare, instructional practice in science and engineering classrooms.

Later in the class period, Mr. Coles provides students with feedback about their display boards based on the visual aesthetics rubric criterion. As students work independently, he provides his assessment of certain students by stating: "I'm not gonna let you slide with that" (Fieldnotes May 28, 2014). Here, he indicated that students' display boards would not meet or exceed the rubric criterion, so he will not let his students "slide" (i.e., submit their projects) without additional revisions. Across both examples, Mr. Coles' pedagogical moves (i.e., familiar communication patterns) acknowledge the cultural and familial spaces learners navigate, ultimately creating synergy between home, community, and the science classroom.

Supporting Identity Development

Next, we focus on examples that demonstrate Mr. Coles' support of academic, racialized, and future professional identity development by leveraging learners' cultural practices (i.e., familiar communication patterns). In the vignette that follows, Mr. Coles begins class by discussing the appearance of students' written work:

> He remarks sarcastically, "God forbid if you're not 100% stereotypical" and "Take pride in your work." He makes the analogy that if somebody had a dirty car, the students would say, "You nasty," yet they are not concerned about the condition of the work they submit. Mr. Coles warns students, "*You* [as African Americans] will be judged on anything you do" because "everyone doesn't see everybody the same [sic]." Mr. Coles states that he will not accept anything "raggedy" and mimics a student formally and carefully handling in work to a teacher because they realize that their schoolwork should be treated like "important business documents." ... He intersperses throughout asides like, "Y'all just don't know," or "I feel like I'm in church."
>
> *(vignette of Fieldnotes, May 19, 2014)*

First, Mr. Coles explicitly states that as African American students, they will encounter teachers and others who will view and judge them according to racial stereotypes. He then refers to *and* mocks (i.e., "God forbid if you're not 100% stereotypical) a common deficit narrative about Black students not taking schooling processes seriously (Bonilla-Silva, 2010; Valencia, 2010). By encouraging students to treat their written assignments like "important business documents," Mr. Coles explicitly addresses how students can resist and push back against this particular racial stereotype, thereby supporting their academic and racialized identity development (Madkins, 2017; Nasir, 2016). His use of phrases such as "I feel like I'm in church" are familiar, cultural referents for *his* students because they are tied to sociohistorical traditions of many Black churches where performative-style discussions of racialized identity development, self-worth, and educational achievement are commonplace (Barrett, 2010; Peele-Eady, 2011).

Thus, Mr. Coles' classroom was a place where students were connected to one another and had opportunities to develop meaningful relationships, saw their home lives as being congruent with their science classrooms, and had explicit discussions about what it means to navigate race as science learners.

Building on Students' Cultural Practices: Supporting Student Learning, Interest, and Engagement in STEM Learning Contexts

As we consider the lessons learned from the learning settings we have described, we return to our three overarching themes, and examine how teachers might teach from a place of deep resonance with these themes. It is important to mention that as we think about implications, we are focused on the lessons learned related to the kinds of process, structure, and interaction we observed in the learning settings we described—*not* direct implications for science and math learning based on essentialized notions of culture and learning. In other words, the learning settings that we describe work precisely because they utilize pedagogical approaches and structures that allow learners to be fully human, are adaptable, and create opportunities for authentic interaction. This is fundamentally different from an approach that makes assumptions about who learners are and what they can do based on racial, cultural, or socioeconomic group membership and teaches them based on those assumptions.

We have highlighted three kinds of process that we argue are key components of learning settings that take the whole-person well-being and learning of learners seriously: fostering meaningful relationships, centering student engagement and interest, and supporting students' identities. In this section, we explore the lessons learned related to teaching practices for each component.

Foster Meaningful Relationships

Importantly, fostering meaningful relationships that we observed in both settings spoke to the importance of cultivating warm, trusting relationships between teachers and learners (even where these roles are fluidly defined) *and* between peers. This required an authenticity in the nature of the learning practice itself, and explicit attention to the building of a learning community where every learner has a valued place. Respect was core to these relationships—in dominoes, respect came from the fluidity of roles and multiple participants having the opportunity to be in a teacher role over time. In the science and engineering classroom, respect came from a genuine expression of care from the teacher, mitigating to some degree the position of power he was in by virtue of the structures of schooling in relation to the students.

Centering Student Engagement and Interest

The practices we studied were spaces where lateral learning occurred—where not only did teachers and learners learn from each other, but where interest was cultivated by connecting to learners' cultural norms, familial conventions, and common ways of being and speaking. In dominoes, we saw this occur frequently as novices and experts taught each other in fluid ways, and where cultural ways of speaking and relating were incorporated into the learning. In the engineering classroom, Mr. Coles made multiple efforts to engage in cultural ways of speaking, reference cultural experiences of learners, and explicitly connect to learners' home lives.

Our point here is that interest and engagement are fostered in spaces where learners get to be both experts and novices; where the knowledge they bring to learning environments is respected; and where community knowledge is built collaboratively in ways that honors the contributions from multiple sources and spaces. This is a very different conception than a teacher-as-knower way of thinking about classrooms. Teaching in this way requires the sophistication to see the unique lenses and strengths that learners bring, and, in turn, to structure interactions in learning spaces such that learners can bring this knowledge to bear. As we saw with Mr. Coles, it can be a challenge to do this within the confines of the norms of schooling environments with respect to the authoritative role of the teachers, but it is possible to disrupt the unidirectional power relations in school, even if just in moments of teaching and learning.

Supporting Identities

And finally, these were spaces where young people could author themselves as learners in ways that honored the richness and range of experiences and skills they brought to classrooms. We saw this occur in a range of ways—from Mr. Coles explicitly discussing the assumptions others often make about race, social class, and science learning, and the stereotypes that learners must contend with, to the implicit assumption in the game of dominoes that learning and cultural linguistic expression go hand in hand. Consistent across these spaces is the importance of learning spaces that allow learners to learn (and to fail) in ways that does not put their competence or intelligence at stake. In these spaces, learners know that their teachers and their peers know they will be capable of engaging in the learning setting in productive—and even additive ways. At times, this work is explicitly connected to race, culture, gender or social class. At other times, these connections are implicit, where just by the very fact that free expression of one's cultural self is honored and encouraged in the learning setting, learners get the message they belong and can learn.

Finally, we reiterate the importance of facilitating student learning in STEM classrooms where teachers engage the three processes we have described. In so doing, teachers can leverage learners' cultural practices and attend to the sociopolitical realities of their learners (i.e., contend with racism insociety and schools) to promote equity and student success. Of the multiple strategies teachers can employ to achieve these goals, we offer a few suggestions based on our own teaching experience and observations of educators across STEM learning environments. First, a critical component of doing this work is self-examination, reflection, and action where educators willingly examine their beliefs about and biases towards students from non-dominant communities (Atwater, Russell, & Butler, 2014; Milner, 2017). In so doing, educators can begin to reconcile their beliefs and related teaching practices to become more equity focused. To learn more about their learners in traditional ways, teachers can interview students one-on-one or in small groups; distribute student interest surveys (digitally, paper); spend time with learners and families outside of school; or conduct home visits in order to learn more about what their students know and do outside school. To really understand students' lives from the perspective of the young person, however, this may require teachers to step outside the familiar role as expert, and to push themselves to experience some of these environments *as their students experience them.* Educators must invite young people to share their expertise with them and others within the learning environment to begin this process.

Educators may also invite classroom or school-wide collaborations with community members and organizations, elders in the local community, or others to strengthen home–school connections. With any of these practices, finding ways to disrupt traditional power relations between schools and communities, and to put young people in the role of experts and learn from them is critical. We encourage educators to try out strategies that work well for them, their learners and families, and school contexts in order to transform STEM learning environments for students from non-dominant communities.

References

Atwater, M. M., Russell, M. L., & Butler, M. B. (2014). Conclusion and next steps for science teacher educators. In M. M. Atwater, M. L. Russell, & M. B. Butler (Eds.) *Multicultural science education: Preparing teachers for equity and social justice* (285–291). New York: Routledge.

Bang, M., Curley, L., Kessel, A., Marin, A., Suzukovich III, E. S., & Strack, G. (2014). Muskrat theories, tobacco in the streets, and living Chicago as Indigenous land. *Environmental Education Research, 20*(1), 37–55.

Barrett, B. D. (2010). Faith in the inner city: The urban Black church and students' educational outcomes. *Journal of Negro Education, 79*, 249–262. Retrieved from http://www.jstor.org/stable/20798347

Bonilla-Silva, E. (2010). *Racism without racists: Colorblind racism and the persistence of racial inequality in America*, 3rd ed. New York: Rowman & Littlefield.

Bryan, L. A. & Atwater, M. M. (2002). Teacher beliefs and cultural models: A challenge for science teacher preparation programs. *Science Teacher Education, 86*, 821–839.

Darling-Hammond, L. (2010). *The flat world and education.* New York: Teachers College Press.

Esmonde, I. & Caswell, B. (2010). Teaching mathematics for social justice in multicultural, multilingual elementary classrooms. *Canadian Journal of Science, Mathematics, and Technology Education, 10*, 244–254.

Foster, M. (1994). Effective Black teachers: A literature review. In E. R. Hollins, J. E. King, & W. C. Hayman (Eds.) *Teaching diverse populations: Formulating a knowledge base.* Albany, NY: State University of New York Press.

Gutiérrez, K. D. & Calabrese Barton, A. (2015). The possibilities and limits of the structure–agency dialectic in advancing science for all. *Journal of Research in Science Teaching, 52*, 574–583.

Gutiérrez, K. D. & Johnson, P. (2017). Understanding identity sampling and cultural repertoires: Advancing a historicizing and syncretic system of teaching and learning in justice pedagogies. In D. Paris & H. S. Alim (Eds.) *Culturally sustaining pedagogies: Teaching and learning for justice in a changing world* (247–260). New York: Teachers College Press.

Gutiérrez, K. D. & Rogoff, B. (2003). Cultural ways of learning: Individual traits or repertoires of practice. *Educational Researcher, 32*(5), 19–25.

Lee, C. D. (2017). An ecological framework for enacting culturally sustaining pedagogy. In D. Paris & H. S. Alim (Eds.) *Culturally sustaining pedagogies: Teaching and learning for justice in a changing world* (261–274). New York: Teachers College Press.

Lincoln, C. E. & Mamiya, L. H. (1990). *The Black church in the African American experience.* Raleigh, NC: Duke University Press.

Madkins, T. C. (2017). Dr. Tia Madkins: Diapers lesson and debrief (Trustey, July 25, 2017). Unpublished video of demonstration lesson. Notre Dame, IN: Notre Dame Center for STEM Education.

Martin, E. P. & Martin, J. M. (1978). *The Black extended family.* Chicago, IL: University of Chicago Press.

Mejia, J. A. & Wilson-Lopez, A. (2017). Sociocultural analysis of engineering design: Latino high school students' funds of knowledge and implications for culturally responsive engineering education. In S. Marx (Ed.) *Qualitative research in STEM: Studies of equity, access, and innovation* (60–81). New York: Routledge.

Meyer, J. A., Mann, M. B., & Becker, J. (2011). A five-year follow-up: Teachers' perceptions of the benefits of home visits for early elementary children. *Early Childhood Education Journal, 39*, 191–196.

Milner, H. R. (2017). Yes, race and politics belong in the classroom: Ten tips for teachers to engage students in difficult conversations. *Education Week.* https://www.edweek.org/ew/articles/2017/08/16/yes-race-and-politics-belong-in-the.html

Mitchell-Kernan, C. (1999). Signifying, loud-talking, and marking. In G. D. Caponi (Ed.) *Signifyin(g), sanctifyin' and slam dunking: A reader in African American expressive culture* (309–330). Amherst, MA: University of Massachusetts Press.

Nasir, N. S. (2016). Designing learning for equity. In *AERA Knowledge Forum YouTube Series*. https://www.youtube.com/watch?v=WfGtG0tD_ag

Nasir, N. S. (2012). *Racialized identities: Race and achievement among African American youth.* Stanford, CA: Stanford University Press.

Nasir, N. S. (2005). Individual cognitive structuring and the sociocultural context: Strategy shifts in the game of dominoes. *Journal of the Learning Sciences, 14,* 5–34.

Nasir, N. S. (2002). Identity, goals, and learning: Mathematics in cultural practice. *Mathematical Thinking and Learning, 4,* 213–247.

Nasir, N. S., Cabaña, C., Shreve, B., Woodbury, E., & Louie, N. (2014). *Mathematics for equity: A framework for successful practice.* New York: Teachers College Press.

Nasir, N. S., Rosebery, A. S., Warren, B., & Lee, C. D. (2006). Learning as a cultural process: Achieving equity through diversity. In K. R. Sawyer (Ed.) *The Cambridge handbook of the learning sciences* (489–504). Cambridge: Cambridge University Press.

Nasir, N. S., Snyder, C. R., Shah, N., & ross, k.m. (2012). Racial storylines and implications for learning. *Human Development, 55,* 285–301.

National Research Council (NRC). (2012). *A framework for K-12 education: Practices, crosscutting concepts, and ideas.* Washington, DC: National Academies Press.

Oakes, J., Welner, K., Yonezawa, S., & Allen, R. (2005). Norms and politics of equity-minded change: Researching the "zone of mediation." In M. Fullan (Ed.) *Fundamental change* (82–305). Amsterdam: Springer.

OUSD Demographics Info: https://dashboards.ousd.org/views/Enrollment/Snapshot?%3Aembed=y&%3AshowShareOptions=true&%3Adisplay_count=no&%3AshowVizHome=no&%3Arender=false#7

Paris, D., & Alim, H. S. (2017). *Culturally sustaining pedagogies: Teaching and learning for justice in a changing world.* New York: Teachers College Press.

Peele-Eady, T. B. (2011). Constructing membership identity through language and social interaction: The case of African American children at Faith Missionary Baptist Church. *Anthropology and Education Quarterly, 42,* 54–75.

Rosebery, A. S., Warren, B., & Tucker-Raymond, E. (2016). Developing interpretive power in science teaching. *Journal of Research in Science Teaching, 53,* 1571–1600.

Shin, M., Calabrese Barton, A., & Johnson, L. (2017). "I am an innovator": Quahn's counternarrative of becoming in STEM. In S. Marx (Ed.) *Qualitative research in STEM: Studies of equity, access, and innovation* (15–35). New York: Routledge.

Smitherman, G. (2012). "If I'm lyin, I'm flyin": The game of insult in Black language. In L. Monaghan, J. E. Goodman, & J. M. Robinson (Eds.) *A cultural approach to interpersonal communication: Essential readings,* 2nd edn (356–364). Malden, MA: Wiley-Blackwell.

Smitherman, G. (1995). Testifyin, sermonizing, and signifyin: Anita Hill, Clarence Thomas, and the African American verbal tradition. In G. Smitherman, (Ed.) *African American women speak out on Anita Hill-Clarence Thomas* (224–242). Detroit, MI: Wayne State University Press.

Vakil, S. (2014). A critical pedagogy approach for engaging urban youth in mobile app development in an after-school program. *Equity & Excellence in Education, 47*(1), 31–45.

Valencia, R. R. (2010). *The evolution of deficit thinking: Educational thought and practice.* London: Routledge.

Ware, F. (2006). Warm demander pedagogy: Culturally responsive teaching that supports a culture of achievement for Black students. *Urban Education, 41*, 427–456.

Warren, B., Ballenger, C., Ogonowski, M., Rosebery, A., & Hudicourt-Barnes, J. (2001). Rethinking diversity in learning science: The logic of everyday sensemaking. *Journal of Research in Science Teaching, 38*, 529–552.

Windschitl, M. & Calabrese Barton, A. (2016). Rigor and equity by design: Locating a set of core practices for the science education community. In D. H. Gitomer & C. A. Bell, (Eds.) *American Education Research Association's handbook of research on teaching*, 5th edn (1099–1158). Thousand Oaks, CA: Sage Publications.

4

"THEY THINK DETROIT IS JUST LITTER": YOUTH CHALLENGING ENVIRONMENTAL INJUSTICE THROUGH PARTICIPATORY RESEARCH AND CIVIC ENGAGEMENT

Enid Rosario-Ramos and Jenny Sawada

Introduction to *Toxic Tour*: Environmental Justice and Civic Engagement

On a Wednesday afternoon in January 2017, youth from local schools had been dropped off at the Detroit Hispanic Development Corporation (DHDC) to participate in after-school programming. After sharing a meal and spending some time in activities of their choice, nine youth met with Enid, the first author, to work on their civic engagement project, which they had titled *Toxic Tour*. The goal of the project was to develop short videos to raise awareness about environmental (in)justice in the city of Detroit. The conversation focused on defining the concept of environmental justice and discussing the specific environmental challenges Detroiters face. While discussing the consequences of long-term exposure to pollution, Enid asked, "How many of you have someone in your family who suffers from asthma or other respiratory issues?" Eight of the nine youth raised their hand. "Dang!" shouted one of them. A conversation ensued about the reasons behind this phenomenon and about how the youth could best use their experiences with pollution-related illnesses to craft an effective message to others about the importance of environmental justice.

This chapter will draw on our research, conducted in partnership with DHDC, to argue that the participation of youth from non-dominant groups in community-based civic engagement programs provides opportunities for them to use and increase their knowledge about social issues that impact their communities, to develop dispositions toward criticality and commitments to social justice, and to learn from others about effective ways to enact social change. We argue that these community-based contexts support youths' growth, both academic, and as informed and active members of their communities. As they work in their projects, they also develop and use important literacy skills, including analyzing relevant texts for understanding issues at stake and crafting compelling messages for target audiences. They do this as they work together with caring adults to address community issues that are both pressing and personal, making these learning experiences especially meaningful (see also Marin, this volume).

DHDC's Legacy of Youth Services and Community Activism

DHDC is a community-based organization that provides services to the Latinx community in Detroit, which is heavily concentrated in the southwestern part of the city. DHDC's founder and director created the agency to address city youths' experiences of violence. Yet, even when violence reduction and prevention is still at the core of its mission, DHDC has widely expanded its offerings to include adult education, youth programs, family-oriented social and educational services, and community organizing. The agency also has a tradition of developing partnerships with individuals and organizations across academia, business, and other community spaces.

Our partnership emerged out of a common commitment to youth civic engagement. After several conversations, we collectively decided that we would address this by developing an after-school program focused on community history (Brecher, 1995) to document the experiences of residents and members of their community. In developing our partnership, we followed the tenets of community-based participatory research, which enables all partners to contribute their expertise, with shared responsibility and ownership; it enhances the understanding of a given phenomenon; and, it integrates the knowledge gained with action to improve the health and well-being of community members, such as through interventions and policy change (Community Action to Promote Health Environments, 2017; see also Rice, 2015).

Thus, we were careful to engage the agency's staff in all decision-making processes, to remain open to having our roles modified to ensure that we were contributing to the agency's functioning (e.g., at times, we had to take a more active role in leading sessions with youth due to staffing challenges), and to allow the goals and needs of the youth program to determine the direction of our research.

During our pilot year (Fall 2015–Winter 2016), the project focused on documenting the lives of families who were scheduled to be displaced as the city began buying the land needed to build the Gordie Howe International Bridge, a new border crossing bridge from Detroit to Ontario. This topic emerged as a pressing issue that impacted some of DHDC's youth directly. A central concern about this construction was the impact on the lives of individuals, including the displacement of residents and businesses, the potential damage to nearby structures during construction, and the expected increase in truck traffic and related pollution. After the pilot year, it became clear that youth saw environmental injustice and their experiences with it as an issue larger than the bridge. During the second iteration of the program (Fall 2016– Winter 2017), we expanded the work to address Detroit's environmental issues more broadly.

Most youth who participated in *Toxic Tour* identified variously as Hispanic, Latina/o, Mexican, and Puerto Rican; we refer to them here as *Latinx*. They ranged from middle-school to high-school aged. These young people had a keen awareness of the challenges that city residents faced. They also understood the narratives that had been created about Detroit, and how these narratives often focused on its problems without discussing its beauty. Moreover, they felt very implicated in the transformation of these narratives, as well as in the transformation of the social conditions they experienced. These youth were well-positioned to grow as knowledgeable and active members of their local communities because their participation in DHDC's programs provided access to a network of people and organizations with a strong legacy of civic engagement (Alexander 2015; Kahne & Sporte 2008). DHDC staff members were central to conversations about the current state and future of the city. They regularly organized and participated in community events to raise awareness about important issues, worked alongside elected officials and other community organizations to impact policy, and developed partnerships with scholars and researchers to influence the direction of research projects in and about the city. Living alongside adults and others who were committed to the city's well-being provided youth with opportunities to participate in collective problem solving around complex issues that often required specialized knowledge.

Framing the Discussion: Valuing Community Knowledge for Social Change

In this chapter, we consider how we can capitalize on youths' language, knowledge, and skills to support their participation in political and civic engagement activities (for other chapters that explore youth civic engagement, see Gallo et al., this volume). We believe that pedagogies that aim to support social change must value youths' ways of knowing and recognize that their communities have a wealth of knowledge that is valuable for their growth and development as agents of change. To guide our discussion here, we consider three distinct, yet interrelated, frameworks. First, we consider critical pedagogy and literacy (Freire, 1970; Luke, 2012; Morrell, 2008) as a framework for understanding ways of engaging youth in critical reflection and transformative action. We draw a connection here to youth participatory action research (YPAR) (Cammarota & Romero, 2009; Schensul & Berg, 2004), as YPAR has been developed and used as an instructional practice that engages young people in investigative and problem-solving processes around local issues. Second, we consider funds of knowledge (Moll et al., 1992), which conceptualizes historically oppressed communities as sources of invaluable knowledge for academic learning and "emphasizes possible intersections and ways to build relationships to support student learning" (Moje, 2007). Specifically, youths' funds of knowledge and cultural contexts provide ways to create bridges to academic knowledge (Lee, 2006). Finally, we look to culturally sustaining pedagogy practices (Paris, 2012) as we consider ways to value and honor the experiences and traditions of youths' communities. This is so, not only as a tool for celebrating and sustaining youths' cultural practices, but also as a call to contribute to sustaining their livelihoods.

Framing Youth Civic Engagement through Critical Pedagogy and PAR

Transformative action and critical pedagogy move in and out of the classroom as part of a legacy of the hard work of communities that have had to fight against violence and oppression, environmental injustice, and economic inequities. Participatory action research (PAR), which Cammarota and Romero (2009) say "involves key stakeholders in a particular site, institution, or community who conduct research for initiating critical changes that produce greater social justice" (p. 54), often partakes in this navigation of multiple learning spaces. Such work provides opportunities for youth to investigate challenging problems that impact them directly in order to provide solutions. PAR can therefore be an effective means of drawing on the skills and knowledges of minoritized youths and communities, as its emphasis lies in "the collaboration of individuals with diverse knowledge, skills, and expertise [which] fosters the sharing of knowledge development" (MacDonald, 2012, p. 40). We were careful to position youth as researchers through YPAR. This placed them in positions of power and authority, as creators of knowledge and as knowers, to privilege their voices and help them develop "leadership capacity ... and use it for social change purposes" (Schensul & Berg, 2004, p. 82).

While much of the research on community-based civic engagement educational programs tends to emphasize the development of skills for political and civic participation, including research and presentation skills (Schensul & Berg, 2004; Cammarota & Romero, 2009), we see language and literacy development as a central component of this work. For this, we draw on Morrell's (2008) definition of critical literacy: the knowledge to "critique social structures and cultural practices" by positioning oneself as an empowered agent in the reading and interpretation of texts (p. 84), including traditional texts, as well as non-traditional texts and representations, such as visuals or sounds. By engaging youth in critically analyzing texts and contexts to produce works of consequence, we hoped to create a bridge between academic literacy practices and disciplinary knowledge and community action, and to argue that critical literacy can be used to inform the design of community-based practices and projects.

In addition to considering youths' critical analyses, we also considered how to take action against inequitable conditions we see in our social worlds. By engaging youth in the development of a counterstory, we challenged them to craft compelling arguments and become agents of political change. This required knowledge and language about social issues, as well as disciplinary knowledge and practices relevant to the project, such as historical inquiry and scientific language. Thus, literacy and language skills were an important component that contributed to civic engagement.

Centering Youth Knowledge: Funds of Knowledge for Civic Engagement

Here, we introduce the term "funds of knowledge," which refers to "historically accumulated and culturally developed bodies of knowledge and skills essential for household or individual functioning and well-being" (Greenberg, 1989; Tapia, 1991; Vélez-Ibáñez & Greenberg, 1989, cited in Moll et al., 1992, p. 133). We can think of this along the lines of "community cultural wealth" (Yosso, 2006). Yosso describes community cultural wealth as comprised of six forms of capital: aspirational, familial, social, navigational, resistant, and linguistic. Each of these informs the ways in which youth from non-dominant groups make sense of texts and contexts. For example, in a discussion about pollution, various youths weighed in, demonstrating their knowledge about their local context and history. One youth said: "Maybe because it's the Motor City and we have a lot of cars and a lot of gas," and another commented that she "had family go to protest the [Dakota Access] Pipeline 'cause my family is also Native American." These examples illustrate the ways in which youth have an understanding of their multiple identities, and they are able to make connections across these contexts, linking issues of environmental injustice from pollution in the Motor City to the Dakota Access Pipeline. Together, these different forms of capital comprise "an array of knowledge, skills, abilities, and contacts possessed and utilized by Communities of Color to survive and resist macro and micro-forms of oppression" (Yosso, 2006, p. 77). Through their work, educators at DHDC leveraged youths' understandings about Southwest Detroit to create bridges to relevant knowledge that may mirror academic knowledge—for example, during discussions about the effects of pollution on community residents' health outcomes— as they cultivated young people's commitment to improving their communities through civic participation. We can draw on this knowledge to understand local issues, but more importantly, this can help us work with youth to understand how they make sense of and address these issues. As researchers or educators who may be outsiders to the communities we work with, it is important to capitalize on the wealth of knowledge and expertise of youth.

Valuing Community Practices to Sustain Livelihoods

There have been various approaches to working with young people which emphasize drawing from their personal knowledge and experiences for instruction. Paris (2012) says that culturally sustaining pedagogies "support young people in sustaining the cultural and linguistic competence of their communities while simultaneously offering access to dominant cultural competence" (p. 95). Culturally sustaining pedagogies were important to this work not only because of principles rooted in political resistance, but also because they were, and continue to be, an important part of sustaining the livelihoods of many Latinx southwest Detroit families.

One means of enacting culturally sustaining pedagogy can be through counterstorytelling. Solórzano and Yosso (2002) define a counterstory as one that challenges mainstream dominant narratives and discourses, often from those who have been marginalized by those in power. Counterstorytelling "can build community among those at the margins of society" (Solórzano & Yosso, 2002, p. 36) through emphasis of experiential knowledge and lived experience. As we explain later in this chapter, youth may already possess views counter to mainstream perspectives about their communities; creating a space for them to share and develop these stories by capitalizing on their knowledge can be an important act of social justice.

What we Have Learned from Youth

Through our work together, youth have taught us that there is a need to remain hopeful when aiming for social change, that it is important to recognize, value, and capitalize on youth knowledge about their own experiences and communities, and that community-based civic engagement projects can be productive spaces for youths' development of knowledge about their communities and strategies for enacting social change.

"Maybe we Can All Come Together": Hope Is Needed for Change

Consistently in our work, youth wrestled with thinking about how to make tangible change in their community, given what they knew about local environmental and socioeconomic injustices, as well as civic and political action. One youth, Nate, said: "I personally think [the Marathon Refinery] is doing the most damage and should be tackled first, but the thing is, I don't really know how feasible that is because ... we are only a couple of people trying to attack a whole corporation ... What do we even do about it, though? 'Cause we can't definitely shoot the Marathon Refinery down 'cause that might destroy the economy."

He later identified examples of what he believed could be done, such as spreading awareness through canvassing and local campaigns from work he had been doing with the agency. He said he believed that "there's power in numbers," which could be an effective way to "branch out" and spread awareness across Detroit. As part of the team, Nate was not only aware of the difficulty of effecting tangible, large-scale social change, but he was also able to consider the nuances of the issue, pointing to knowledge about the local economy, as well as thinking about ways in which we could productively use community resources to make their voices heard.

Other youth also expressed knowledge about the importance of making one's voice heard for social change. Estela expressed the importance of "making our voices bigger," noting that: "They, Obama kind of paid attention to the people who was ... trying to stop the [Dakota Access] Pipeline stuff so, it could work, but our president now is a little more stubborn so you gotta work harder." There is a recognition here of sociopolitical contexts, and an understanding of the importance of making one's voice heard in order to move toward transformative action.

Yet working toward social justice can be daunting and frustrating. The journey may lead to success at times, but failure is also part of the process. DHDC youth travelled the road from helplessness to hope often, at times in one single conversation. During times when some felt helpless, it was their peers and adult leaders who helped them see the possibility of doing something positive. During a conversation where youth were discussing the potential limits of their voices for changing environmental conditions in the city, Tanya, one of the youth said: "Why you all gotta be so negative? I think that's the problem. One person's like 'oh, my voice is too small,' then everybody's like, 'my voice is too small.' So, the more you doubt it then it doesn't get anywhere."

Tanya was pushing back on a conversation that was more focused on stating the limits of youth agency than on asserting their ability to make social change. After some back and forth, they seemed to agree that raising their voices individually might not be enough, but if they worked together, they could have an impact. As Daniel stated: "As individuals our voice is quite small but as you see with the [Dakota Access] Pipeline, once a bunch of people got together and rallied together, they were, you know, more people were paying attention 'cause there was a larger group with the same idea."

Our meetings often became opportunities to discuss the potential as well as the challenges of our own agency. Being able to hope for change and to imagine oneself as agentive has been an essential component of youth participation in DHDC programs. That said, youths' hope was rarely unquestioned, as they often found opportunities to discuss with honesty the potential and the limits of their efforts. We believe that this awareness allowed them to strategically make decisions about how to best use their skills. Yet, hope alone is not enough. Youth also had to develop nuanced understandings of the situations they hoped to address.

"Maybe because it's the Motor City": Identifying and Countering Master Narratives

Youth frequently expressed awareness of local issues and the importance of community voice, particularly around perceptions surrounding Detroit. They were acutely aware of the master narratives about their city, often pointing to Detroit's "reputation" as part of the reason for many of its problems. Nate noted: "Its reputation is crap … The idea of, 'We're going to put a new coal plant' and instead of throwing a dart to a map, how about we say, 'Go there to Detroit' because its reputation is already bad, one more bad thing is not going to make any news."

This demonstrates an understanding about the negative views that non-residents may have of Detroit. In a video trailer that youth developed with staff, youth participants focused on what they believed were dominant perceptions of Detroit. Xavier said: "They think that Detroit, when they hear the name, is a bunch of crimes and gang violence, and everything."

In a peer interview included in the same trailer, Vincent expressed: "I think they're building the [Gordie Howe International] Bridge because they think Detroit is nothing. They think Detroit is just litter." Over the course of this work, youth seemed to have developed an in-depth understanding of how the positioning of the city and its residents as disposable may have been related to the careless actions contributing to pollution and environmental injustice. Furthermore, youth often discussed how they viewed these negative narratives about the city as tightly connected to the perceptions about its residents, mainly people of color and families living in poverty.

In spite of these narratives, youth recognized the lived experiences of those affected by the bridge construction. At the beginning of this project, though they were aware of many of the social injustices and dominant perceptions of their community, some youth, such as Ben, "didn't believe" that residents of their community would be displaced, or they believed that the bridge would be beneficial for reducing traffic. After conducting interviews with community members and drawing on their experiential knowledge (Solórzano & Yosso, 2002) around issues related to health and displacement, Ben began rethinking his position about the costs and benefits of building the bridge:

JENNY: Why don't you like the bridge? What changed your mind?

BEN: It's like they're taking away their past.

JENNY: What do you mean?

BEN: Yeah, it's like, they're destroying their houses and their lives … That's all their memories and they're just taking it away.

Youth were able to make sense of such complex issues based on their lived experiences. When the agency's youth organizer introduced the issue of environmental justice to a small group, they may have felt it was difficult to understand at first; they asked for clarification about the definition of "environmental justice," and after a short explanation, they were quickly able to draw conclusions and express their understandings based on their experiences in Detroit. In particular, Miri expressed her understanding that environmental injustice has to do with one's social status:

Y.O: Environmental justice is really the fight against the inequitable distribution of pollution and its associated effects.

NATE: Would you please explain that word?

MIRI: Simplify.

Y.O: Yeah. So, basically the idea is that if you are of a lower socioeconomic status, generally speaking, you will pay, or you will face a bigger burden of pollution than would your friends of another socioeconomic bracket. So to put it—

MIRI: Nobody cares about minorities … You're poor, so we're going to give all the pollution to you because you don't have the money or the power to do anything about it.

Conversations about race, class, and migratory status were common during our sessions. Youth often discussed their awareness of how living in a community with high concentrations of poverty, people of color, and immigrant families meant that their values, beliefs, and experiences were often misrepresented or made invisible. Yet, conversations also made evident that they had developed counternarratives challenging mainstream views about Detroit. These counternarratives showed a complex perspective of the city. On one hand, youth narratives often emphasized the beauty and goodness of the city, focusing on beloved businesses, parks, and Detroiters they respected and appreciated. DHDC itself was often mentioned as one of the great things about Detroit. On the other, young people also recognized the challenges that Detroit was facing. They could identify pressing issues including a struggling economy, crime, violence, poverty, lack of access to quality educational programs, and, of course, pollution. Even when they could name these issues as problems that served as dominant representations of the city, youth also spoke of the invisibility of the plight of Detroiters. These perspectives spoke to the nuanced knowledge that youth had about the ways in which narratives and policies that often did little to contribute to their well-being benefited more privileged individuals and communities. However, even when they discussed how they felt unheard, unseen, and uncared for, they remained committed to raising their voices, and they had developed knowledge and skills central to civic engagement.

"We Can do Petitions": Strategies for Civic Engagement

As youth engaged in completing the project, they often offered their knowledge about community organizing strategies. The following conversation illustrates their knowledge about strategies for raising awareness:

SEAN: We can do petitions.

ENID: Ok, petitions.

SEAN: Community events, like if I see something free, like free hot dogs and come to this event to hear about, what you call it, the environment, I would go. And then, like, you could also have entertainment there.

ENID: All right, we have a recruitment strategy for our events.

DANIEL: Are you trying to relay your message or entertain people?

SEAN: Well, at least you are getting your point across. 'Cause if someone gives me some free food …

Youth, at times jokingly, used their knowledge about other community efforts, as well as their personal experiences (e.g., preference for events with free food), to come up with plans for raising awareness about environmental (in) justice. Even when they conceded that changing environmental policy was a daunting task, they were committed to finding ways of spreading their message with the hope that increased awareness would lead to collective action. Their discussions showed that they had developed important knowledge about ways to galvanize support for their agendas. Some of their suggestions mirrored strategies used by adults in the agency, including hosting events where meals were shared, and inviting stakeholders to engage in conversation.

One of the goals of the project was to create a video to share information and raise awareness about current and future actions that could potentially exacerbate the already harmful effects of pollution in the city of Detroit. Youth knew that they had to create a message that was not only accurate, but also compelling. During a conversation about their personal experiences with respiratory issues, Sean and Tanya offered:

SEAN: I feel like we should have hope and when we do our video about it, like some, if they feel comfortable with it, talk about how they had to deal with it, like deal with asthma because of pollution and stuff so that other people can hear them. Like, say I have asthma and he was talking about asthma, like "yeah, that happens to me" and maybe I want to help other people.

TANYA: Personal experiences touch other people, I feel like it does.

This discussion about how to use personal experiences to raise awareness showed that youth had developed important literacy skills related to how to effectively engage an audience. Sean emphasized the importance of crafting the message with a hopeful tone, suggesting that it was important for audience members facing similar health issues to identify with the people in the video and feel compelled to help others in similar situations.

Furthermore, youth understood how to investigate issues to gather more information that might help them make their case and raise awareness. For example, Nate drew on some of the knowledge he developed over the course of the project to consider possible courses of action:

"We went up to that park, that area, the park across from Marathon? Marathon plant. We went over there and we had big masks on, that way nobody got any pollution and stuff ... We could go, say, to an area that is less polluted and isn't by any power plants or big polluters and we can check the wildlife ... not the wildlife but like the trees and stuff and see how they're affected ... I found out all this stuff goes in the air and gets mixed with the clouds and the rain and they make rain acidic ... but, it kills the trees and stuff."

A guest speaker—an environmental lawyer frequently involved in efforts to address issues around Detroit—had recently discussed these local issues with a few of the youth. Nate was drawing from the work for *Toxic Tour* as well as his further developed knowledge from the guest speaker about how the environment is affected by power plants and polluters in the area. In his view, this plan of activities could help us gather important evidence to craft a compelling argument. In doing so, youth hoped we could illustrate the inequitable treatment of southwest Detroit by drawing direct comparisons through the visual juxtaposition of a clean Michigan park with a southwest Detroit park.

Youth also demonstrated knowledge about routes of action that were perceived as less accessible based on their community's resources. During our discussions, we sometimes questioned why Detroit was the site of so many environmental hazards, and whether such pollution concentrated in a single area was legal, because we certainly believed it was inequitable. Miri believed that "some people just don't care and it's hard to make them care" about the issues in Detroit because, like many of her peers, she believed that Detroit's demographics and outsider perceptions of the city played a role in informing policy and legislation.

MIRI: Some people are treated differently; some people have different environments depending on their race.

NATE: Yeah, just like income …for example, the bridge, people with low income can't do things like hire a lawyer or stuff like that.

Here, Miri and Nate discussed the extensive and unfair financial burdens that may especially affect non-dominant groups because of the unequal distribution of environmental hazards disproportionately affecting areas such as Detroit, but also because of the unequal distribution of financial and political resources to fight against these injustices. Despite recognizing that some venues of action felt inaccessible to individual residents, youth often reiterated the importance of gathering as a community and raising awareness in order to collectively raise their voices.

When one conversation felt hopeless because it felt as though tackling social policy was too daunting, a recognition of the importance of action and a glimmer of hope arose when the youth organizer pressed them to consider why it mattered:

NATE: It's never going to happen 100% for everything to be equal and fair.
Y.O: So, why bother?
NATE: Because it's not always going to be exactly how you want it but you can better it and make small or big strides towards your main goal or realistic goal. 'Cause I think we can all agree that it's never going to be that way, 'cause it's all, there's always going to be a big guy and always going to be a little guy, but you can try and meet someone in the middle.

Here, Nate not only expressed hope, but the knowledge that compromise is often a necessary part of the process for social change. He recognized that drastic and immediate changes may not be feasible in a short timeline, but by giving up the fight entirely and settling for inaction, they would be losing hope for any change coming to their community. This also suggests a recognition of youths' agency and power to act. Despite knowing how Detroit was perceived and the issues faced by their community as a result of inequitable and oppressive structures, youth continued to recognize the ways in which we could contribute in the fight toward equity.

Cutting across Learning Spaces: Civic Engagement in Communities and Schools

While looking at videos, audio recordings, fieldnotes, and transcripts of our interactions with youth, we were often left in awe of their brilliance. Even when many narratives about youth from non-dominant groups in general, and youth from Detroit in particular, tend to position them either as problems to be solved, or as victims of their environments, we have found the young people at DHDC to be committed, agentic, and knowledgeable. They were not only well-positioned to enact change, but were often determined to be informed and active members of their communities (Ginwright, Cammarota, & Noguera, 2005). We believe that their knowledge and agency was, in part, the result of their participation in a space where caring adults had created a strong legacy of community and civic engagement (Kahne & Sporte, 2008). Both new and long-term participants in the agency spoke with great respect and appreciation about the opportunity to be at DHDC, in many cases because of the projects they worked on, but also because of the people they developed relationships with, and the experience of sharing a space, a meal, or a game with others.

We recognize that calls for bridging community-based literacies and practices to academic knowledge are often difficult to answer as these two kinds of setting often have distinct goals, characteristics, and routines that impact how learning occurs. Community organizations are often grounded in goals toward making a local difference in the areas they serve. The DHDC youth programs, for example, were centered around the development of youth civic engagement and leadership skills. Thus, even though community-based organizations' work is sometimes limited by access to resources such as funding, they often have not only the freedom, but also the urgency to develop projects that have a direct impact in local communities. Furthermore, community-based organizations navigate different contexts related to educational standards and learning expectations. As a result, learning activities are often designed to engage and keep the interest of youth—who have the option of not attending programs—and their implementation can be flexible enough to account for youth's shifting interests.

Yet, we have found that, frequently, the skills needed for informed civic participation cut across learning spaces and are developed and deployed both in community-based realms as well as within schools. One could argue that, for example, the knowledge and skills necessary for successful participation in a social studies classroom are similar to those needed for engaged participation in community activism. Furthermore, effective activism often draws from school-based knowledge within and across disciplines. Environmental activism is a perfect example of how political skill merges with academic knowledge in order to demand the improvement of the quality of lives of local residents. Effective advocacy in this case requires a depth of knowledge about a) environmental science, b) collection and interpretation of environmental justice data, c) historical trends related to urban development, d) ways to best engage a range of stakeholders—including policymakers, local residents, community leaders, the press, and others—and e) crafting compelling messages for diverse audiences. Thus, we argue that as youth travel across educational spaces, they may bring with them the knowledge and skills they have accrued through their participation in multiple learning contexts.

Nevertheless, school-based narratives about youth literacy learning and development are often based on discussions of test scores that too frequently focus on what young people do not know or cannot do. This is particularly true for youth from non-dominant backgrounds. These narratives may leave many educators in schools feeling like their goal is to remediate, rather than draw from, youth knowledge. In our experience, we have seen that the work that youth engage in while participating in community-based youth programs matches, and at times surpasses, the complexity of thought that is traditionally expected in schools. For example, participation and engagement in such community-based and activism projects requires complex skills, such as addressing not just one audience, but simultaneously engaging multiple stakeholders with different experiences, points of view, and agendas. Also, the goals of the work go beyond intellectual growth and academic performance as assessed by any individual teacher; they include a belief that community work should lead to social change, as well as a commitment to acting on behalf of one's community. In that sense, the work always seems high stakes, as it involves not just one's intellectual growth, but the betterment of a community. Moreover, civic engagement work often cuts across disciplinary boundaries, requiring knowledge of local history, natural science, social sciences, and the intersections of these academic fields with personal and community knowledge.

Therefore, it is important for educators across community and school-based spaces—particularly those concerned with youth development as informed and active citizens—to draw from and leverage all the knowledge related to civic participation that youth bring to projects of social change. Our work suggests that there is much that we can learn from community-based organizations' commitment to young people's development as scholars and civically minded individuals. Their work, and youth participation in it, indicates that young people from non-dominant backgrounds have the capacity, and often the motivation, to deeply engage with rigorous intellectual work, particularly when such work relates to the realities of the communities they belong to and/or care about. Thus, we encourage educators in schools, and other educational spaces, to design and implement curricula that integrate inquiry-based and participatory learning with the goals of social justice.

We offer the Equitable Futures Project—a collaboration between Michigan's Oakland Schools Intermediate School District and the University of Michigan's School of Education—as an example. Equitable Futures rethinks civil rights education by engaging high from both institutions have designed a project-based unit to teach about the Civil Rights Movement by connecting it to educational injustices currently faced by school students across multiple schools in three southeast Michigan school counties districts in the investigation of social injustices impacting their region. For the project, a team of educators communities in the local region. Then, professional learning opportunities are provided for local participating teachers to learn about social justice education and project-based learning. Teachers use the curricular materials provided and their newly developed and/or refined instructional practices to guide their students through an investigation of both the historical antecedents and current effects of local injustices. As they complete their investigations, students are encouraged to draw from the lessons of the Civil Rights Movement to develop action plans for the problems they investigated. The unit culminates in a youth conference that brings together students and teachers across the participating schools and districts to discuss their projects and share their insights, while they also learn about the diverse communities they live in. Similar to DHDC, Equitable Futures engages young people in the investigation of complex problems. Understanding and addressing these regional problems requires the development of complex interdisciplinary knowledge, as well as skills related to critical literacy and civic engagement.

Our work in community-based organizations has taught us a lot about the language and literacy skills that young people develop and deploy as they move across contexts. As scholars whose work is often located at the intersection of schools and community spaces, we bear witness to youth's deep knowledge about their experiences and their communities, their eagerness to contribute to social justice, and their willingness to engage in difficult work alongside caring adults. In the United States, we continue to see examples of this brilliance appear in our national consciousness as young people fight for gun control, criminal justice reform, and educational justice. We argue that these characteristics provide caring and justice-committed educators with important tools for engaging young people in projects and learning activities that encourage them to leverage the knowledge that they have developed as they move across spaces in order to tackle complex issues of important consequences for people and communities in local and more global scales. Our hope is that we have offered an example to illustrate that young people are capable of and are motivated by complex problem solving in the context of civic engagement projects. We encourage educators in and out of school contexts to leverage such talent to encourage youth to further grow and develop both as scholars and as active members of their communities.

References

Alexander, D. (2015). It's not what you know it's who you know: Political connectedness and political engagement at the local level. *Journal of Sociology, 50*(4), 827–842.

Brecher, J. (1995). *History from below: How to uncover and tell the story of your community, association, or union.* New Haven, CT: Commonwork.

Cammarota, J. & Romero, A. (2009). A social justice epistemology and pedagogy for Latina/o students: Transforming public education with participatory action research. *New Directions for Youth Development, 123*(1), 53–65.

Community Action to Promote Healthy Environments (2017). *What is community-based participatory research?* Retrieved from http://caphedetroit.sph.umich.edu/resources/community-based-participatory-research/

Freire, P. (1970). *Pedagogy of the Oppressed.* New York: Continuum.

Ginwright, S., Cammarota, J., & Noguera, P. (2005). Youth, social justice, and communities: Towards a theory of urban youth policy. *Social Justice, 32*(3), 24–40.

Greenberg, J. B. (1989). Roots of the whole-language movement. *The Elementary School Journal, 92,* 113–127.

Kahne, J. & Sporte, S. (2008). Developing citizens: The impact of civic learning opportunities on students' commitment to civic participation. *American Educational Research Journal, 45*(3), 738–766.

Lee, C. D. (2006). 'Every good-bye ain't gone': Analyzing the cultural underpinnings of classroom talk. *International Journal of Qualitative Studies in Education, 19*(3), 305–327.

Luke, A. (2012). Critical literacy: Foundational notes. *Theory into Practice, 51,* 4–11.

MacDonald, C. (2012). Understanding participatory action research: A qualitative research methodology option. *Canadian Journal of Action Research, 13*(2), 34–50.

Moje, E. (2007). Developing socially just subject-matter instruction: A review of the literature on disciplinary literacy teaching. *Review of Research in Education, 31*(1), 1–44.

Moll, L. C., Amanti, C., Neff, D., & Gonzalez, N. (1992). Funds of knowledge for teaching: Using a qualitative approach to connect homes and classrooms. *Theory Into Practice, 31*(2), 132–141.

Morrell, E. (2008). Critical literacy as social praxis. In *Critical literacy and urban youth: Pedagogies of access, dissent, and liberation* (185–203). New York: Routledge.

Paris, D. (2012). Culturally sustaining pedagogy: A needed change in stance, terminology, and practice. *Educational Researcher, 41*(3), 93–97.

Rice, K. (2015). *Community based participatory research principles.* Retrieved from http://caphedetroit.sph.umich.edu/resources/community-based-participatory-research/

Schensul, J. & Berg, M. (2004). Youth participatory action research: A transformative approach to service-learning. *Michigan Journal of Community Service Learning, 10*(3), 76–88.

Solórzano, D. G. & Yosso, T. J. (2002). Critical race methodology: Counter-storytelling as an analytical framework for education research. *Qualitative Inquiry, 8*(1), 23–44.

Tapia, J. (1991). *Cultural reproduction: Funds of knowledge as survival strategies in the Mexican American community.* Unpublished doctoral dissertation. University of Arizona, Tucson, AR.

Vélez-Ibáñez, C. G. & Greenberg, J. (1989). *Formation and transformation of funds of knowledge among U.S. Mexican households in the context of the borderlands.* Paper presented at the annual meeting of the American Anthropological Association, Washington, DC.

Yosso, T. (2006). Whose culture has capital? A critical race theory discussion of community cultural wealth. *Race, Ethnicity, and Education, 8*(1), 69–91.

5

LEVELING THE POLITICIZED EXPERIENCES OF CHILDREN FROM MIXED STATUS FAMILIES: CONNECTIONS TO CIVIC EDUCATION IN ELEMENTARY SCHOOLS

Sarah Gallo, Holly Link, and Jessica Somerville

Elementary school classmates from mixed status Mexican immigrant and African American families were meeting in an after-school group in Pennsylvania when Ben and Santi, both from Mexican immigrant families, began talking about Ben's father's deportation case. This was the month before the 2012 presidential elections and Ben reasoned his undocumented family members should try to acquire fake identifications to vote against Mitt Romney, who had threatened to send back families who were not born "here." During whole-group storytime Ben shared his family's immigration struggles with this trusted group, and he and Santi warned how, if Romney were elected, Romney would knock on every door in their town to send away people who were not born "here." They re-broached the topic of voting rights and Chantel, an African American classmate, talked about her involvement in her church to help inform community members about proposed voter identification laws that would disproportionately impact people of color. Chantel also admitted that she was not born "here," but in a neighboring state, and Ben warned that Romney would also send her back.[1]

This opening vignette demonstrates the ways that fourth graders from a range of racial and immigration backgrounds drew on meaningful political experiences from their lives to collaboratively engage in civic education. Some of the concepts were in formation; they had to figure out the consequences of state versus international borders among other things. At the same time they demonstrated

---

1 We use pseudonyms for names of locations and names of research participants.

dexterity in coalition building across their differences as well as naming civic issues that shaped their communities. Indeed, this informal educational interaction, along with the other examples in this chapter, provide fruitful opportunities to learn from young students across a range of educational spaces in order to reimagine civic education for elementary school students living in communities where issues such as family documentation status are at stake. To do this, we explore how educators can better validate and incorporate children's politicized experiences to meet the goals of civic education while simultaneously supporting students to develop critical understandings of these issues.

In this chapter, we argue that elementary school civic education can and should build on students' politicized educational experiences. We propose validating and incorporating—or leveling (Martínez, Montaño, & Rojo, this volume)—these knowledges for civic education. By recognizing and incorporating their experiences for academic goals, civic education can move beyond learning sanitized versions of U.S. history, government, voting, or volunteering. In this way, children's knowledge and experiences can meet top-down assessment goals while fostering pathways for all students to develop critical understandings of civic life in which they work towards change as civically engaged members of their communities (see Rosario & Sawada, this volume).

Expanding what Counts as Civic Education

Traditionally civic education has focused on civic knowledge, or facts about U.S. history and government. Prototypical civic engagement practices, such as voting or community service activities, are often aimed at helping those who are positioned as less fortunate (Rubin, 2007). Yet such narrow definitions of civic education tend to be reflective of white middle class practices and overlook the range of knowledges that non-dominant students bring to their civic learning (Dabach, 2015; Duncan-Andrade, 2007; Rubin, 2007, 2012). We instead believe it is important to expand our approaches to civic education so that we can build on the civic experiences and real-world concerns that diverse students bring to our classrooms.

Careful examinations of what counts as civic education are particularly important for educators working with students from immigrant, undocumented, and mixed status families (Callahan & Muller, 2013; Dabach, 2015; Seif, 2010). Such students may be less familiar with traditional U.S. civic knowledge and may have loved ones whose documentation status bars them from participating in typical civic engagement practices celebrated in school-based civics. Yet students from immigrant families, including those who have undocumented family members, bring a breadth of civic engagement experiences and awareness about political issues that impact their daily lives in profound ways (Gallo, 2016; Gallo & Link, 2015). As U.S. classrooms are usually comprised of students from a range of backgrounds and statuses, teachers can take on difficult yet important roles in brokering the civic knowledge and experiences that diverse students bring to bear on their learning (Dabach, 2015).

Despite children's engagement in civic life, we do not know much about civic education in elementary schools. This is partially because most civic education research has occurred in high schools and middle schools (e.g., Callahan & Muller, 2013; Dabach, 2015; Duncan-Andrade, 2007; Rubin, 2007, 2012). This scholarship has brought attention to the process of identity formation during adolescence, as well as to students' transition from adolescence to adulthood. We also do not know much about civic education for elementary school students because the term "civic education" is rarely used. Although the National Council for Social Studies names "civics and government" as one of the four areas to be covered, civic education tends to be referred to as "social studies" (Hinde, 2008). And although it is a core academic subject, social studies have taken a backseat to math and reading under high stakes testing (Hinde, 2008; Kahne & Sporte, 2008). Yet, there are additional ways across the elementary school curriculum that civic education is instilled. Developing skills needed for participation in a democracy has long been a goal of U.S. education, and most elementary schools seek to accomplish this through "character education programs" (Hinde, 2008, p. 78). Such programs, which are often talked about as the core values of the school, help students foster the ability to understand other points of view, work together, follow rules, and build other "citizenship skills" (Hinde, 2008, p. 78).

What we Mean by Civic Education

We define civic education as interactive educational practices that level students' politicized experiences and authentic concerns while also developing understandings of their rights and responsibilities as community members. In order to explore the ways that elementary school students from diverse backgrounds engage in civic education, we tailor Rubin's four principles for meaningful civic learning (Rubin, 2012, p. 9). We also add a fifth principle for working with students from undocumented or mixed status families (where some family members have U.S. documentation, and some do not).

> #1 *Build on students' experiences*: This focuses on the content of learning. Civic education should not be about filling students' heads with civic knowledge, or facts about U.S. history or government. Instead, it should open up spaces for students to draw on their own experiences to collaboratively learn from and with one another. Unlike traditional civic education, this point of departure assumes that all students have noteworthy civic experiences to contribute to their classmates' learning.

#2 *Include key issues and controversies*: Rather than focusing on relatively sanitized notions of U.S. history or government, civics education should incorporate topics shaping the political arena and students' everyday worlds. These topics are often dismissed as political in schools, but it is important to recognize that everything we teach is political (Bartolomé, 1994; Freire, 1970); it is often when we, as educators, move against the status quo that it *feels* political. As the students in the opening vignette illustrate, it is often adult educators who feel uncertain about broaching such topics, not young people who are already aware of the key roles these issues play in their lives.

#3 *Provide opportunities for interactive student learning*: This focuses on the forms or participation structures for learning. Civic education should not be about the memorization of facts and systems—instead it requires taking risks of sharing and learning from ideas and experiences, searching for new perspectives, and applying them in new ways. It includes "discussion, analysis, critique, and research skills" (Rubin, 2012, p. 9). We would add that this is particularly important among groups of students of various immigration statuses and backgrounds because it provides spaces to humanize, sympathize, and build coalitions to address key issues in civic life that are often silenced or pathologized in the media.

#4 *Build meaningful knowledge of students' rights and responsibilities*: When educators carefully open up spaces to build on students' civic knowledges that are connected to their real-world concerns, students will likely bring in their politicized experiences that are often silenced. Building from Rubin (2012), we seek to highlight the inclusion of politicized experiences. Elsewhere we have written about these experiences, which we call students' politicized funds of knowledge, or the real-world experiences, knowledges, and skills that young people develop and use across educational spaces that are often positioned as taboo or unsafe to incorporate into classroom learning (Gallo & Link, 2015).

#5 *Carefully consider labels and terms*: We have added this as a fifth principle in order to highlight how terms that are often assumed to be neutral can take on different meanings for students living in contexts where family documentation status shapes their lives. For example, although Rubin (2012) uses phrasing such as "rights and responsibilities as citizens" in her framework, we instead suggest minimizing the use of terms such as "citizen" within civic education, except when used as a springboard to question the unequally distributed legal rights of those with and without official U.S. citizenship. When "citizen" is used as an assumed reality or endpoint for all students and their families, it can unintentionally foster circumstances in which students from undocumented families discount their civic experiences as relevant or valuable.

In the remainder of the chapter, we use these five principles to illustrate the successes and challenges that two educators encountered as they engaged in civic education. We end this chapter by returning to these principles to imagine additional pedagogical approaches to engage in meaningful civic education with elementary school students from non-dominant backgrounds.

How we Learned from Students and Educators

The examples in this chapter come from students and educators in a Pennsylvania town and a city in Ohio. Schools in both locations worked with a growing number of Latinx immigrant and African American families.

Marshall, Pennsylvania, is a suburb of approximately 35,000 people with a Latinx school population that increased from 2% to 25% between 1990 and 2010. We learned from students and educators in these schools during a five-year ethnography in which we followed one cohort of children from Mexican immigrant families with mixed documentation status. Children attended Grant Elementary, a K-4 English-medium school of over 400 students with relatively equal numbers of African American and Latinx students. Grant teachers were primarily white, middle-class women who spoke only English. School curricula followed scripted programs that focused on preparation for standardized testing.

Nepi, Ohio, is a large Midwestern city whose growing population includes significant numbers of immigrants and refugees from around the world. Latinx students made up 9% of the student body across the large urban district and the examples from this school come from a year-long ethnography in a fourth grade social studies classroom at Chivas Bilingual Elementary. About half of the students were Latinx children and most of the other students were African American. Their teacher, Señora Valencia, like many of the teachers in the school who were originally from Latin America, had taught in both Latin America and the United States for over 30 years. History and government units were part of a statewide social studies curriculum that was tied to an English-medium standardized test. Although classroom talk occurred in both Spanish and English, content was mostly taught through English to prepare students for testing.

In Marshall, during our five-year ethnography Sarah and Holly spent time with a cohort of students from Mexican immigrant families at home and school from kindergarten through fourth grade. To document their educational practices, we used ethnographic approaches such as weekly participant observation, video recording of routine activities, and interviews. When children were in third and fourth grades, Holly also met weekly with students at the public library. During this time, children described their social worlds through digital storytelling and participated in audio- and videorecorded interviews and group conversations on various topics they selected. In Chivas Bilingual Elementary, Jessica drew on similar ethnographic approaches within Señora Valencia's fourth grade classroom for about an hour each week, but did not spend time in students' homes. The examples presented here focused on the ways family immigration status directly and indirectly shaped students' participation in civic education within mixed status classrooms.

Students' and Educators' Engagement in Civic Education

In this section, we discuss examples from Marshall and Nepi that illustrate how children experience and understand immigration status and tie it to civic education. We highlight the pedagogical moves that educators can draw on to open sometimes difficult conversations around these topics.

Students' Understandings of "Illegal" Immigration

One afternoon in the spring of Grant students' fourth grade year, the topic of immigration came up during a group discussion with Holly (white, non-Latinx)[2] at their weekly library meeting. The fourth graders (Rebecca, white; James, African-American; Abi, Mexican; Ben, Mexican; Marisol, Mexican; Princess, Mexican American) had been talking about what it meant to be "racist." To provide an example, Rebecca, the only white non-Latinx student in the group, referenced Mexican immigration to the United States. In the discussion that ensued, Mexican students drew from their politicized funds of knowledge to explain why their families had come to the U.S. and to describe the experiences of border crossing. This first excerpt shows how children both drew from and responded to broader stereotypes about Mexican immigrants.

4	Rebecca:	A lot of people don't like Mexicans because they say they shouldn't be
5		coming here because they're illegal and they get mad about it and kids
6		say "well I'm not supposed to be friends with you."
7	James:	Why is it [they] even moving here then? What's the point?
8	Rebecca:	'Cause they need jobs.
9	Abi:	Mmhm they don't pay them in Mexico (pause).
10	Holly:	Does anyone want to answer that question?
11	Abi:	Some people might come from Mexico because it's really hard to get
12		money and feed their families.
13	Ben:	'Cause there's not many jobs there plus they kill people there.

2 We use the broad label of Latinx when referencing the general demographics of participants in our studies. Yet whenever known, we used individual students', teachers', and authors' self-descriptors to describe their race and ethnicity, which is included in parentheses after their name.

The beginning of this discussion shows how children were grappling with key issues and controversies in civic life (#2), issues that while pertinent to their daily experiences were not approached in their weekly social studies lessons at school. Pedagogical moves included supporting conversation around these issues as they emerged. For example, Holly recognized Abi's interest in providing an answer but uncertainty if she should continue. During a pause, Holly stepped in with a question that shifted the focus from a single student (Abi) to invite all students to contribute a response, if they were interested (line 10). This move helped shift the focus away from an individual who was carefully considering how she broached this personal topic. It also validated the topic and promoted building on students' own experiences with civic life (#1) to explore what they had heard in the media. These exact moves were not pre-planned, but rather came about through supporting children as they engaged in conversation with each other.

As the conversation developed, students continued to explore and name reasons for Mexican immigration and began to talk explicitly about border crossing (lines 11–22).

14	James:	If ya'll don't have money to pay your house or your bills but have
15		money to come here on the plane. You know how much money it costs?
16	Marisol:	Planes cost a lot of money and I've been there. It costs like a thousand.
17	Holly:	Does anybody know how they come if they don't come in planes?
18	Ben:	I don't know what it's called in English, but it's *la frontera* [border].
19	Abi:	First it took me like an airplane to the border, but it was really hard
20		because we needed to stay away from the polices. We used to walk
21		only in the night because in the day (pause).
22	Holly:	Do you remember it?
23	Abi:	Every time you gotta crawl, my hands were bleeding.
24:		Why?
25	Ben:	Because there were snakes, spiders, animals, nails, rocks.

Here three children from Mexican immigrant families (Marisol, Ben, and Abi) shared their expertise and experiences with James and others as he continued to ask about the reasoning and logistics of immigration and border crossing. In this case, the three collaboratively contributed to their peers' learning through sharing general knowledge and personal narrative of border crossing (#1). Through an adult supporting and extending the conversation, and deferring to the children as experts, students were able to bring in their own politicized experiences on a topic that was often silenced in the classroom (#1, #2, #4). At the same time, children's stories were humanized and Abi was comfortable enough to take a risk in sharing details about her border crossing (#3).

Through a close look at Holly's pedagogical moves here, we see how she carefully tailored her questioning to reflect students' desires to disclose how border crossing had touched their own lives. Through the use of "they" rather than "ya'll" (which James had used) in the beginning, Holly oriented to an overall discussion about immigration when she invited students to share their knowledge about border crossing, thus providing the space to talk about immigrants in general, rather than focusing on specific people in the room (line 17). After Abi decided to disclose her personal experiences of crossing the border (lines 19–21), Holly again used the pause in the discussion to personally invite Abi to continue (line 22), a move that validated and supported Abi's contribution. Throughout, Holly was attentive to how students from mixed status families were engaging in the topic, helping to create distances of safety if they were not providing clear signals that they wanted to disclose personal experiences, as well as encouragement to continue if they did.

Because the topic of border crossing is controversial, often receiving negative attention in the media and increasingly in daily life, children from immigrant and nonimmigrant backgrounds needed an opportunity to discuss and explore it together. This involved risk-taking and difficult moments as the conversation continued.

26	James:	Ya'll comin illegally, that's not right. I know it's to make money and
27		take care of your family, but how come only some of the family gonna
28		go? So they gotta suffer until ya'll make money. Why they go with ya'll
29		then?
30	Holly:	James is bringing up some interesting points. He's wondering why you
31		can't bring your whole family.
32	Princess:	Because you have to cross the border.
33	Holly:	It's a really hard journey.

In line 16, James began his question by voicing an anti-immigrant sentiment through his use of the word "illegally" and his explicit statement that "that's not right." But he also showed new understanding about reasons for immigration and touched upon family separation, an issue that affected many of his peers. In the moment, Holly was unsure of whether or how to respond to the first part of James' comment and chose, instead, to emphasize his question (lines 30–31). Looking back, she wished she had addressed this comment explicitly. At difficult moments like these there is no easy formula for responding, and educators can feel discomfort or uncertainty with how to proceed. While it might be easier to simply shut down conversation, we argue that doing so would reinforce silence around an issue that greatly affects many children's daily lives and schooling. Instead, we urge educators to facilitate conversations that allow children to discuss and analyze key issues in civic life that connect directly to their own concerns and lived experiences, (#3) yet in ways that students are in control of when they disclose personal experiences on such topics. For example, in this conversation Holly did not ask Ben to share about his family's situation, but looked for ways to support him when he decided to do so. This also involved facilitating children's dialogue about immigration based on what they understood and wanted to know. And although not taken up here, it is also important to look for opportunities to support students in questioning the broad labels that are used, such as "illegal," (#5). Such conversations are not easy but may help children develop deeper understandings of key issues and controversies in civic life.

The discussion around immigration and border crossing continued for another ten minutes. Abi and her Mexican and Mexican American peers shared their expertise and personal experiences on these issues and some of their nonimmigrant peers defended Mexican families' decisions to cross the border. The following week, Holly facilitated a discussion on immigration using materials from the Teaching Tolerance website,[3] which provides resources for educators to address issues around equity, diversity, and justice. This allowed children to continue exploring immigration through a more critical lens and with more specific learning goals around civic education in ways that centered on their own experiences and understandings. In the following example, we show how similar themes were taken up in a social studies classroom in Ohio.

Immigration, Presidential Elections, and Balances of Power

The day after the 2016 Ohio primaries with Trump and Clinton, Señora Valencia (who identified as Hispanic) opened the social studies lesson by asking students if they had watched the news. Most of the students were African American, including Leeyana and Keyarra, and a few students, such as Paola and Silas, came from families where one or both parents were from Latin American countries. After students shared their knowledge regarding the elections, Señora Valencia posed a question indirectly connecting the news topic of immigration with the curricular topic of branches of government.

1	SraV:	Could a president come and say, "you know what, from now on, nobody
2		can come to our country? I want to say that you are going to wake up at
3		five in the morning and go to work til midnight." Could he do that? Why
4		not? From what you know and from what we talked already, why couldn't
5		he do that? Paola.
6	Paola:	Because that would—unfair for other people to work really hard, cuz

3 http://www.tolerance.org

7		sometimes some people—
8	Leeyana:	We don't get paid that much.
9	Paola:	Some people's parents work so hard to get—to raise money for something,
10		but it wouldn't be fair if other people couldn't come to our country.

Señora Valencia opened space for students to share their knowledge, experiences, and perspectives through two integrated pedagogical moves. She used examples (immigration and long work hours) that related to critical issues in many students' civic lives (#2) and she introduced these examples through a question rather than statement. Here, Señora Valencia did not use the term "immigration," but rather described the process of not being able to "come to our country" (line 2). Thus she provided a humanizing definition of the term to help children think about people's lived experiences. A second generation immigrant, Paola, brought these two themes together in her response, stating that barring immigration "wouldn't be fair" and Leeyana used "we" to position herself among a group that receives low wages. As Señora Valencia continued the lesson, she drew on both students' politicized experiences and prior civics lessons.

11	SraV:	From what we learned, could the president just have all the power in the
12		country to say, "I can do this, you need to do that." Could a president do
13		that?
14	Keyarra:	No, not really. He can't have too much a law but they —the legislature— have
15		to say "Yes, we're gonna make this a law," and he has to look at the
16		Constitution to decide what we can make the law.
		(SraV high fives Keyarra and discussion continues for a few minutes.)
17	Silas:	The three branches—one cannot have too much power.
18	SraV:	(*High fives Silas.*) So, there's a balance in the three branches of the
19		government, so nobody can just do whatever they want. They have to do
20		the check and balance. If they have too much power, they might go into a
21		situation where things are not fair for everybody.

Señora Valencia facilitated a connection between students' earlier expressed concerns with presidential power and the civics lessons on the system of checks and balances, and by doing this built students' knowledge of rights and responsibilities that directly connected to their own concerns (#4). To facilitate the connection, she posed a question about students' concerns, but began by explicitly requesting that students draw "from what we learned" (line 11) to answer her question. Señora Valencia then closed the discussion by explicitly tying a concept (fairness) brought up by students to a curricular concept (checks and balances).

Like the Marshall students in the opening vignette of the chapter, students in this lesson also raised the issue of voting rights. Silas argued that: "Kids should have the right to vote." Keyarra built on this with "I'm going to start a petition" and she and Silas continued the discussion of a petition for children's right to vote as they left the classroom. Like many non-dominant elementary school students throughout our studies, students here oriented toward activism and change as meaningful civic engagement practices, rather than traditional voting rights or volunteering that prevail in white middle-class curricula and communities. Indeed, a focus on protest and petitions were integrated into Señora Valencia's curriculum. This included connecting the 18th-century protests around the Boston Massacre to modern-day protests against presidential administrations and, as Señora Valencia explained to us, the importance of teaching students "how you participate as a citizen," which included "the ability to create a petition and how to reach your representatives."

Facilitating space for students to make connections between their personal experiences, current events, and the curriculum was a central practice in Señora Valencia's approach to civic education. One key pedagogical choice she made the following academic year was to cover the civics unit in the fall of 2016 to coincide with the elections, as many of the controversial issues from the Trump and Clinton campaigns deeply affected her students' lives. This move facilitated teaching civics and current events in an integrated manner, and opened space for students to contribute their civic experiences and knowledge.

Rather than shying away from controversial civic topics and students' politicized experiences, Señora Valencia looked for ways to authentically address students' questions. For example, she emphasized how the issue of immigration always arose in her class, with kids having questions about "how you become legal, why there are illegal people, and things of that nature … because they hear about that subject, but they don't know exactly how it works." Pedagogically she prioritized drawing on her own immigration experiences when students posed questions. As an immigrant who had gone through the legalization process, she shared this to illustrate different processes while being careful to never put individual students in a position in which they felt they had to disclose their own immigration experiences, although some did so voluntarily. She also recounted some of the more recent forms of activism she had noted from Latinx families, such as detailed letters in Spanish explaining that they had not sent their children to school in solidarity with the "day without an immigrant" in 2017. Reflecting on the varying backgrounds of students in her classrooms, she emphasized how the topic of "immigration is big and they see each other. They are friends. So they are very empathetic with each other's realities in that sense." These classroom friendships can be a starting point for students to build coalitions around shared issues and concerns in their communities, including voting rights and living wages. Señora Valencia illustrated the importance of educators opening up spaces to include key issues that matter to students (#2), creating interactive spaces in which students learn to empathize with each other's experiences (#3), and carefully fostering opportunities to allow students to bring their politicized civic experiences to bear on their learning (#1).

Reflections on Pedagogical Practices

The examples in this chapter counter important myths about civic education. They show that non-dominant students, including elementary school students from a range of immigration statuses, are civically engaged and that students from differing immigration statuses and racial backgrounds can safely engage in conversations regarding their politicized experiences. Yet to validate and incorporate these experiences for civic learning we need to rethink what counts as civic education. We illustrated how the five principles discussed here (tailored from Rubin, 2012) provide a framework to develop meaningful civic education at the elementary school level. Our examples show how two educators have begun to achieve this, and in this final section we offer additional suggestions.

Learning from Children's Politicized Experiences

While we understand that elementary teachers are beholden to social studies curricula that are based on historical facts, geographical information, and relatively decontextualized government processes, it is important to find ways to tie civic education to the topics and experiences that are central to students' lives. As these findings show, undocumented immigration was a central topic of concern and interest to elementary school students from a range of backgrounds. Rather than silencing this topic, both educators found ways to broach it in careful and productive ways. In Pennsylvania, Holly made intentional pedagogical moves by tailoring her questions to allow spaces for students with undocumented family members to address the difficult questions posed by peers when they signaled they felt safe responding to such inquiries. She also followed up with a session on immigration from Teaching for Tolerance. In Ohio, Señora Valencia drew on her own immigration experiences to answer students' questions and provided an example of immigration bureaucracy's policies and procedures. She also posed questions that facilitated connections between students' concerns and experiences and their civics curriculum. It is important to note that in both spaces these educators had relationships of *confianza* [deep trust] with students and carefully invited students to share their politicized knowledges related to immigration if they so chose, but never forced students to talk about their family's immigration experiences (see Gallo & Link, 2015). No one starts out as an expert and it is through experience, deeply listening to and engaging with children around their politicized experiences, and seeking out resources that teachers will become more adept at leveling the experiences of their students.

For educators seeking specific pedagogical activities related to leveraging students' politicized experiences, Rubin (2012) offers many discussion-, writing-, project-, role play-, and research-based classroom activities that can be tailored for K-6 classrooms. For example, daily/weekly "social studies journals" provide an opportunity for students to express their opinions and connect their personal experiences to civics issues in the curriculum.

Engaging Students in the Tensions of Citizenship Terminology

Throughout both schools there were difficult and unresolved tensions of how terms such as "American," "citizen," and "illegal" were used by students and educators. Indeed, in curricular materials, the media, and everyday talk, these terms are often utilized in unquestioning ways. Yet our long-term work with students from non-dominant backgrounds has shown us that they can cause exclusion, fear, and silencing in educational spaces. For example, the term "illegal," common in much media discourse, was used by students in Marshall, and by students and Señora Valencia in Nepi, and we have noted it is sometimes unquestioningly used by caring educators looking to support immigrant students. Yet this term blurs the lines between not having official U.S. documentation (which is often referred to as illegality) and criminality, and thus can lead to subconscious thoughts that people without official U.S.documentation are bad or less important than U.S. citizens (see Gallo & Link, 2016). Instead, we encourage educators to engage students in critical discussions about these terms and to consider alternatives such as "from the U.S." for "American", "community members" for "citizens", and "undocumented" for "illegal" immigrants. We encourage teachers to consider how such terms can foster more inclusive conversations and learning.

Rethinking "Good Citizen" Character Education Report Cards

Many elementary schools emphasize the development of certain values throughout their curricula, pedagogies, and behavior management systems that are often reinforced by behavioral report cards sometimes framed in terms of being "good citizens." Yet many of the values emphasized in these evaluations are reflective of white middle-class civic engagement and overlook the practices that many non-dominant students bring to their classrooms and need to survive and thrive as young people of color (see Gallo, 2017). In addition, when behavior report cards in elementary schools are talked about as "good citizenship," this terminology can unintentionally instill fear in families with undocumented members (Mangual Figueroa, 2011).

Alternatively, what if "working together" were conceptualized as "coalition building," a practice through which Latinx and African American students collaboratively responded to civics issues that affect their and/or their peers' daily lives? Seeds were planted for this kind of practice in both Marshall and Nepi as educators engaged in dialogue with and learned from children. And what if "helping others" were to include components of "activism," such as joining local movements around voting rights, immigrant rights, and petition writing that were part of many non-dominant students' regular practices. These forms of political action are common among immigrant and other non-dominant students. These examples illustrate that adults have a great deal to learn from young people's civic engagement, and that elementary school curricula that proactively validate and incorporate students' politicized experiences are central. Indeed, as our current political climate illustrates, these may be the very civic skills that are needed to improve our democratic society in which all of us, including our undocumented neighbors, are crucial members.

References

Bartolomé, L. (1994). Beyond the methods fetish: Toward a humanizing pedagogy. *Harvard Educational Review*, *64*(2), 173–194.

Callahan, R. M. & Muller, C. (2013). *Coming of political age: American schools and the civic development of immigrant youth*. New York: Russell Sage Foundation. Retrieved from http://muse.jhu.edu

Dabach, D. (2015). "My student was apprehended by immigration": A civics teacher's breach of silence in a mixed citizenship classroom. *Harvard Educational Review*, *85*(3), 383–412.

Duncan-Andrade, J. M. R. (2007). Urban youth and the counter-narration of inequality. *Transforming Anthropology*, *15*(1), 26–37.

Freire, P. (1970). *Pedagogy of the oppressed*. New York: Herder & Herder.

Gallo, S. (2017). *Mi padre: Mexican immigrant fathers and their children's education*. New York: Teachers College Press.

Gallo, S. (2016). Humor in father-daughter immigration narratives of resistance. *Anthropology & Education Quarterly*, *47*(3), 279–296.

Gallo, S. & Link, H. (2016). Exploring the borderlands: Elementary school teachers' navigation of immigration practices in a new Latino diaspora community. *Journal of Latinos and Education*, *15*(3), 180–196.

Gallo, S. & Link, H. (2015). "Diles la verdad": Deportation policies, politicized funds of knowledge, and schooling in middle childhood. *Harvard Educational Review*, *85*(3), 357–382.

Hinde, E. R. (2008). Civic education in the NCLB era: The contested mission of elementary and middle schools. *Journal of Curriculum and Instruction*, *2*(1), 74–86.

Kahne, J. E. & Sporte, S. E. (2008). Developing citizens: The impact of civic learning opportunities on students' commitment to civic participation. *American Educational Research Journal*, *45*(3), 738–766.

Mangual Figueroa, A. (2011). Citizenship and education in the homework completion routine. *Anthropology & Education Quarterly*, *42*(3), 263–280.

Rubin, B. C. (2012). *Making citizens: Transforming civic learning for diverse social studies class-rooms*. New York: Routledge.

Rubin, B. C. (2007). "There's still not justice": Youth civic identity development amid distinct school and community contexts. *Teachers College Record, 109*(2), 449–481.

Seif, H. (2010). The civic life of Latina/o immigrant youth: Challenging boundaries and creating safe spaces. In L. R. Sherrod, J. Torney-Purta, & C. A. Flanagan (Eds.) *Handbook of Research on Civic Engagement* (445–470). Hoboken, NJ: John Wiley & Sons.

6

LINKING CHURCH AND SCHOOL: LANGUAGE AND LITERACY PRACTICES OF BILINGUAL LATINX PENTECOSTAL YOUTH

Lucila D. Ek

Entering the Community

On my drive to the Pentecostal church, at the end of the freeway exit, I catch a red light at a busy intersection where the only pedestrian is a Latino vendor who sells oranges, peanuts, and flowers to the stopped cars. Driving further up the street today, I am immediately confronted with a variety of sights and sounds. Businesses, offices, and billboards announce their wares in English, Spanish, and Korean reflecting a few of the languages spoken in this community. Given the diversity of linguistic codes, this area provides an interesting and rich site in which to study literacy practices and the children who participate in them.

The roar and honking of cars mingle with the rhythmic sounds of hip-hop, salsa, and roc-en-español that come from open car and store windows. At the intersection, an insistent and urgent voice cuts through the noise. A man dressed in a suit stands at the corner, microphone and Bible in hand, preaching loudly in Spanish, invoking *Dios nuestro Señor* (the Lord Our God). I leave him and his voice behind as I round the corner and approach the church. The final billboard I see is in the church's parking lot. The large red sign with white lettering in English and Korean is a remnant from the last business that was housed here, "Pico Building Supply." The transformation of this building from a construction supply store to a Pentecostal church reflects a community that is constantly in transition.

A small sign depicting a picture of a cross with a curving flame marks *La Iglesia* (the church), a small storefront Latinx immigrant Pentecostal church in Los Angeles, California. I enter through the side door on the first floor. The space reminds me of a garage, complete with overhead sliding metal gates in the front and back. The pastor gives his sermon from the front of this room. He stands behind a brown pulpit that faces several rows of pews covered with brown wood and green cloth. The front door of the church opens onto a busy street. Passersby, overhearing the songs and prayers, often peer curiously into the room.

Introduction

Education scholars highlight religious settings as important sites for language and literacy learning (de la Piedra, 2010; Fader, 2001; García-Sánchez, 2010; Klein, 2009; McMillon and Edwards 2000; Moore, 2013; Moss, 2004; Zinsser, 1986). Much of the scholarship (Baquedano-López, 1997; Farr, 2000; Wellmeier, 1998; see also Pacheco & Morales, this volume) on Latinx religious literacy practices centers on Catholics as the majority of Latinx affiliated with a religious institution are Catholics. Fifty-five percent of Latinxs identify as Catholic and 22% are Protestant including 16% who identify as Evangelical (Pew Research Center, 2014). In addition, one in four Latinx adults identified as a former Catholic (Pew Research Center, 2014). These demographics call for greater attention to be paid to non-Catholic institutions including Pentecostal churches as they are an important part of life for a significant sector of Latinx immigrants in the U.S.

This chapter draws from a four-year ethnography of a Central American and Mexican immigrant Pentecostal church *La Iglesia* (pseudonym) located in southern California that examined how Pentecostal children and youth were socialized to language, literacy, and morality. Practices at the church mediated the children and youth's language and literacy development in Spanish while socializing them to particular notions of right and wrong. For this chapter, I focus on the literacy practice of reading the Bible as a way to understand church practices that students engage in that can be leveraged in the public school. I am not arguing to link church ideologies to schools, but rather to show how church practices could inform school lessons in productive ways to foster students' literacy knowledge and skills. (See also Pacheco & Morales, this volume.)

Schools, having long enforced a separation of church and state, may not recognize the literacy skills that many families cultivate from the practice of reading the Bible. Understanding what such reading looks like, the values, relationships, and practices that shape it, may help teachers to leverage and expand children's understanding of literacy—different ways of reading both the word and the world. In addition, because church literacy practices socialize the children and youth to moral ways of being and doing, they can inform how schools also transmit moral values and beliefs to students. This chapter explores a particular approach to Bible reading deployed in this Pentecostal church. While the specific practices engaged in this church may differ from those used in other Pentecostal churches (Leon, 1998), Pentecostal churches in general place great emphasis on Bible reading (Walsh, 2018). Other religious groups may also emphasize the reading of ancient, sacred texts, so some consideration of the language that youth are exposed to in such readings is important. I recognize that there may be differences in other religious contexts, but a significant number of immigrants, especially from Guatemala, have adopted Pentecostalism and thus it is important to understand these particular practices. To better understand the literacy practices at *La Iglesia*, I draw from sociocultural theories that integrate language, literacy, and culture.

Ways of Seeing Language, Literacy, and Culture

Sociocultural theories of literacy (Vygotsky, 1978), the language socialization paradigm (Schieffelin & Ochs, 1986), and cultural modeling (Lee, 2003, 2006) offer productive lenses for studying teaching and learning in religious institutions and in schools. These views reconceptualize literacy as not only reading and writing but as a social practice that is ideological, contested, and situated. Language socialization posits that people acquire language and culture in everyday interaction (Duranti, Ochs & Schieffelin, 2011; Garrett & Baquedano-López, 2002; Ochs, 1991; Ochs & Schieffelin 1984, 2017). Novices are socialized by more expert members to and through language. Because language is the preeminent tool for participating in literacy practices, it is the medium through which children are socialized to literacy. As students participate in literacy practices, they acquire skills and knowledge about how to participate in culturally appropriate ways and at the same time acquire values, beliefs, norms, worldviews, and identities (Ek, 2009; Sterponi, 2007; Zentella 2005). At the Pentecostal church, the youth learned to read religious texts, particularly the Bible, in specific ways that transmitted certain beliefs and norms about literacy, morality, and community.

My theoretical frame also draws from Cultural Modeling (Lee, 2003, 2006) to examine how language and literacy practices are embedded in larger cultural contexts. The Cultural Modeling framework complements the language socialization paradigm in that Cultural Modeling also analyzes students' everyday language practices (Lee). In addition, an important aspect of Cultural Modeling involves how talk and participation are organized. Furthermore, a Cultural Modeling framework identifies analogous relationships between the modes of reasoning and discursive practices of disciplinary work and those of everyday life.

Scholarship on Church Literacy

Sociocultural theories, language socialization, and Cultural Modeling have proved productive for studying the literacy practices of Latinx students. Scholarship has found that these students engage in rich language and literacy practices in and across home, school, and community spaces (Bauer & Gort, 2012; González, Moll, & Amanti, 2005; Orellana, 2006, 2009; Orellana & Reynolds, 2008; Reyes, 2012; Reyes & Azuara 2008). Researchers from various disciplines including education, anthropology, and religious studies have recognized the significance of churches as sites for learning. Much research on church literacy has largely focused on adult participants (Isaac, 2005; Isaac, Guy, & Valentine 2001). Research by Hones (2001) found that church facilitated literacy acquisition in both Hmong and English for a Hmong refugee by providing a safe and comfortable environment and by including Hmong culture and traditions. Hence the church can play a valuable role in developing literacy skills in both native and second languages. Farr (2000) and Farr and Dominguez Barajas (2005) found that Mexican Catholic women in Chicago claimed authority for themselves through their church literacy practices. Another study that also focused on adults was Moss' (2001, 2004) research that found that the sermon in African American churches constituted a community text.

A related body of work has examined the language and literacy learning of children and youth in religious institutions. Baquedano-López (1997) studied how *doctrina* (catechism) socialized Mexican immigrant children to ethnic identities through the use of the narrative of Our Lady of Guadalupe. Specifically focusing on the differences between church and school environments, McMillon and Edwards (2000) studied a Sunday school for preschoolers in an African American Baptist church. They found that their focal child was a "superstar" at church whereas in his preschool his behavior was socially unacceptable. The student was an active participant in such church literacy practices as recitation, retelling stories, and reading. Emdin's (2016) research on teaching practices in a Black church gives rise to a Pentecostal pedagogy that can serve as a model for teachers of urban youth of color in schools.

Pentecostalism and La Iglesia

La Iglesia, which is part of the denomination of the Church of God, reflects the ongoing rise of Pentecostalism in Latin America and in the United States (Levitt, 2009; Stoll, 1990). Globally, the larger Pentecostal movement has about 280 million members (Walsh, 2018). In the United States, there are approximately 20 million Pentecostals out of 152 million Protestants and much of the growth can be attributed to communities of color (Walsh, 2018). Around the turn of the century when I conducted my study, in the United States, there were approximately, "3,500 Catholic parishes where mass is celebrated in Spanish and 7,000 Hispanic/Latino Protestant congregations, most of them Pentecostal or evangelical in theology" (Warner & Wittner, 1998, p. 6). At the time, out of 37 million Latinos living in the United States, nearly five million were either Pentecostal or Charismatic (Walsh 2003).

Although predominantly Mexican, the community where *La Iglesia* was located experienced a large inflow of Central American immigrants during the 1980s (Hamilton & Chinchilla, 2001). *La Iglesia's* church membership was comprised of approximately 70% Central American (Guatemalan, Salvadoran,

Honduran, and Nicaraguan) and about 30% Mexican. Most of the children and youth at the church were born in the U.S., and the few born in Latin America came to the United States as very young children. The church offered religious services and activities throughout the week to its working-class Central American and Mexican members. Monday through Saturday, the church was opened in the evenings to offer such activities as Bible study, prayer services, youth groups, and women and men's groups. On Sundays, the main church day, services were held both in the mornings and in the evenings. The Sunday school classes for the children and youth were offered in the mornings.

Researching the Pentecostal Youth Class

The Sunday school classes for the children and youth took place for two hours and the youth class was comprised of on average ten Guatemalan, Salvadoran, and Mexican youth between the ages of 11 and 24, but teenagers constituted the majority. Five girls and four boys attended the class consistently for the first three years that I was a participant observer there. Of these nine students, seven were in high school and two were in middle school. Three of the students came from Mexico, three from Guatemala, and three from El Salvador. Two main teachers taught the Sunday school classes and the Pastor guest taught when needed. Tommy who grew up in Guatemala and came to the U.S. as a teenager was one of the Sunday school teachers.

I conducted an ethnography of *La Iglesia* from October 2000-April 2004 focusing on the *clase para jovenes* (youth class.) The majority of my visits took place between March and December 2001 and some follow-up visits were conducted in 2002. Over the course of the year, I attended 30 youth classes. My fieldnotes recorded what I saw, heard, and experienced in the field (Emerson, Fretz, & Shaw, 1995). I also video - and audiorecorded whenever possible to capture the participants' talk.

Making Sense of Data

My qualitative analysis (Miles & Huberman, 1994) was an ongoing process. Specifically, I read through all of my fieldnotes several times, coding to identify salient themes, patterns, and relationships (Emerson, Fretz & Shaw, 1995). I looked for values, practices, and norms. I typed up summaries of the videorecordings and transcribed audiotapes that I then coded. I transcribed and analyzed key interactions using discourse analysis. My analysis focused primarily on the interactions around the literacy events, centering specifically on how religious texts were read, discussed, and interpreted. There were 18 lessons that were centered around a Biblical story. Literacy events involve talk-in-interaction around written text and have social interactional rules for the type and amount of talk (Heath, 1983). Further analysis was conducted on how the students took up these literacy events, their language uses, and instances where they resisted their teachers' or the Biblical arguments.

Socialization to Church Literacy

I made my way up the narrow staircase that leads to the room marked with a sign proclaiming *Clases para jóvenes* (youth class). Inside, a small dark brown teacher's desk faced the four rows of tables and brown plastic chairs. Wall decorations included a T-shirt with a picture of the Bible on it and "SOUL FOOD" written across the book. On the wall at the front of the room was a white dry erase board. This board was used to display the *temas* (themes) and the *textos para memorizar* (texts for memorizing) that organized each literacy lesson.

Sunday school teachers organized the learning so that students could have multiple opportunities to engage in practices valued by the church and to make sense of and appropriate the texts and principles. Students were engaged in literacy activities, such as the recitation of Bible verses as well as more interactive sessions where they could discuss their own interpretations of readings. The teacher opened the class by presenting the guiding *tema* (theme) and a *texto* (text) on the dry erase board. The teacher then led the prayer, followed by the singing of hymns. Lecture followed, and prayer and hymns closed the day's lesson. These activities took place primarily in Spanish.

The Authority of the Bible

The primary religious written text used at the church was the Bible which the Pentecostal community considered *la palabra de Dios* (God's word). In Pentecostalism, the Bible is "the infallible word of God and the sole authority for theological doctrines" (Walsh, 2018, p. 1). As members of the community of Pentecostals, the children and youth needed to learn to use the Bible in designated Christian ways as defined by *La Iglesia*. They were expected to bring it with them to every Sunday school class. The youth have acquired their own Bibles and found ways to individualize them. One of the girls, for example, covered her Bible in dark blue denim. Each person had to have the text in front of him/her during Bible readings. During the lessons, students followed along in their Bibles. A few times I saw students take notes.

Other written texts at the church included religious lesson books, such as *La Senda Juvenil* (The Youthful Path), which also reinforced the norms, values, and beliefs of the Pentecostal church. A member of the community of *La Iglesia* had to recognize and display proper deference to authority, including textual authority. During a lecture, Tommy, one of the Sunday school teachers, pointed out the differences between Catholics and Pentecostals, and said about Catholics: *Ellos no tienen tanto la autoridad (de) la Biblia como nosotros.* (They do not have the authority of the Bible as much as we do.) Relationships between Catholics and

Protestants have long been marked by mutual suspicion and tension (Walsh, 2003, p. 31).

Tommy emphasized to the Pentecostal students the powerful role that the Bible had and should have in their lives. As God's word, the Bible was imbued with a moral authority that was communicated to the youth repeatedly. Students received explicit messages that they were responsible for following what the Bible asked them to do. As Tommy stated: *Nosotros somos responsables por lo que está en la Biblia.* (We are responsible for what's in the Bible.) Teachers and the Pastor often framed their statements with *La Biblia dice* (the Bible says) or *La Biblia habla de* (the Bible talks about) to convey the truth and incontestability of their remarks. These ways of talking about the Biblical text underscored the close relationship between the written and oral word, almost blurring the distinction.

Students were assigned the Bible readings for moral development and not to become better readers. The Biblical narrative was an important medium in the youth's socialization to the moral knowledge and values that the elders wanted them to have. Tommy warned the students: *Cuando uno deja de leer la Biblia, … viene el Diablo y aprovecha para hacerse la suya.* (When one stops reading the Bible, … the Devil comes, takes advantage, and does whatever he wants.) The goal at *La Iglesia* was that children and youth become good Christians (Ek, 2005). Themes of the Bible upheld good Christian values: helping others; honoring, serving, and obeying God; resisting temptation; not being hypocritical; and being chaste. The moral dimensions of the practice are important to consider and I do so in other work (Ek, 2009), but in this chapter, I focus on the language and literacy demands in order to identify analogies with the literacy practices that are cultivated in schools.

Reading as a Collective Community Practice

Different activities were used to familiarize the children with the organization of the Bible books and chapters. These activities included games, reciting the Bible books in order, and copying the names of the books in order. Finding the book, chapter, and verse to be read quickly was a skill that facilitated the students' engagement in the reading. Tommy also assigned the students to write one part of the Bible each Sunday at home. Teachers constantly encouraged, asked, and instructed students to read the Bible daily as part of their Christian activities outside of church. Tommy directed them to preface their reading by talking to God and asking: *Señor háblame.* (Lord, speak to me.)

Through their participation in literacy practices, students learned *La Iglesia*'s specific practices for reading the Bible, which occurred in one of three ways: 1) the teacher read the Bible himself with the students quietly following in their own Bibles; 2) the teacher selected one student to read a certain verse or verses; or 3) all read the Bible taking turns to read a verse. The teacher might also ask students to read a certain verse all at the same time, an example of how students were socialized to choral reading. Tommy once remarked that reading aloud together helped the less fluent readers fully participate in the literacy event and helped them acquire more fluency. At the same time, choral reading primarily emphasized collectivity and community.

To illustrate how students engaged in the literacy practice of Bible reading, I analyze one literacy event that took place during one of Tommy's lessons. On this day, Tommy selected a narrative from the book of *Hechos* (Acts) that focused on the *dones* (gifts) that God can give to his disciples, one of which was the ability to tell whether people are lying. In the story, a husband and wife try to cheat God and are severely punished. During the lesson, Danny, Rocio, Laura, Carla, Ana, Eduardo, and Amalia (pseudonyms) were all students in the class:

Segment #1

Tommy:	1	**En esta ocasión Dios le dió a los apóstoles el dicernir (reading)** *On this occasion God gave the apostles the ability to discern*
	2	**si lo que estaban diciendo era verdad o era mentira.** *whether they were telling the truth or a lie*
	3	**Es el Capítulo cinco del versículo uno al diez. (thumbing through Bible)** *It is Chapter five from verse one to ten.*
	4	**Okay, go ahead° (to student)**
Danny:	5	**(reading) Mas un varón llamado Ananías** *But a certain man named Ananias,*
	6	**con Safira, su mujer, vendió la posesión.** *with Sapphira his wife, sold a possession,*
Rocío:	7	**¿Cuál?** *Which one?*
Tommy:	8	**(Es el) cinco: dos.** *It's five:two.*
Rocío:	9	**Y defraudó el precio (sabiéndolo) también su mujer** *And kept back part of the price, his wife also being privy to it,*
	10	**y trayendo una parte (la puso) a los pies de los apóstoles.** *and brought a certain part, and laid it at the apostles' feet.*
Student	11	**cinco:tres** (whispering to me) five: three

In this transcript, the teacher begins the Bible reading (lines 1–5). Through literacy events such as this one, students learned that each person took a turn to read a verse that facilitated the turn-taking. Students also knew that the Bible was organized by numbers, which they used as a guide and reference. This organizational system is different from other texts the students encounter but at the church children and youth have learned how the system is set up and are able to find the readings quickly, almost automatically. They also know multiple ways of stating the verses both in the longhand (as in line 3) and shorthand (as in lines 8 and 11).

Through their participation, the youth were being socialized to the community's norms of reading that emphasized collectivity. Because the Bible readings were divided into verses and students knew that they could each read a verse, there was minimal interruption of the narrative as students read. The interruptions of the flow of the narrative in lines 7–8 and 11 occurred when students asked what verse was next or when they and the teacher offered help to students or to me, the researcher. As a novice to the community, I was not familiar with the organization of the Bible books and so was slow to find the reading. I usually had to look in the table of contents to find the page number of the book being read. The students were often helpful in guiding me as in line 11.

Learning the Bible's Register

The Sunday school teachers afforded the children and youth rich experiences reading the Bible, a complex literary text. An important part of the students' literacy learning in the class was the literary, archaic Spanish register to which they were exposed. The next segment of the transcript demonstrates the students' reading of this register:

Segment #2

Ek	12	**Y dijo Pedro, "Ananías, (Reading)**
		And Peter said, "Ananias,
	13	**¿por qué llenó Satanás tu corazón**
		why hath Satan filled thine heart
	14	**para que mintieses al Espíritu Santo**
		so that you lied to the Holy Ghost
	15	**y sustrajeses del precio de la heredad?**
		and extracted part of the price of the property?
Laura	16	**Um, reteniéndola ¿no se=no se te queda-quedaba a ti**
		Retaining it, was it not thine own
	17	**y vendida no estaba en tu poder?**
		and after it was sold, was it not in thine own power?
	18	**Por qué pusistes [sic] esto en tu corazón.**
		why hast thou conceived this thing in thine heart?
	19	**No has mentido a los hombres sino a Dios."**
		thou hast not lied unto men, but unto God."

The youth knew that the language of the Bible is not the same as how they talk. During one lesson, Tommy reading a verse asked them: *¿Por qué en esos tiempos escribían así? ¿Por qué hablaban así?* (Why did they write like that in those times? Why did they speak like that?) Junior, one of the boys, responded: "It's like a code." Students were also aware that there were different versions of the Bible, such as when Danny brought one written in a more modern Spanish. These kinds of metalinguistic question are incredibly powerful in raising students' metapragmatic awareness. Students have the opportunity to reflect on the language and behavior that are appropriate to use in specific contexts and in particular interactions. Specifically, they become more aware about different linguistic styles or (registers) for different audiences, for different purposes, and for different social situations. Students also learned about how language changes over time.

Vocabulary and grammar

Through their reading of the Bible, the students learned a literate vocabulary that they were less likely to encounter in everyday talk. The register included such words as *defraudó* (defraud) (line 9), *dicernir* (discern) in (line 1), *heredad* (property), and *reteniéndola* (retaining) (line 16). As demonstrated by the transcripts above, these Latinx children and youth engaged in vocabulary building activities on a weekly basis (and sometimes more) in their church. These experiences counter persistent claims that poor and working-class children develop a "language gap" or vocabulary gap in the language acquisition process that contributes to their educational failure (Avineri et al., 2015).

The literary register of the Bible also frequently included complex and rare tense forms of the subjunctive mood. The transcript includes *mintieses* (line 14) (you lied) and *sustrajeses* (line 15) (you extracted). This subjunctive form is not often used as the more common is *mintieras* (you lied) and *sustrajeras* (you extracted). Thus, these students were being exposed to two different ways of forming the subjunctive, a difficult verbal mood to learn that is often not used among second generation Latinos/as in the U.S. (Otheguy & Zentella, 2007).

As students read the text, they talked about it in their own vernacular ways. For example, as Laura, who was Salvadoran, read the text, she said *pusistes* (line 18) (you put), which is a non-standard form of the standard *pusiste* (you put). This form of *pusiste* is very common all over the Spanish-speaking world including among Mexicans and Central Americans living in California. As previously mentioned, the Spanish Bible uses Spanish forms and vocabulary that the children and youth did not use in their everyday interactions. When making sense of the text, they put it in their own ways of speaking. In this way, they effectively translated between more formal and informal registers. These examples of lexicon and verb tense and moods show a few of the complexities embedded in this literacy practice and highlight that these intricacies may often present more at church than in Spanish texts found at school.

Making Meaning of Complex Texts

During these literacy events, the teachers' main concern was the students' understanding of the moral narrative and not the accuracy of the reading. There were several miscues and it was difficult to hear some of the students yet Tommy did not correct the students nor tell them to read in a louder voice. As the next segment illustrates, Tommy prompted the students to co-construct a real-life example of the story to facilitate their comprehension:

Segment #3

Tommy:	50	**Pero estos dos, eh=eh ¿cómo es qué se llaman?**
		But these two, what are their names?
Students:	51	**Ananías–**
Tommy:	52	**Ananías y Safira. Ellos eran un matrimonio**
		Ananias and Sapphira. They were a married couple.
	53	**y ellos tenían, hazte cuenta ellos tenían una granja.**
		and they had, pretend they had a farm.
	54	**Ellos vinieron y lo vendieron (.)**
		They came and they sold it.
	55	**Imagínense que ( ) en dólares.**
		Imagine that ( ) in dollars.
	56	**¿Cuánto es una buena cantidad para una granja ( )**
		How much is a good price for a farm ( )
	57	**no tan grande, una pequeña?**
		that is not that big, a small one?
Adalia:	58	**Five thousand?**
Tommy:	59	**Like, o.k., let's say no–**
Student	60	**Fifty thousand**
Tommy:	61	**Lo que vale un carro nuevo del año.**
		The price of a new car.
Adalia:	62	**Twenty-six thousand, no I don't know.**
Students	63	**( )**
Tommy:	64	**thirty thousand dollars ( ).**
	65	**Hazte cuenta que la granja costó thirty thousand dollars.**
		Pretend the farm cost thirty thousand dollars.
	66	**Entonces ellos vinieron y dijeron**
		Then they came and said
	67	**"Wow, nos dieron buen dinero con esta–por esta granja**
		Wow they gave us good money with this–for this farm
	68	**que nosotros teníamos, 30 mil dólares.**
		that we had, thirty thousand dollars.
	69	**¿por qué no agarramos 10 mil dólares**
		why don't we take 10 thousand dollars.
	70	**y sólo damos 20 mil dólares?**
		and only give 20 thousand dollars."

This segment shows how Tommy helped the archaic and formal text make more sense to the kids. Strategically, Tommy changed the Biblical farmhouse to a car, more interesting and familiar to these urban youth. Tommy asked students to pretend that the couple had a farm (line 53) and asked about how much a farm (line 56) or a car (line 61) would cost. In this way, he further brought the narrative into the present and, at the same time, engaged the students. Tommy scaffolded students' comprehension with the meaning-making activity that helped the youth relate to the Biblical action. Hence, Tommy was doing exactly what schoolteachers often ask students to do with complex texts. A key linguistic resource used in this part of the interaction was codeswitching. Students responded to Tommy's questions in English (lines 58, 60, 62), which he accepted, and he too switched between Spanish and English (lines 59, 61, 64).

Linkages to Schools and Classrooms

Connections to the Common Core State Standards

As the teachings at *La Iglesia* show, Tommy socialized the Pentecostal youth to literacy skills. Through Tommy's lessons, the students demonstrated literacy competence in a variety of ways: participant structures, registers, and semantics. Also, church literacy practices built students' lexicon in Spanish as well as their capacity for textual analysis, evaluation, and interpretation. Schools can leverage these language and literacy skills to meet state literacy standards.

As the data demonstrate, the Pentecostal students engaged in many experiences of reading and making sense of literary texts written in an archaic formal register. These literacy demands for the youth at *La Iglesia* have important connections to the academic literacy development that takes place in public schools, particularly as articulated in the Common Core State Standards in English Language Arts (CCSS-ELA). The CCSS-ELA provide guidelines for English Language Arts and literacy with the goal that students in K-12 will acquire the literacy skills and concepts required for entering college and career (Common Core State Standards for English Language Arts/Literacy, 2018, p. 46). These skills spiral through the K-12 curriculum and build on one another.

The CCSS-ELA asks that students read increasingly complex texts. The Bible is written in very complex language, and Biblical narratives expose students to vocabulary, grammar, and themes not commonly used in everyday talk. At *La Iglesia*, Tommy used various strategies to scaffold students' comprehension of the text. He used figurative language when he asked students to imagine a contemporary scenario of the protagonists' cheating the apostles (Segment #3, lines 53–70). Tommy also facilitated discussions about the texts. Through their talks about characters, settings, and plots, the Pentecostal students were able to identify key themes of the Bible narratives. An important component of these class discussions was that both the Sunday school teacher and the students used varieties of Spanish and English as well as codeswitching to make sense of the texts (Segment 3). These practices can further connect to the CCSS in literacy that call for engagement in collaborative discussions with teachers and classmates for comprehension. Moreover, the Pentecostal teacher's and students' use of their various linguistic resources links to Speaking and Listening Standards including that students learn to "adapt speech to a variety of contexts and tasks" (Common Core State Standards for English Language Arts/Literacy, 2018, p. 46).

La Iglesia's literacy practices can prepare students for another CCSS-ELA standard that calls for students to "analyze how a modern work of fiction draws on themes, patterns of events, or character types from myths, traditional stories or religious works such as the Bible" (p. 37). Students at the secondary level encounter many works of fiction, such as Shakespeare's writings, that draw from the Bible. Furthermore, students' engagement with themes and characters from religious texts in public classrooms can open up opportunities to discuss and explore the secular values of school and the moralizing socialization of church literacy.

Contrary to the church, at school, the explicit goal is socialization to literacy without awareness of socialization to morality through literacy. Yet, it is important to recognize that reading the Bible socialized the Pentecostal youth to morality and that other texts also transmit moral ideologies. Classroom teachers can be mindful of the socializing power of the texts and curricula that socialize students not only to literacy but also to notions of what is good and right in the world. To do this, teachers can first cultivate their own awareness of the moralizing discourses that are found in texts and organize lessons for students to develop skills for recognizing, understanding, and critically interpreting these ideologies. Doing so can allow educators to open up spaces for students to question or reinterpret texts. For example, teachers can explicitly ask students what values and beliefs are texts' authors arguing for, whether they agree or disagree, how they feel about these beliefs, and to compare them to their home and church values.

However, teachers can also attend to the different ways in which texts assume authority (or not) in different institutional contexts. As my study showed, for the Pentecostal youth, the Bible is *the* authoritative text. Other kids will have different experiences and expectations about the relationship of texts to "truth" and authority and the questioning of truth and authority can result in tensions that need to be explored. It is also important to recognize that students must navigate between these spaces of friction. Emdin's (2016) research in an African American Pentecostal church offers an approach for grappling with tensions and emotions in the classroom. He calls for a Pentecostal pedagogy that can meet students' cultural and emotional experiences. Teachers can create safe spaces where students can express their perspectives and "identify, discuss, and express emotion" (Emdin, 2016, p. 54). A Pentecostal pedagogy also calls for affording students opportunities to be leaders in the teaching and learning that takes place. Such an approach requires that teachers take on a learner role.

Conclusion

This chapter has demonstrated how Latinx immigrant Pentecostal youth are socialized to literacy through their Sunday school lessons. The particular approach taken to Bible reading in the Pentecostal church I studied emphasized the skills of reading, comprehension, and vocabulary building. The Pentecostal youth were exposed to a distinct formal, literary register of Spanish that can link to the more specialized registers they may encounter in literary works in schools and can be leveraged for developing students' understandings of literature. Children and youth who attend other Pentecostal churches whether bilingual or monolingual might have similar experiences because the reading of the Bible is a core practice for many evangelical groups (Walsh, 2018).

An important finding from my church ethnography is that Latinx bilingual immigrant students are exposed to low-frequency "academic" Spanish vocabulary and register, and engage in discussions of complex, archaic texts recounting events that take place in a particular historical and social context. This church language may be more complex than the language they encounter in school texts in both English and Spanish. For example, some of the Latinx students at the church who were in ESL programs engaged in higher level language and literacy practices at church than in their high school (Ek, 2008/9). Yet, immigrant children are often and erroneously believed to have very little exposure in their communities to the kinds of formal linguistic register and study of literary texts that are valued in schools.

Teachers can leverage these kinds of church funds of knowledge (González, Moll, & Amanti, 2005; Mercado, 2005) and make connections to the Common Core State Standards in English Language Arts/Literacy. For example, many works of western literature both classic and modern contain Biblical allusions. When reading Dante's *Inferno* and Steinbeck's *East of Eden*, teachers might ask students about their understandings of heaven, hell, and paradise. To increase students' understanding of Toni Morrison's *Song of Solomon*, teachers might also ask students to make connections between characters found in the book, Pilate, Hagar, and First Corinthians, and their Biblical counterparts. Furthermore, students' skills and knowledge acquired in church and leveraged in classrooms can also help them acquire conceptual knowledge in other content areas including science (Bravo, Maldonado, & Solis, forthcoming). Thus, the more knowledge educators attain about Latinx home and community language and literacy practices the sturdier the bridges that they can build between their students' lives and school disciplinary knowledge.

References

Avineri, N., Johnson, E., Brice-Heath, S., McCarty, T., Ochs, E., Kremer-Sadlik, T., Paris, D. (2015). Invited forum: Bridging the "language gap". *Journal of Linguistic Anthropology, 25*(1), 66–86.

Baquedano-López, P. (1997). Creating social identities through doctrinal narratives. *Issues in Applied Linguistics, 8*(1), 27–45.

Bauer, E. B. & Gort, M. (Eds.). (2012). *Early biliteracy development: Exploring young learners' use of their linguistic resources.* New York: Routledge.

Bravo, M., Maldonado, S. & Solis, J. L. (forthcoming). Addressing complexities of science texts to facilitate English-language learners' conceptual development. In M. Kuhn, M. J., & J. Halladay (Eds.). *Developing conceptual knowledge through oral and written language.* New York: Guilford Press.

Common Core State Standards for English Language Arts/Literacy (2018). Retrieved from http://www.corestandards.org/wp-content/uploads/ELA_Standards1.pdf

de la Piedra, M. T. (2010). Religious and self-generated Quechua literacy practices in the Peruvian Andes. *International Journal of Bilingual Education and Bilingualism, 1*(13), 99–113.

Duranti, A., Ochs, E., & Schieffelin, B. B. (Eds.). (2011). *The handbook of language socialization, Vol. 72.* Chichester: John Wiley & Sons.

Ek, L. D. (2009). "It's different lives": A Guatemalan American adolescent's construction of ethnic and gender identities across educational contexts. *Anthropology & Education Quarterly, 40*(4), 405–420.

Ek, L. D. (2008/2009). Language and literacy in the Pentecostal Church and the public high school: A case study of a Mexican ESL Student. *The High School Journal, 92*(2), 1–13.

Ek, L. D. (2005). Staying on God's path: Socializing Latino immigrant youth to a Christian Pentecostal identity in Southern California. In A. C. Zentella (Ed.) *Building on strength: Language and literacy in Latino families and communities* (77–92). New York: Teachers College Press and California Association for Bilingual Education.

Emdin, C. (2016). *For White folks who teach in the hood … and the rest of y'all too: Reality pedagogy and urban education.* Boston, MA: Beacon Press.

Emerson, R., Fretz, R., & Shaw, L. (1995). *Writing ethnographic fieldnotes.* Chicago, IL: University of Chicago Press.

Fader, A. (2001). Literacy, bilingualism and gender in a Hasidic community. *Linguistics and Education, 12*(3), 261–283.

Farr, M. (2000). Literacy and religion: Reading, writing, and gender among Mexican women in Chicago. In J. K. Peyton, P. Griffin, W. Wolfram, & R. Fasold (Eds.) *Language in action: New studies of language in society* (139–254). Cresskill, NJ: Hampton Press.

Farr, M. & Dominguez Barajas, E. (2005). Mexicanos in Chicago: Language ideology and identity. In A. C. Zentella (Ed.) *Building on strength: Language and literacy in Latino families and communities* (46–59). New York/Covina, CA: Teachers College Press/California Association for Bilingual Education.

García-Sánchez, I. M. (2010). The politics of Arabic language education: Moroccan immigrant children's language socialization into ethnic and religious identities. *Linguistics and Education, 3*(21), 171–196.

Garrett, P. B. & Baquedano-López, P. (2002). Language socialization: Reproduction and continuity, transformation, and change. *The Annual Review of Anthropology, 31,* 339–361.

González, N., Moll, L. & Amanti, C. (2005). *Funds of knowledge: Theorizing practices in households and classrooms.* Mahwah, NJ: Laurence Erlbaum Associates.

Hamilton, N. & Chinchilla, N. S. (2001). *Seeking community in a global city: Guatemalans and Salvadorans in Los Angeles.* Philadelphia, PA: Temple University Press.

Heath, S. B. (1983). What no bedtime story means: Narrative skills at home and school *Language in Society*, *11*(1), 49–76.

Hones, D. F. (2001). The word: Religion and literacy in the life of a Hmong American. *Religious Education*, *96*(4), 489–509.

Isaac, E. P. (2005). The future of adult education in the urban African-American church. *Education and Urban Society*, *37*(3), 276–291.

Isaac, E. P., Guy, T., & Valentine, T. (2001). Understanding African-American learners' motivations to learn in church based adult education. *Adult Education Quarterly*, *52*(1), 23–38.

Klein, W. L. (2009). Turban narratives: Discourses of identification and difference among Punjabi Sikh families in Los Angeles. In A. Reyes and A. Lo (Eds.) *Beyond yellow English: Toward a linguistic anthropology of Asian Pacific America* (111–130). Oxford: Oxford University Press.

Lee, C. D. (2006). "Every good-bye ain't gone": Analyzing the cultural underpinnings of classroom talk. *International Journal of Qualitative Studies in Education*, *19*(3), 305–327.

Lee, C. D. (2003). Cultural modeling: CHAT as a lens for understanding instructional discourse based on African American English discourse patterns. In A. Kozulin, B. Gindis, V. S. Ageyev, & S. M. Miller (Eds.) *Vygotsky's educational theory in cultural context* (256–268). Cambridge: Cambridge University Press.

Leon, L. (1998). Born again in East LA: The congregation as border space. In R. S. Warner & J. G. Wittner (Eds.) *Gatherings in diaspora: Religious communities and the new immigration* (163–196). Philadelphia, PA: Temple University Press.

Levitt, P. (2009). Roots and routes: Understanding the lives of the second generation transnationally. *Journal of Ethnic and Migration Studies*, *35*(7), 1225–1242.

McMillon, G. T. & Edwards, P. A. (2000). Why does Joshua "hate" school … but love Sunday school. *Language Arts*, *78*(2), 111–120.

Mercado, C. I. (2005). Seeing what's there: Language and literacy funds of knowledge in New York Puerto Rican homes. In A. C. Zentella (Ed.) *Building on strength. Language and literacy in Latino families and communities* (134–147). New York: Teachers College Press.

Miles, M. B. & Huberman, A. M. (1994). *Qualitative data analysis*, 2nd edn.). Thousand Oaks, CA: Sage.

Moore, L. C. (2013). Qur'anic school sermons as a site for sacred and second language socialisation. *Journal of Multilingual and Multicultural Development*, *34*(5), 445–458.

Moss, B. J. (2004). A literacy event in African American churches: The sermon as a community text. In M. Farr (Ed.) *Ethnolinguistic Chicago: Language and literacy in the city's neighborhoods* (137–159). Mahwah, NJ: Lawrence Erlbaum Associates.

Moss, B. J. (2001). *A community text arises: A literacy text and a literacy tradition in African American churches*. Cresskill, NJ: Hampton Press, Inc.

Ochs, E. (1991). Socialization through language and interaction: A theoretical introduction. *Issues in Applied Linguistics*, *2*(2), 143–147.

Ochs, E. & Schieffelin, B. (2017). Language socialization: An historical overview. In P. A. Duff & S. May (Eds.) *Language socialization* (3–16). Amsterdam: Springer.

Ochs, E. & Schieffelin, B. B. (1984). Language acquisition and socialization: Three developmental stories. In R. A. Shweder & R. A. LeVine (Eds.) *Culture theory: Essays on mind, self, and emotion* (276–320). Cambridge: Cambridge University Press.

Orellana, M. F. (2009). *Translating childhoods: Immigrant youth, language, and culture*. New Brunswick, NJ: Rutgers University Press.

Orellana, M. F. (2006). Building on the translating experiences of immigrant youth for academic literacies. In E. W. Ross & V. O. Pang (Eds.) *Race, ethnicity, and education* (1–27). Westport, CT: Praeger Publishers.

Orellana M. F. & Reynolds, J. F. (2008). Cultural modeling: Leveraging bilingual skills for school paraphrasing tasks. *Reading Research Quarterly, 43*(1): 48–65.

Otheguy, R. & Zentella, A. C. (2007). Language and dialect contact in Spanish New York: Toward the formation of a speech community. *Language, 83*(4), 1–33.

Pew Research Center. (2014). The shifting religious identity of Latinos in the United States. Pew Research Center, Washington DC. Retrieved from http://www.pewforum.org/2014/05/07/the-shifting-religious-identity-of-latinos-in-the-united-states/

Reyes, I. (2012). Biliteracy among children and youths. *Reading Research Quarterly, 47*(3), 307–327.

Reyes, I. & Azuara, P. (2008). Emergent biliteracy in young Mexican immigrant children. *Reading Research Quarterly, 43*(4), 374–398.

Schieffelin, B. B. & Ochs, E. (1986). *Language socialization across cultures.* Cambridge, MA: Cambridge University Press

Sterponi, L. (2007). Clandestine interactional reading: Intertextuality and double-voicing under the desk. *Linguistics and Education, 18*(1), 1–23.

Stoll, D. (1990). *Is Latin America turning Protestant?: The politics of evangelical growth.* Berkeley, CA: University of California Press.

Vygotsky, L. (1978). *Mind in society.* Cambridge, MA: Harvard University Press.

Walsh, S. A. (2018). *Pentecostals in America.* New York: Columbia University Press.

Walsh, S. A. (2003). *Latino Pentecostal identity: Evangelical faith, self, and society.* New York: Columbia University Press.

Warner, R. S. & Wittner, J. G. (Eds.) (1998). *Gatherings in diasporas: Religious communities and the new immigration.* Philadelphia, PA: Temple University Press.

Wellmeier, N. (1998). Santa Eulalia's people in exile: Maya religion, culture, and identity in Los Angeles. In R. S. Warner & J. G. Wittner (Eds.) *Gatherings in diaspora: Religious communities and the new immigration* (97–122). Philadelphia, PA: Temple University Press.

Zentella, A. C. (2005). *Building on strength: Language and literacy in Latino families and communities.* New York: Teachers College Press.

Zinsser, C. (1986). For the Bible tells me so: Teaching children in a fundamentalist church. In B. Schieffelin & P. Gilmore (Eds.) *The acquisition of literacy: Ethno-graphic perspectives* (55–71). Norwood, NJ: Ablex.

7

FIGURATIVE LANGUAGE IN RELIGIOUS COMMUNITY CONTEXTS: OPPORTUNITIES TO LEVERAGE AND EXPAND BILINGUAL YOUTH'S LINGUISTIC REPERTOIRES

Mariana Pacheco and P. Zitlali Morales

In this chapter, we draw on a multiyear ethnographic study of the religious language and literacy practices in which one bilingual youth participated at the church service she attended with her family on a weekly basis. Our analysis focuses on the routine and typical language practices and discourses that characterized activities such as sermons, prayers, and songs. Our detailed analysis reveals that figurative and metaphorical language practices created opportunities for bilingual children and youth to participate in and experience the complex and nuanced ways that members of this Christian community constructed their relationship with God. Specifically, we focus on the figurative and metaphorical language practices they employed as they engaged with religious texts. We then make connections to the Common Core State Standards to demonstrate that the language practices in which bilingual children and youth already engage in their out-of-school lives can align with our expectations for language use and skills in the classroom.

Background

Mariana first met Ximena[1] during her ethnographic study at a community-based teen newspaper in a mid-sized Midwestern community where she was one of few Latina/o high school students in the program (Pacheco, 2014, 2015). The study lasted about three years and data collection involved participant observation methods, including field notes, audio recordings, document collection, in-depth

---

1 All names are pseudonyms.

interviews, and photography (Creswell, 2009; Emerson, Fretz, & Shaw, 1995). Ximena was 15 years old at the start of the study and a Spanish-English bilingual with Spanish as her home language. She had participated in an early-exit transitional bilingual program but had experienced the majority of her schooling in English. In high school, she was a relatively successful student and participated in many extracurricular activities (i.e., track, dance clubs, etc.), including the teen newspaper. She was outgoing and open and extremely committed to doing well in school, which required a great deal of effort and energy on her part because the academic and (English) language demands were an increasingly overwhelming fact of school. Across three years of getting to know Ximena and her family, it was clear that Christianity and her Christian identity played an important role in their lives. One Halloween, for example, Ximena was one of the few students who did not wear a costume or go trick-or-treating because, she said: "It's against my religion." This refrain was common. Her family regularly attended church services on Sunday mornings that lasted between two to six hours, depending on particular special events and holidays.

Ximena participated in a range of linguistic and discursive practices outside of school. This chapter focuses on an analysis of religious discourses and practices at the United Church of Christ (UCC) as documented in field notes and transcribed audio recordings. We attend to those routine and typical patterns of using language during sermons, singing and choir performances, and prayers that the Christian church community valued. Since these discourses and practices occurred in the context of a religious community, we attempt to infer meaning and significance from the immediate particular interactional context of participation (Baquedano-López, 2001; Wuthnow, 2011; see also Ek, this volume), rather than a deep historical analysis of religious texts and institutions. In other words, we focus analytically on what these uses of language meant and signified to the community, although we acknowledge that they change over time and with the ebb and flow of members.[2]

We recognize numerous reasons for educators to perhaps raise issues regarding the acknowledgement and place of religious discourses and language practices in schools. For example, attempts to more fully understand students' linguistic repertoires may require an appreciation of the religious communities and constituent practices (i.e., songs, prayers) in which students participate. In ostensibly secular schools, educators may have legitimate concerns about properly honoring and integrating these practices in a school context that may include students from many different religious backgrounds or no religious background at all.

We believe, however, that serious efforts to explore and build on the linguistic and cultural resources non-dominant students bring to the classroom must

---

2 My (Mariana) positionality as a Catholic was relevant because I observed with "new eyes" some unfamiliar practices, such as the spontaneous chiming in and witnessing during sermons.

consider their engagement with religious discourse practices and texts, as these experiences are important sources of learning for many young people. For example, Baquedano-López (2001) illustrates that in the context of religious education (i.e., *doctrina*) classes, teachers constructed extended narratives that linked the past and present to socialize Mexican immigrant Catholic children to a collective social experience, ethnic and racial identities as "dark-skinned peoples," and an affiliation with an oppressive and colonial Mexican past. Additionally, researchers have documented that Black communities engage in call-and-response practices, for example, that have deep historical roots in the traditional African worldview (Daniel & Smitherman, 1976; Foster, 2001; Smitherman, 2000). While call-and-response is enacted in both religious and secular life, it nonetheless links "speakers" and "listeners" into a unified, holistic movement constituted by interactive, interdependent, and spontaneous communicative processes.

Clearly, many students participate routinely in different types of religious community in their out-of-school lives, and these communities engage with language and literacy in significant and specialized ways. Concerns about local responses to the acknowledgement of students' participation in religious communities notwithstanding, it is important for practitioners and educators to recognize and attempt to leverage these students' out-of-school skills in ways they might similarly leverage their literacy performances (Skilton-Sylvester, 2002) and translation experiences (Orellana, 2009; see also Reynolds & Orellana, this volume). In arguing for the social scientific importance of religious talk and discourses to understand constructions of social life, Wuthnow (2011) contends:

> [T]reatments of lived religion have argued for the importance of examining practices in everyday life, and discussions of spirituality have noted the extent to which religious meanings and identities are constructed from multiple repertoires rather than adhering to particular creedal formulations.
> *(p. 15)*

Thus, in our analysis, we assert that youths' language use in religious contexts employ multiple discursive practices (e.g., narratives, call-and-response) that are valuable resources and have deep significance for understanding the meanings and identities they index.

It is important for practitioners and educators to consider as well that the deep meanings and identities these discourses and literacy practices have for community members could not be replicated fully in places such as classrooms. The fundamental goal, however, is to enhance our awareness about non-dominant students' knowledge of language forms, styles, discourses, and varieties outside of school and to explore the sociocultural processes by which students come to understand their deep meanings across out-of-school contexts (Morales, 2016; Pacheco, 2009). And while these meanings change over time as communities and their members change as well, we emphasize the importance of teachers examining the daily and regular language practices of their students, in order to recognize them and draw on them. Here we illustrate how practitioners and educators might approach religious discourses and practices in the classroom by highlighting the repertoire and resources of one case study youth.

Site Description

The United Church of Christ (UCC) was located about 30 minutes away from Ximena's family home in a middle-class area on the west side of a mid-sized Midwestern city that had been experiencing demographic shift. While the Euro-American/white population in the city remained relatively stable, the population of Latino migrants and immigrants—mostly from Mexico—had been growing since about 2000. Of import, the UCC was responsive to this demographic shift. The UCC website stated that it was "comprised of people from many different backgrounds and cultures. [...] We are a multi-cultural, international, bilingual fellowship of believers. All of our services are in both English and Spanish."[3] The UCC was housed in a large brown building and surrounded by a sizeable parking lot. Inside, the main worship room had relatively bare walls with minimal decorations, except for a couple of simple, large crosses. There were usually around 150 members and about 50 children in attendance for Sunday services. On entry into the UCC, participants greeted one another with large smiles, warm embraces and handshakes, and greetings in Spanish and English, such as white community members addressing Ximena and her family with a boisterous *¡Bueynos díuz!*[4] Gradually, individuals filed into the large meeting room with dark-wooded pews that stretched across the room and faced the pulpit.

During Sunday services, the founding pastor (Pastor Mark) and the Spanish-speaking associate pastor (Pastor Roberto) stood on a raised platform, wore wireless microphones pinned to their suit jackets, and spoke to Spanish- and English-speaking members scattered throughout the room. When guest speakers attended (for example, when Pastor Wesley who recently returned from a missionary trip to Haiti), bilingual youth volunteered to translate consecutively into Spanish. When children participated in the Christmas performance, they all sang bilingual songs. Still, due to Mark's position as a co-founder and long-time pastor, he typically initiated sermons, choir and singing activities, and shifts from activity to activity (e.g., potlucks)—rarely the other way around. According to Pastor Roberto, the UCC leadership recognized that bilingual youth used more English such that they would tune out of a Spanish-language service, or, *no van a poner atención* (they're not going to pay attention). Also, they sought to

3 We do not reference the website to protect the anonymity of the church organization.
4 The spelling of *¡Buenos dias!* has been modified to reflect an Anglicized pronunciation.

accommodate a growing number of mixed-race and mixed-language couples; Pastor Roberto, for example, was married to a white woman who spoke Spanish as a second language. Finally, they sought to accommodate mixed-language families like Ximena's that included Spanish-dominant parents and English-dominant children. Bilingualism, then, was normative.

Church activities were largely—although not exclusively—coordinated and facilitated by adults. Both children and youth participated in the majority of activities. Even though the very young children were escorted to the youth ministry classroom, older children and youth worshipped alongside their parents and hence had ongoing opportunities to participate in central and observable ways. They participated in call-and-response, singing, guest-speaking events, Bible readings, sermons, choral singing, and so on. In the next section, we analyze the circulating discourses and practices that characterized the UCC community and that provided ongoing opportunities for participants—and children and youth in particular—to appropriate them for their own purposes and goals in future activity (Rogoff, 1995, 2003).

We need to make a note here about the ways we represent the bilingual languaging practices in this religious community of practice. In some cases, the English and Spanish translations were projected on the wall of the UCC. When the congregation was led in singing worship songs, for example, the English and Spanish lyrics were projected on a white wall and both verses were sung by the congregation. During sermons, however, Pastor Roberto engaged in concurrent translation, meaning that he translated Pastor Mark's English-language sentences and phrases in the moment-to-moment such that his translations often focused, of course, on the meaning and substance of Pastor Mark's remarks (Orellana, 2009; Valdés, 2003). In the examples that follow, we represent the translations as they were documented at the UCC, in transcripts of audiorecordings, field notes, or photos and drawings. In cases where Pastor Roberto elaborated or deviated slightly from Pastor Mark's utterances, we indicate our own translations of phrases, clauses, or sentences in brackets for our readers. Our goal is to ensure that readers can access the full range of language practices that were made available in the UCC religious community.

Everyday Learning at UCC

During church services, Ximena participated in numerous practices that utilized figurative and metaphorical language to substantiate meaning and significance for the religious worshiping community. These practices facilitated ways to enact a particular Christian identity as well as ultimately to expand Christianity and God's word. These interactions demonstrated the discourses and practices that the religious community valued in that they were patterned, routine, and characteristic of everyday life on Sundays during church services, youth ministry, performances, potlucks, and special events. Moreover, they were enacted by a variety of participants (pastors, choir members, guest speakers, community members, and, to a lesser extent, children and youth) in both English and Spanish.

It is important to emphasize that children and youth were regularly exposed to these figurative and metaphorical language practices and could, therefore, appropriate them for their own purposes as a consequence of their participation in the everyday life of the church community. Following Rogoff (1995, 2003), students—by virtue of their varied forms of engagement in different religious communities—come to acquire these language forms and discourse norms over time and as their participation in the community changes. In this way, these language practices become linguistic resources that students might capitalize in the service of future—if yet unknown—purposes and goals. While we may or may not be able to document precisely what practices bilingual children and youth appropriate over time, the important point is for practitioners and educators to consider the varied, contextualized, and community-specific language experiences that students bring to the classroom. These linguistic resources may remain untapped if we do not explore them intentionally in the service of literacy learning and development.

In the next two sections, we address two particular themes: (1) the figurative language forms used to venerate God and to worship collectively and (2) the figurative language forms used to link bodies symbolically to God. These themes emerged during our data analysis of language practices across sermons, prayers, and songs as we sought to identify the normative and patterned ways that figurative language—in English and Spanish—was used to index Christianity and community at the UCC. Certainly, these two distinct ways to employ figurative language are related as the ways the religious community venerated and worshipped God was highly consistent with the ways they symbolically linked individual bodies to God. However, our analysis demonstrated that the body and its functions (e.g., breathing) had salient importance as church members both acknowledged God as the creator of all living things and positioned themselves as being in service to Him. We turn now to these examples.

Figurative Language to Venerate and Worship

One of the dominant language practices that pervaded sermons, prayers, Sunday school, and songs was the use of metaphorical language to venerate God and profess His[5] greatness and power in worshipers' lives. These utterances expressed particular ideas, affirmations, and feelings directly to God, particularly with regard to appreciating His creations, seeking salvation, and expressing their

---

5 We have chosen to conceive of God as masculine and to capitalize pronouns referencing Him to reflect this Christian community's practice. However, we acknowledge that we are writing in a cultural-historical moment in which gendered pronouns are being reconceptualized.

thankfulness. In the following song lyrics, which were projected on a wall, symbolism was used extensively:

Jesus, mighty God	*Cristo, fuerte Dios*
Our rock, our fortress, our defense	*Mi roca y fortaleza es*
Your conquering arm will be our strength	*Tu diestra es mi sostén*
Oh, God of power and rightness	*¡Oh! Dios de justicia y poder*
Every free will[6] trembles at Your name	*Los amigos tiemblan ante ti*
	(The friends)

First, in this excerpt, "mighty," "rock," and "power and rightness" symbolized God's power and strength as unbreakable and unyielding, while in the expression "every free will trembles at Your name," symbolism has the effect of capturing the fear and trepidation embodied among worshipers. Beyond this symbolic representation of strength, use of the words "fortress," "defense," and "conquering" realized a war metaphor. The effectiveness of war metaphors depends on effective conceptual frameworks for thinking about abstract and complex situations but they also invoke emotional sway in their construction of good–bad/evil, right–wrong, and soldiers–pacifists (see Flusberg, Matlock, & Thibodeau, 2018). In this religious context, this war metaphor constructs the congregation as a shared and unified voice as everyone in the room sings along. Moreover, it positions the congregation as being on the "we are good, right, soldiers" side of the (Christian) war but simultaneously asserts that God—particularly His "conquering arm"—will be their strength and primary defense against bad/evil, wrong, and those who ignore and decline to soldier in the (Christian) war. Given that metaphor is so prevalent in canonical and contemporary literary works, it seems that bilingual youth like Ximena whose out-of-school lives include routine participation in religious communities might bring varied experiences with metaphors to the high school classroom.

Third, the bilingual dimension of this example illustrates a key point. That is, undertaking these metaphorical language practices in two languages potentially expands the linguistic forms, styles, registers, and varieties accessible and available to children and youth, including Ximena. Specifically, expressions such as "your conquering arm" were translated as *tu diestra* when the literal translation of *un brazo conquistador* might have sufficed. Instead, Pastor Roberto employed *tu diestra*, which is a very literary and slightly archaic form of referring to God's arm and, metaphorically, to God's powerfulness. Further, *tu diestra* is a familiar expression for references to Jesus sitting at the right side of God; thus, the expression "Christ sitting at the right hand of the Father" would translate as *Cristo sentado **a la diestra del Padre***. Thus, *tu diestra* and *a la diestra* are extremely familiar in religious discourse and contexts.

---

6 In this instance, "free will" was translated by Pastor Roberto as "the friends."

Additionally, this example illustrates that these moment-to-moment translations often resulted in expanded bilingual repertoire. For example, the phrase "power and rightness"[7] was translated to *justicia y poder* (justice and power), such that "rightness" was translated as "justice." Therefore, in the case of bilingual children and youth, their participation in religious communities expanded their knowledge of English and Spanish forms, particularly when acts of translation were the norm. Like Ek (this volume), we believe these specialized discourses in Spanish could be extremely helpful resources for practitioners and educators committed to further leveraging—and expanding—bilingual youths' linguistic repertoires.

Figurative Language to Link Bodies to God

In this section, we share examples of figurative language practices that linked the bodies of individual parishioners to the spirit of God, Jesus Christ, and the Lord. We selected representative language practices that explicitly spoke specifically to the body and/or to bodily movements, such as dancing and breathing, and that were employed among adults, youth, and young children in different contexts (i.e., Sunday school, sermons, etc.). These practices included forms of language that invoke the body as a witness, in service to the Lord, and as a symbol for Jesus Christ. In the examples that follow, figurative and metaphorical language were used strategically to link the physical existence of parishioners to an otherworldly power that is perceived to work in/through the body.

The first example is taken from a transcript of an audiorecorded sermon that involved simultaneous translation between the English-speaking pastor (Pastor Mark) and the Spanish-speaking pastor (Pastor Roberto). As was common, they stood on the platform in the center of the worship room, holding microphones, and Pastor Mark led the sermon whereas Pastor Roberto translated Pastor Mark's statements, also often elaborating on these statements in Spanish. This short excerpt illustrates how figurative language constructed the Holy Spirit as both moving on parishioners' bodies and evoking joyous dancing.

PASTOR MARK: The spirit of the Lord moves on my heart.
PASTOR ROBERTO: *El espíritu de Dios se mueve en mí.*
[moves in me]
PASTOR MARK: Let there be a shout of joy.
PASTOR ROBERTO: *Demos un grito de júbilo.*
PASTOR MARK: I will dance as David danced.
PASTOR ROBERTO: *Bailaré como David bailó.*

---

7 In most contexts, "rightness" could be translated as *corrección*.

First, this figurative language (in English and Spanish) constructed the spirit of the Lord as "moving on" the heart whereas Pastor Roberto constructed the spirit as "moving *in* me" in his Spanish translation. Through the constructions of "moving on" and "moving in," bilingual youth like Ximena participated in language practices that figuratively indexed the body as a witness to the power of the Holy Spirit.

Additionally, this example illustrates that the prepositional phrases "moving *on*" and "moving *in*" are used to construct the spirit of the Lord as the active subject and worshippers' bodies and souls as rather passive recipients of these otherworldly actions. These prepositional phrases are employed to index the power of the spirit that "moves" bodies and souls. Similar usage of the passive voice can be found in academic textbooks across different subjects and in history textbooks in particular (Schleppegrell, Achugar, & Oteíza, 2004). By bringing attention to these discursive regularities in particular genres, teachers can increase students' metalinguistic awareness as well as knowledge of particular disciplinary literacies. In contrast to the construction of parishioners as passive subjects, similes were used in the utterance "I will dance *as* David danced" to indicate that parishioners could actively dance and come to embody—and *be*—David, even if temporarily. In this way, individuals are simultaneously constructed as social agents who can potentially come to fully embody the spirit of King David, a historical biblical figure known for his passion for God. These examples illustrate, then, that youth participants were exposed to and participated in figurative language forms that simultaneously constructed active and passive relations and that could be helpful in creative and academic writing tasks.

In a second example, metaphorical language was employed to address feet in symbolic ways. One common expression was "I lay my life down at your feet" wherein the phrase "lay my life down" in this religious context symbolizes worshipers submitting their lives and themselves fully and wholeheartedly to Jesus. While feet carry us in the material world, this metaphorical language employs "feet" to symbolize cleanliness and purity based on the common image of Jesus cleaning the disciples' feet, for example, as well as heeding Jesus' command to serve others. Other sentiments such as "We dance for you, Jesus" and "We sing for you, Jesus" similarly invoked bodily actions (i.e., dancing and singing) to enact their subservience and submission to Jesus.

Even autonomous breathing and more specifically, breath, was constructed as being in service to the Lord through metaphorical language. In an excerpt of a lengthy audiorecorded sermon, the two pastors professed that "everything that has breath will praise the Lord" as they implored their fellow parishioners to feel their own breath:

PASTOR MARK: Everybody in this place, put your hand up in your face.

PASTOR ROBERTO: *Todos pongan la mano en frente de su boca.*

PASTOR MARK: Now, blow in the air.

PASTOR ROBERTO: *Ahora, soplen.*
PASTOR MARK: What is that?
PASTOR ROBERTO: *¿Que es eso?*
PASTOR MARK: That's breath.
PASTOR ROBERTO: *Eso es su aliento. Dice que usted puede respirar.*
[He says that you can breathe.]
PASTOR MARK: And everything that has breath will praise the Lord.
PASTOR ROBERTO: *Y dice que todo lo que respire, lo que tenga aliento, alabe al señor.*
[And he says that everything that breathes, that which has breath ...]

Pastor Mark and Roberto use the metaphorical language of "everything that has breath" to command living beings in the world, by virtue of breathing and with or without consciousness or will, to praise the Lord. Note the significance here of the verb phrase "will praise" to index their own power to declare that all living and breathing beings will be in service to the Lord. This metaphoric language that invokes an autonomous bodily function can further be interpreted as reifying the belief that the Lord created the heavens and earth; that is, since He created everything living and breathing on Earth, we must in turn praise Him.

Finally, figurative language was employed in the Sunday school program with adolescents and young children. While Ximena's parents typically expected her to praise alongside them upstairs in the worship room, she occasionally accompanied her younger brother in the basement. The classroom walls were covered with a Christian-inspired alphabet: for example, "Dd" was associated with "Depart from evil and do good." During one observation, the male teacher (Mr. Ortiz) primarily used figurative language and personification to help children and several youths complete a project titled "Jesus is My House," as he facilitated a discussion about Jesus' body parts and what they symbolized for Christians "if our house was a temple." In this regard, houses symbolized a place of worship that was ostensibly intended to serve Jesus. At the outset, Mr. Ortiz had distributed a picture of a large house. He then instructed students to draw body parts throughout the structure to represent particular aspects of what it meant to be a good Christian. He employed phrases such as "windows are our eyes to see," "ears can represent vents where air comes in and out," and "the mouth can be the door" throughout the activity. In this Sunday school context, Jesus' body parts symbolized the different parts of a house. Similarly, personification was employed to give houses human abilities such as the ability to see, hear, and speak. The task as well required students to represent this symbolism in their art project. Thus, in socializing children and youth to worship as Christians, normative practices included varied types of metaphorical and figurative language, including the use of similes, comparisons, and personification across Spanish and English.

Discussion and Connecting to Common Core State Standards

By analyzing the language practices of the UCC religious community, we have identified Ximena's participation in figurative and metaphorical language practices, which reflected one aspect of her broad and varied linguistic repertoire, as discussed in Pacheco (2015) in more detail. These language practices were evidenced throughout participant observations at the UCC during Sunday services and activities documented in field notes, transcribed audiorecordings, and primary documents. We analyzed the most common forms, styles, registers, and varieties that pertained to the routine ways that figurative and metaphorical language constituted everyday activities and routines to venerate God and to link the body to God, Jesus Christ, and the Lord. These language practices included personification, symbolism, similes, and metaphors, as well as passive sentence constructions that strategically used prepositions to enact Christian beliefs and values. Even though children and youth participated as observers and co-worshippers, these language practices were available to them for appropriation in the future and for novel goals and purposes (Rogoff, 1995, 2003).

Literacy researchers have encouraged teachers to examine the language practices that youth already engage in, in order to leverage those students' language skills and understandings (Martínez, 2010; Orellana, Martínez, Lee, & Montaño, 2012; Orellana & Reynolds, 2008). Martínez (2010) (see also Martínez et al., this volume) explicitly made connections between middle school students' use of Spanish and English codeswitching or "Spanglish" and the California language arts content standards. One of the sixth grade writing standards requires that students demonstrate awareness of audience and purpose. Martínez explained that audience awareness was a skill these bilingual youths already possessed when they switched between languages, as well as registers, even communicating subtle nuances of meaning (p. 125). Similarly, Ximena experienced familiarity with and engagement in rhetorical practices using figurative and metaphorical language that could be leveraged in classroom settings, particularly language arts classrooms.

In this section, we suggest some productive ways that classroom practitioners could build on the discourses and practices we analyzed, across content areas, even as we simultaneously encourage practitioners to continuously explore their bi/multilingual students' always already expanding linguistic repertoire (Martínez & Morales, 2014; see also Molle et al., 2015; Zentella, 2005). The figurative language practices with which Ximena was already familiar due to her engagement with her church on a regular/weekly basis clearly relate to the standards in the language arts section of the Common Core State Standards (CCSS). These posit that students need not only to understand the underlying linguistic structures across disciplines but also to use more discipline-specific communication rules within each discipline.

Requirements for understanding and using figurative language can be found across the grade levels, from fourth grade through high school. The K-5 College and Career Readiness (CCR) anchor standards for reading are broader standards that students are required to demonstrate and that are delineated with more specificity by grade level. Under "vocabulary acquisition and use," they state: "Demonstrate understanding of figurative language, word relationships, and nuances in word meanings."

A teacher who was familiar with the language and discursive practices in which Ximena and her family engaged at church could draw on this knowledge to remind students that they already are familiar with metaphors from out of school literacy practices such as reading the Bible. Teachers might point out that students who read the Bible encounter metaphors all the time, and create opportunities for students to make those connections to the metaphors they encounter in literary texts. We emphasize, however, that it is not necessary for teachers to have full knowledge of the different religions and their corresponding primary texts (e.g., the Vedas, Qur'an, Bible)—and their more archaic uses of figurative and metaphorical language—represented among their students. Rather, we encourage teachers to invite students to share what they understand about these distinctive language forms from their engagement in religious communities and with religious texts.

Another example of a standard that could be connected to Ximena's life experiences is the following K-5 CCR anchor standard for language under "knowledge of language": "Apply knowledge of language to understand how language functions in different contexts, to make effective choices for meaning or style, and to comprehend more fully when reading or listening."

This standard is similar to emphasizing the importance of audience awareness, as in the California writing standards Martínez (2010) addressed, and communicating subtleties in meaning. Teachers could draw on the discourse practices of students such as Ximena to call attention to the different vocabulary and style choices they employ in different contexts such as church, school, or other home–community spaces where they spend time with friends. (See also chapters by Ek and García-Sánchez, this volume.)

Understanding figurative language and nuances in word meanings are important aspects of both reading and language that are included in the CCSS at the K-5 school level and that continue through high school level. The CCR anchor standards for reading (grades 6–12) under "craft and structure" include the following statement: "Interpret words and phrases as they are used in a text, including determining technical, connotative, and figurative meanings, and analyze how specific word choices shape meaning or tone."

Oral language can be analyzed as text, and as bilinguals, students have access to distinct sets of text in two languages that can be compared for nuances in meaning. In the example described of figurative language linking bodies to God, the two pastors use different phrases to evoke similar meanings. Pastor

Mark describes the spirit of the Lord moving *on* his heart, while Pastor Roberto (in Spanish), states that the spirit of God moves *in* him. Translation exercises have been used to raise students' metalinguistic awareness and understanding of language features (Jiménez et al., 2015). Comparing phrases across languages for nuanced meaning would be another language activity in connection to the standards and in support of students' academic language development. However, since the use of figurative and metaphorical language were linked to the religious discourses in which Ximena engaged regularly, students like her might benefit from recognizing these connections. That is, teachers can help students continue to develop their competencies by exploring their out-of-school lives.

Finally, in the CCSS, students are tasked with analyzing what they are taking in, via reading. The reading standards for literature (grades 11–12) under "craft and structure" state:

"Determine the meaning of words and phrases as they are used in the text, including figurative and connotative meanings; analyze the impact of specific word choices on meaning and tone, including words with multiple meanings or language that is particularly fresh, engaging, or beautiful. (Include Shakespeare as well as other authors.)"

As discussed previously, Ximena's use of figurative language and other rhetorical devices were skills that could help her recognize these same language uses in the context of school and school-based texts. The standards offer Shakespeare as a suggested author, but a teacher could choose from myriad other authors; in fact, teachers knowledgeable of their students' out-of-school lives and activities could use written examples produced by students to analyze figurative language.

Conclusion

We have described the routine language practices and discourses in which Ximena engaged through her participation at church. These practices and discourses revealed some particular language and literacy skills that students are expected to understand and demonstrate in school. Students can benefit from ongoing support from teachers who can make explicit the skills embedded in these everyday practices, making connections to the school-based literacies articulated in the standards. Language arts teachers especially can support bi/multilingual students like Ximena in fully appreciating their vast knowledge of how figurative language works and the vocabulary they can access across Spanish and English.

According to the CCSS website, the ELA/literacy standards are intended "to prepare students for life outside the classroom" and ultimately, promote "a vision of what it means to be a literate person who is prepared for success in the 21st century. We argue that to prepare 21st century citizens, researchers and practitioners must consider the skills and content knowledge students may have developed outside of school, particularly bi/multilingual youths. Indeed, bi/multilingual who have had the opportunity to acquire and develop unique repertoires of language and literacy across languages and speech communities possess the linguistic and intellectual resources to help educators enact this vision." (Quoted from http://www.corestandards.org/ELA-Literacy/.)

References

Baquedano-López, P. (2001). Creating social identities through *doctrina* narratives. In A. Duranti & P. Shipton (Eds.) *Linguistic anthropology: A reader*, 2nd edn. (364–378). Malden, MA: Blackwell Publishing.

Creswell, J. W. (2009). *Research design: Qualitative, quantitative, and mixed methods approaches*. Thousand Oaks, CA: Sage Publications.

Daniel, J. L. & Smitherman, G. (1976). How I got over: Communication dynamics in the Black community. *Quarterly Journal of Speech, 62*(1), 26–39.

Ek, L. D. (2009). "It's different lives": A Guatemalan American adolescent's construction of ethnic and gender identities across educational contexts. *Anthropology & Education Quarterly, 40*(4), 405–420.

Ek, L. D. (2008). Language and literacy in the Pentecostal church and the public high school: A case study of a Mexican ESL student. *The High School Journal, 92* (2) 1–13.

Emerson, R. M., Fretz, R. I., & Shaw, L. L. (1995). *Writing ethnographic fieldnotes*. Chicago, IL: University of Chicago Press.

Flusberg, S. J., Matlock, T., & Thibodeau, P. H. (2018). War metaphors in public discourse. *Metaphor and Symbol, 33*(1), 1–18.

Foster, M. (2001). Pay Leon, pay Leon, pay Leon paleontologist: Using call-and-response to facilitate language. *Sociocultural and historical contexts of African American English, 27*, 281.

Hull, G. A. & Schultz, K. (Eds.) (2002). *School's out: Bridging out-of-school literacies with classroom practice*. New York: Teachers College Press.

Hull, G. & Schultz, K. (2001). Literacy and learning out of school: A review of theory and research. *Review of Educational Research, 71*(4), 575–611.

Jiménez, R. T., David, S., Pacheco, M., Risko, V. J., Pray, L., Fagan, K. et al. (2015). Supporting teachers of English learners by leveraging students' linguistic strengths. *The Reading Teacher, 68*(6), 406–412.

Martínez, D. C., Morales, P. Z., & Aldana, U. S. (2017). Leveraging students' communicative repertoires as a tool for equitable learning. *Review of Research in Education, 41*, 477–499.

Martínez, R. A. (2010). *Spanglish* as literacy tool: Toward an understanding of the potential role of Spanish-English code-switching in the development of academic literacy. *Research in the Teaching of English, 45*(2), 124–149.

Martínez, R. A. & Morales, P. Z. (2014). ¿*Puras groserías?*: Rethinking the role of profanity and graphic humor in Latin@ students' bilingual wordplay. *Anthropology and Education Quarterly, 45*(4), 337–354.

Molle, D., Sato, E., Boals, T., & Hedgspeth, C. A. (Eds.) (2015). *Multilingual learners and academic literacies: Sociocultural contexts of literacy development in adolescents*. New York: Routledge.

Morales, P. Z. (2016). Transnational practices and language maintenance: Spanish and Zapoteco in California. *Children's Geographies, 14*(4), 375–389.

Orellana, M. F. (2009). *Translating childhoods: Immigrant youth, language, and culture.* New York: Rutgers University Press.

Orellana, M. F., Martínez, D. C., Lee, C. H., & Montaño, E. (2012). Language as a tool in diverse forms of learning. *Linguistics and Education, 23*, 373–387.

Orellana, M. F. & Reynolds, J. F. (2008). Cultural modeling: Leveraging bilingual skills for school paraphrasing tasks. *Reading Research Quarterly, 43*(1), 48–65.

Pacheco, M. (2015). Bilingualism-as-participation: Examining adolescents' bi(multi)lingual literacies across out-of-school and online contexts. In D. Molle, E. Sato, T. Boals, & C. Hedgespeth (Eds.) *Multilingual learners and academic literacies: Sociocultural contexts of literacy development in adolescents* (135–165). New York: Routledge.

Pacheco, M. (2014). Nepantleras in the New Latino Diaspora: The intersectional experiences of bi/multilingual youth. In C. Grant & E. Zwier (Eds.) *Intersectionality and urban education: Identities, policies, spaces & power* (97–123). Charlotte, NC: Information Age Publishing, Inc.

Pacheco, M. (2009). Expansive learning and Chicana/o and Latina/o students' political-historical knowledge. *Language Arts, 87*(1), 18–29.

Rogoff, B. (2003). *The cultural nature of human development.* New York: Oxford University Press.

Rogoff, B. (1995). Observing sociocultural activity on three planes: Participatory appropriation, guided appropriation, and apprenticeship. In J. V. Wertsch, P. Del Rio, & A. Alvarez (Eds.) *Sociocultural studies of mind* (139–164). New York: Cambridge University Press.

Schleppegrell, M. J., Achugar, M., & Oteíza, T. (2004). The grammar of history: Enhancing content-based instruction through a functional focus on language. *TESOL Quarterly, 38* (1), 67–93.

Skilton-Sylvester, E. (2002). Literate at home but not at school: A Cambodian girl's journey from playwright to struggling writer. In G. A. Hull & K. Schultz (Eds.) *School's out: Bridging out-of-school literacies with classroom practice* (61–90). New York: Teachers College Press.

Smitherman, G. (2000). *Talkin' that talk: Language, culture and education in African America.* New York: Routledge.

Valdés, G. (2003). *Expanding definitions of giftedness: The case of young interpreters from immigrant communities.* New York: Routledge.

Wuthnow, R. J. (2011). Taking talk seriously: Religious discourse as social practice. *Journal for the Scientific Study of Religion, 50*(1), 1–21.

Zentella, A. C. (Ed.). (2005). *Building on strength: Language and literacy in Latino families and communities.* New York: Teachers College Press.

8

CENTERING SHARED LINGUISTIC HERITAGE TO BUILD LANGUAGE AND LITERACY RESILIENCE AMONG IMMIGRANT STUDENTS

Inmaculada M. García-Sánchez

Introduction

In this chapter, I discuss ways in which linguistic anthropological analysis can help schools teach language(s) in ways that center immigrant children's multi- or bilingual strengths rather than their, often exaggerated, language deficits. I consider how immigrant children's everyday language practices and cultural funds of knowledge (Moll, 1992) in their peer groups and communities can be used as central features in language programs that pursue pluralist outcomes. For this purpose, I analyze the linguistic repertoires Moroccan immigrant children in Spain use in school and out-of-school settings to identify commonalities across formal and informal learning contexts. Building on a broad comparative frame, in which I sketch the basic contours of what these children are being asked to do in school with what they are already doing in two common everyday practices—playing with peers and language brokering for adults—I suggests how immigrant students' everyday language practices outside school can be powerful tools for academic language development.

I develop the idea that cultivating Moroccan immigrant students' metalinguistic awareness about historical linguistic connections between Spanish and Arabic is one of the strategies that would enhance their knowledge of cultural and formal properties of both languages, while validating their multilingual repertoires in a way that disrupts sociolinguistic inequalities based on ideological constructions between "home" and "academic" languages. Furthermore, I argue that designing curricula that attend to both formal properties of languages and indexical orders (Silverstein, 2003) underlying linguistic hegemony and hierarchization can create a learning environment conducive to building what I call *linguistic resilience* among immigrant students, a sense of affirming confidence in their multilingual abilities that can transcend monolingual notions of educational success. Attention to metalinguistic strategies that make explicit shared linguistic heritage and language contact phenomena can be important entry points to destabilize monolingual literacy programs, centering and honoring immigrant students' linguistically hybrid lived experiences. (For additional descriptions of immigrant students' rich experiences with language and literacy hybridity, see, in this volume, D'warte, Enciso, Martínez et al., Pacheco & Morales, and Reynolds & Orellana.) Although this ethnographic case features varieties of Spanish and Arabic, the strategies discussed here can also be useful for language education in other immigrant contexts (and even in postcolonial nations) where the multiple languages in young people's repertoires have come into significant contact and end up influencing each other in profound ways due to historical, political, and economic reasons related to (linguistic) colonialism, migration, slavery, and other forms oppression that underlie contemporary migration processes.

This chapter speaks to the power and the promise of an applied linguistic anthropology perspective to help teachers and schools reimagine language and literacy education for immigrant children in ways that help overcome the rigid, and often pernicious, dichotomous framings that inform educational approaches to academic language development: whether those framings have to do with "home" and "school" linguistic practices, which are seen as *discontinuous* and *incommensurate*; or whether those distinctions have to do with the sociocultural and political boundaries of named national languages, (in this case Spanish and Arabic) which are still seen as pure, stable, and completely distinct from one another, an enduring legacy of the language ideologies associated with Herderian nationalism.[1]

Previous Work I am Building on

I bring into critical dialogue three theoretical frameworks: sociocultural studies of literacy, linguistic anthropology, and Cultural Modeling-inspired research (Lee, 2007). Although these three perspectives have much to offer one another, they have rarely been considered together because of traditional disciplinary boundaries.

In situating literacy as a social and cultural practice in which language is a powerful mediating tool (e.g., Scribner & Cole, 1978; Street, 1993), sociocultural studies have documented the rich repertoires individuals engage in as a central means of sharing knowledge in communities of practice (Gutierrez & Rogoff, 2003). An unfulfilled promise of this literature, however, is how everyday language practices shape children's processes of academic language acquisition. While this work has implied the potential role that everyday

---

1 Herderian nationalism refers to a notion of national belonging based on monocultural and monolingual ethnolinguistic homogeneity.

interactions and language practices can play in providing a strong foundation for children's encounters with academic work and texts (e.g., Heath, 1983), efforts to specify this relationship have been forestalled by a persistent ideological dichotomy between orality and literacy in western academic traditions (Bauman & Briggs, 2003). It has also been impeded by educational approaches that see immigrant children's everyday language practices as socially functional but of little value for academic tasks (see Rosa & Flores, 2017 for a recent critique of those approaches). As part of my analysis, I will examine similarities between immigrant children's everyday language practices and the language tasks they are expected to perform in schools.

Second, much work within linguistic anthropology and sociolinguistics has detailed the rich linguistic and literacy practices of a wide range of non-dominant linguistic communities (e.g., Alim, 2004; Labov, 1972; Zentella, 1997). In documenting this linguistic dexterity, this work has helped counter deficit views of the verbal abilities of non-dominant groups. This scholarship has also helped to explain obstacles to non-dominant students' development of academic literacy, by identifying discontinuities between participation structures, literacy practices, and pragmatic use of language in communities and educational institutions (e.g., Delpit, 1995; Heath, 1983; Philips, 1983). However, as we discuss in the Introduction to this volume (García-Sánchez & Faulstich Orellana), it is important for researchers to also identify clearly similarities and generative points of continuity between home/community-school that can be productively centered and expanded on in schools.

The Cultural Modeling paradigm precisely focuses on finding robust points of continuity between the skills that non-dominant youth themselves use in their lives outside the classroom and the modes of reasoning emphasized in disciplinary modes of thinking (Lee, 1997, 2007). Lee's research on the multiple rhetorical uses of the practice of signifying among African American youth detailed how hybrid spaces, which allow students to tap into their full linguistic repertoires, could be generated in literature classrooms.

In this chapter, I am using Lee's notion of "metacognitive strategies," which seek to cultivate overtly the skills young people are already deploying in their everyday language use. I build on recent applications of Cultural Modeling to how literacy practices are shaped in U.S. migration contexts (Orellana & Eksner, 2006; Orellana & Reynolds, 2008), and relate these developments with the traditions of interactional sociolinguistics and linguistic anthropology to examine similar processes for immigrant children outside the U.S.

In bringing together these perspectives, I show how Moroccan immigrant children are already engaging in language practices in their peer groups/communities that are analogous to those that are promoted in schools. I further suggest how the communicative skills that these children already possess can be used as a strength in their academic language development. The goal is not for immigrant children to leave behind their everyday bilingual practices in favor of the standard monolingual practices preferred in schools, but for them to expand all of their linguistic repertoires.

I also stand in solidarity with recent formulations of *culturally sustaining pedagogies* (Paris & Alim, 2017), which seek to center and foster linguistic, literate, and cultural pluralism as part of schooling for positive social transformation (pp. 12–13). In keeping with this approach to schooling, I argue that language and literacy education of Moroccan immigrant children in Spain needs to begin with the assumption that we are enriching the linguistic and literacy horizons of children who already possess sophisticated multi-/bilingual competencies rather than with the assumption that we are remedying deficits of children who have limited proficiency in academic Spanish. Assuming competence and sophistication form the ideological basis of an approach to curriculum and instruction that fosters linguistic resilience among immigrant students.

Studying Learning Contexts in Immigrant Children's Lives

The analysis below builds on a longitudinal language socialization-inspired ethnography documenting the linguistic repertoires displayed by Moroccan immigrant children in Spain, aged 8–11, across social contexts. Because one of the main goals of this study was to get a holistic sense of the sociocultural and linguistic matrix of these children's lives as they negotiated processes of difference and belonging in their multiple communities (García-Sánchez 2014),[2] I documented, via videotaping and participant observation, the daily interactions in which the children engaged in a variety of contexts, including familial, institutional (their academic and social life at the public school, Koranic lessons at the local mosque, track and field training sessions), and neighborhood play with friends. This breadth gave me the opportunity to examine Moroccan immigrant children's language practices, communicative resources, interpretive strategies, and modes of reasoning in both formal and informal learning contexts.

For this chapter,[3] I compare the literacy practices that Moroccan immigrant students engaged in at the public elementary school, with two types of language practice outside school. Because of this research priority, of all the academic activities I observed in the public school, I focused especially on my videorecordings of a Spanish

2 For more detailed information on the methodology used in the larger study, see García-Sánchez (2014), particularly Chapter 3 (pp. 61–87). This research was supported by funding from a Wenner-Gren Foundation Individual Dissertation Research Grant (Grant # 7296), from a Harry and Yvonne Lenart Foundation Graduate Research Travel Grant, and from a UCLA Center for European and Eurasian Studies Summer Dissertation Research.
3 This research project was supported by a National Academy of Education/Spencer Foundation Post-doctoral Fellowship (2012–2013) and by a Temple University Summer Research Fellowship.

language and literacy enhancement pull-out program (akin to ESL programs in the U.S.) in order to illuminate the literacy skills and tasks immigrant children are expected to perform in the classroom. As for the out-of-school contexts, I examined immigrant child language-brokering activities at the local health center and neighborhood peer play. Language brokering was chosen because it is a common, but unique, way in which immigrant children use their linguistic knowledge to speak, read, write, listen on behalf of others, and which requires sophisticated deployment of their multilingual skills (Orellana, 2009). Play was chosen because unsupervised peer interaction is a prime context to study how immigrant children use the multiple codes available in their linguistic repertoires to structure their own peer cultures and learning environments (García-Sánchez, 2005, 2010). These two out-of-school activity settings give us a fairly complete and representative picture of the skills that Moroccan immigrant children routinely display in their everyday language use. They are also useful to show the wide range of language experiences, beyond the familial, that immigrant youth encounter out of schools.

Using linguistic anthropology-inspired microanalysis of social interaction (Goodwin, 2018; Philips, 2013), I analyzed immigrant children's language use across contexts, paying particular attention to: (a) type of linguistic or communicative practice; (b) literacy strategies, or modes of reasoning; (c) forms of participation/participants (including how relationships among participants are shaped by the structure of the activity setting, both context and sociocultural expectations); and (d) goals of the activities.

Moroccan Immigrant Children's Communicative Practices Outside School

Learning and Teaching How to Play with Peers

Observing Moroccan immigrant children peer groups during play in local parks and playgrounds, I documented their wide variety of activities, such as pretend-play, marbles, soccer, hopscotch, jump rope games, singing nursery rhymes and traditional and popular songs, clapping rhymes, tag and other chasing games. Children's communicative ecology was rich and varied: word play/puns, reciting, gossiping, arguing and negotiating parameters of the game, teasing and bantering, explaining game rules, describing moves, giving tips and directions. Children's efforts to negotiate play often involved complex modes of reasoning, such as making abstract rules visible and concrete, accompanying descriptions with physical enactments and demonstrations, and creating a local structure of attention that facilitated attunement to other people's actions. One of the most salient features that all these linguistic and literacy practices had in common was their *hybrid multilingual and multimodal flexibility*, which refers to children's creative combination of different languages and non-verbal channels to accomplish a variety of communicative functions.

Children's communicative practices were characterized by hybrid sociocultural and linguistic practices, mostly between Spanish and Moroccan Arabic. For example, in the jump rope game interactions I videotaped, girls would often alternate between jump rope songs in Spanish and Moroccan Arabic. This seamless incorporation of different languages and gaming traditions during play had the effect that over the course of a series of game rounds, no child would feel left out. In this way, children's participation affordances were maximized, since children knew they could draw on any linguistic and semiotic resources in their communicative repertoires.

Semiotic flexibility in forms of participation and interaction lent itself to relatively egalitarian participation framework among the children. This was important because of the multi-age and the multi-expertise character of the peer groups, which often included children with different histories of immigration and with varying degree of knowledge and expertise with Spanish and Moroccan linguistic practices. Such dynamic structural configuration allowed for interchangeable expert/novice participation roles that encouraged all children to feel like they had something to contribute and that promoted self-affirming forms of competent participation among the children. This flexibility in communicative strategies and participation frameworks was key to accomplishing the goals of peer group activities, which usually involved achieving shared intersubjective understandings of how to play games, maximizing collaboration among players, and being able to resolve conflicts.

In order to give a more vivid idea of how all these dimensions play out in immigrant children's actual everyday social interactions, I reproduce below a typical example of neighborhood play. This particular example features a group of Moroccan immigrant girls teaching one another how to play hopscotch, a traditional game that they were are all familiar with, but one that different girls knew different versions of, a common occurrence in diverse immigrant children peer groups (García-Sánchez, 2005). For this reason, it is common to find teaching scenes that involve players describing moves, demonstrating explanations, and giving advice to other players. What follows is an abridged version of an analysis I developed elsewhere (García-Sánchez, 2017). Participants included Wafiya and Worda, two nine-year-old girls who had been living in Spain for five years at the time I made these recordings. Wafiya and Worda attended fourth grade at the same elementary school and ran together for the local track-and-field club. They spent most of their out-of-school time together, either training, playing, or hanging out.

Example # 1 starts right after Worda loses her turn. Wafiya starts her turn, but after completing a round, she is not quite sure how she should proceed and asks Worda to help her (line 2). From line 3 through 8, Worda shows Wafiya the correct way of traversing the grid for her next move. This explanation, however, is not easy; Worda needs to describe not only the intricacies of the move but also what Wafiya's posture must be and in what specific place in the grid that move has to occur in order for it to be valid. As the transcripts and frame grabs below show, Worda makes visible this fairly abstract description for her friend through the flexible and strategic deployment of a complex form of *multimodal translanguaging;* a combination of bilingual (Spanish and Moroccan Arabic) and paralinguistic (e.g., gestures, body positioning, the hopscotch grid) resources that allows for successful participation in play from children with different levels of bilingual communicative competence

Example # 1
Key: Spanish (Regular Font); Moroccan Arabic (***Bold Italics***)
English Glosses (**Bold**)

Participants: **Worda**   **Wafiya**   **Sarah**   **Salma**   **Leila**

1 WORDA: No te rías eh?
            Don't laugh, ah?

            (2.1)

2 WAFIYA: Vamos Worda, tú. Ven aquí (.) primero
            Come on, Worda, you. Come here (.) first

3 WORDA: Salto o piso? (.) Salto
            Jump or step? (.) Jump

4 WAFIYA: ***nnaqqazha***
            I jump it

            (2.0)

5 WORDA: Ahora te pones así=
            Now you position yourself like this

            =y tiras a la primera sin salirte de-
            and throw (it) at the first without exiting from—

6 WORDA: *KhaSSak ddiri hak šuf hanaya*
           You have to do like this, look here

7 WORDA: *tarmiha allawla o ddiri hak*
           Throw it to the first and do like this

8 WORDA: **[*thazziha o twalli***
           [You pick it up and you come back

Worda is positioned as an expert; a position rarely accorded to children in school. And, almost like an instructor would, Worda tells Wafiya how she has to position herself, how she has to throw the marker, and how she has to traverse the grid, first in Spanish (line 5) and then in Moroccan Arabic (lines 6, 7, and 8). In carefully sequencing her verbal directions, Worda occupies the relevant spaces in the grid that the deictics "así"/"hak" (this, respectively in Spanish and Moroccan Arabic) and "hanaya" (here, in Moroccan Arabic) are indexing. Throughout these turns, Worda is performing her description verbally, through the use of her bilingual resources, and simultaneously using sequences of body displays, such as embodied demonstrations to make visible for other players how the moves should be executed. These forms of multimodal translanguaging mediate complex linguistic, social, and cognitive activities that are crucial to achieve shared understandings. For example, the girls construct a local cognitive structure of attention that requires mutual attunement to linguistic cues and embodied demonstrations. This structure demands that Wafiya confirm that she has understood Worda's explanation. In lines 9 and 10, Wafiya performs a multimodal demonstration of understanding, which is organized in terms of how well she can redo what was just described.

9 WAFIYA: *[wah,wahonwalli*
           [yeah,yeah and I come back
           (3.0)
10 WAFIYA: *nwalli alhiha*
           I go back there

11 WORDA: *wah nwalli alhiha maši nnakkaz Hatta*
     assadas
     Yes, go back there don't jump until the sixth

     matkharžiš man assadas
     don't exit from the sixth

Another feature that facilitates peer learning in play is how these girls go about establishing the rules of the game. Rather than having a preformulated script explained at the beginning as the rules of the game, the girls are coming to have shared and increasingly more complex understandings of these rules as the local environment of the interaction makes available new moves and new possibilities. Girls' local interactional organization thus resembles other learning situations that involve starting with something at the lower level and only later, after gaining mastery of a set of subskills, come to understand new aspects of the activity in which they are participating in relation to the larger picture. Table 8.1 presents a snapshot of immigrant children's ways with words in peer play contexts. I highlight how many of the communicative practices and modes of reasoning used to give/follow precise directions and to check/demonstrate understanding, as in the previous example, are all skills highly valued in schools.

Learning and Translating at the Doctor's

Moroccan immigrant children translated for their families on a regular basis, particularly at home, usually official paperwork and letters for their parents and

TABLE 8.1 Ways with words in peer play contexts

Linguistic/Communicative Practices	Literacy Strategies/Modes of Reasoning
<ul><li>Codeswitching</li><li>Word play</li><li>Explaining</li><li>Describing</li><li>Giving directions</li></ul>	<ul><li>Making abstract rules visible and concrete</li><li>Enacting</li><li>Demonstrating</li><li>Attunement/attention to other people's actions</li></ul>
Forms of Participation	**Goal(s) of the Activity**
<ul><li>Horizontal participation frameworks</li><li>Flexible expert/novice roles</li><li>Flexible multilingual and multimodal participation</li></ul>	<ul><li>Achieving intersubjective understandings of how to play the game</li><li>Maximizing collaboration</li><li>Overcoming conflicts</li></ul>

neighbors; at school, where they were sometimes unofficially recruited by teachers to translate for newly arrived Moroccan classmates; and at the local health center, mediating between their families and doctors. Immigrant children display many sophisticated linguistic practices when translating in two (sometimes three) languages, such as para-/rephrasing, summarizing, describing, and narrating. Also, among the many literacy and cognitive strategies children exhibit when language brokering, I highlight those that schools seek to cultivate (see also Table 8.2): good listening and memory skills, illustrating with examples, being able to differentiate main ideas from secondary points, transcultural competencies, such as cross-cultural perspective taking (Guan et al., 2014), and meta-pragmatic awareness involving strategic decision making in translation, such as style shifting for different interlocutors or deciding how much information to translate and when. While the participation frameworks in language brokering are more hierarchical than the peer play examined above, this is mitigated by two facts. One is that the child's bilingual knowledge is seen as an asset crucial to the success of the encounter. The second is that children and adults are active contributors to the interaction, pooling different kinds of expertise to make meaning collaboratively (cf. Eskner & Orellana, 2012).

As an illustration of how these interactional features could typically unfold in language brokering encounters, I reproduce below an excerpt in which a Spanish pediatrician is trying to determine the reasons for the lack of effectiveness of a boy's treatment. Fatima, a nine-year-old neighbor, is acting as translator between the boy's mother and the doctor. What follows is a reanalysis of an excerpt that I also analyzed elsewhere for different purposes (García-Sánchez, 2014). Example # 2 begins with the doctor asking the mother how long the

TABLE 8.2 Using (multi-)/bilingual knowledge to speak on others' behalf

Linguistic/Communicative Practices	Literacy Strategies/Modes of Reasoning
• Translating • Paraphrasing • Summarizing • Describing • Narrating	• Illustrating with examples • Listening skills • Memory skills • Transcultural/cross-cultural skills • Metapragmatic awareness about interlocutors' communicative needs
Forms of Participation	**Goal(s) of the Activity**
• Hierarchical participation frameworks • Flexible expert/novice roles • Distributed competence • Child's bilingual knowledge as asset	• Clear communicating about patients' health needs

boy has been taking one of the medicines she had prescribed. When Fatima attempts to translate the mother's answer in line 4, and cannot find the right translation for "boxes," and looks up, performing a wordsearch.

Example # 2
Key: Spanish (Regular Font); Moroccan Arabic (***Bold Italics***)
English Glosses (**Bold**)

Participants:	Doctor	Fatima	Mother

1 DOCTOR: Cuánto tiempo tomó?
For how long did he take them?

2 FATIMA: ***šHal min- šHal howwa išrab fhadik?***
For how long- how long did he drink that?

3 MOTHER: ***šrab tlata delakraTan, tlata del paket***
He drank three boxes, three packages

4 FATIMA:

Tres- cómo se llama?
Three- how is it called?

tres botellas que se había comprao
Three bottles that were bought

5 DOCTOR: Tres cajas
Three boxes

6 MOTHER: Huhm Huhm ((making a rectangular shape
with her hands and nodding))

7 FATIMA: Sí
Yes

   As she performs the wordsearch, Fatima is drawing with her hands the rectangular box shape of the medication container, even though she subsequently comes up with the word "botellas" (bottles). The doctor, however, who knows that that kind of medication comes in boxes, offers a correction in line 5: "Tres cajas" (three boxes). 'Ali's mother who has been monitoring the interaction ratifies this correction in line 6 and also starts nodding and drawing with her hands the rectangular shape of a box, with Fatima also acknowledging the correction in line 7.

A crucial aspect I want to highlight in this example is the strong ethos of collaboration between doctor, child language broker, and mother that allows them to arrive at the exact understanding, a key goal in medical interactions, where successful treatment is often predicated on clearly communicating patients' needs and symptoms. The collaborative endeavor begins as soon as Fatima indicates with her hesitation that she is having trouble with the translation task: the doctor may not know Moroccan Arabic, but she possesses medical knowledge about how medicines are dispensed and about her own patients; the mother many not know much Spanish, but she has real-world experience about the medicines she has herself been giving to her son; Fatima may have very limited amounts of medical and caretaker knowledge, but she has the bilingual knowledge that makes it possible for other interlocutors to bring in other kinds of expertise. The way in which they pool these resources and the multimodal participation affordances brought to bear in the interaction are reminiscent of the dynamic way in which competence and expert/novice roles are distributed and reassigned in peer play. These structural arrangement and participation affordances not only maximize possibilities for successful communication, but also enhance the learning opportunities of child language brokers. Table 8.2 provides a summary of how immigrant children use their (multi-)/bilingual knowledge to speak on behalf of others.

Realities and Possibilities of School Literacy

The rich communicative practices described in these two out-of-school activity settings, with peers and community adults, contrast with Moroccan immigrant children's more marginal participation in formal learning environments; participation that was often laced with educators' overt concerns about the children's deficiencies, particularly in school academic literacy. Teachers in the school were most concerned with those Moroccan students who were placed in the *Programa de Educación Compensatory* (Compensatory Education Program), a pull-out Spanish language enhancement program for immigrant students, colloquially referred to as *la clase de apoyo* (the support class), whose very name and nickname bespeak the deficit discourses about Moroccan immigrant children's perceived linguistic deficits. What makes this contrast more jarring is that, as I describe above, there is indeed a high degree of overlap between what children are already doing outside of the classroom (see Tables 8.1 and 8.2) with the communicative practices, modes of reasoning, and literacy strategies that immigrant children were expected to master at school.

There were also, however, significant differences that put in sharp relief the tensions of trying to leverage in the classroom what children are doing outside of school. In this section, I grapple with some of those tensions. Identifying the nature and demands of academic language tasks, such as the design of the task itself and the design of the social organization of the classroom, are key in understanding these differences. Conceived as a monolingual (Spanish-only) literacy program with a heavy emphasis on formal properties of language and technical literacy strategies, its pull-out nature (children would leave their regular classrooms for several hours a week to study Spanish in the support class) underscored how decontextualized literacy was understood to be. Literacy was conceptualized as a subset of skills relating to reading, writing, and arithmetic. Literacy was taught for literacy's sake, with literacy tasks neither embedded as part of larger real-life-like goals nor as part of larger content area learning goals.

In terms of participation and social organization in the classroom, perhaps it is not surprising to find hierarchical participation frameworks, with a more rigid expert (=teacher) and novice (=students') role distribution. This is despite the fact that, much as in the peer groups, in these classes there were often children with different immigration histories and different levels of expertise in Spanish and Moroccan language varieties. Yet, because children were seldom viewed as a source of expertise and because the emphasis was on children's individual engagement with texts, children were rarely allowed to help other children; for the most part, that was considered "cheating." Meaning making and comprehension were considered an individual endeavor, not a collaborative process like at the doctor's office or during peer play. The most consequential difference, however, is that in this literacy program children's bilingual expertise was neither valued nor encouraged; neither was it allowed to be used to solve linguistic/literacy tasks. Rather, citing outdated theories of linguistic transfer in bilinguals, most teachers in the program adhered to the premise that it was detrimental for the children's academic Spanish development to use any Moroccan Arabic while in *la clase de apoyo*. Given the hybrid nature of children's linguistic practices in every other context of their social lives (including other school settings), it must have felt very unnatural to them not to be able to use their Arabic skills in the language and literacy classroom, judging by how often children were chastised for using Moroccan Arabic unwittingly. These differences make it difficult to identify opportunities in the classroom that would be amenable to modification in favor of task designs that could capture what children are doing out of school, particularly when doing so would necessitate fundamentally reframing deficit ideologies about immigrant children's linguistic competencies, as well as convincing schools that Spanish and Arabic do not inhabit separate linguistic, social, and cognitive realms for the children.

The following example illustrates most of the characteristics I have just described. While I cannot claim that this example is representative of all the activities children did in the support classroom (since children participated in many other activities, such as computer-based literacy tasks, reading-comprehension worksheets, flash-card based literacy tasks, arithmetic workbooks, etc.), it is typical of the monolingual, decontextualized, non-collaborative ethos that was used to teach grammar and vocabulary. Example # 3 is an abridged version of a much longer lesson featuring an important topic in the teaching of Spanish as a second language: morphological derivation, or the process of forming new words by adding prefixes and suffixes to existing words. The lesson focused on morphemes associated with the semantic field of professions (-ero/era; -or/ora) and with corresponding workplaces (-ería).

Example # 3
Professions and Morphological Gender Derivation Language Activity:

Participants: **Teacher** **Omar** **Nada** **Ahmed** **Rim**

1 TEACHER: A ver y: cómo se llama:: la persona: (.)
que vende pescado?
**Let's see and how is it called the
person (.) who sells fish**

(0.6)

Cómo se llama?
How is it called?

2 AHMED: Enferma
The patient (lit. sick one)

3 TEACHER: No
No

4 (RIM/OMAR): °La de pescado-
° **(The person) of the fish-**

5 OMAR: Pesca[dero
fish [seller-male

6 TEACHER: [Pescadero y si es una chica?=
**[Fish seller-male and if it is a
girl?=**

7 OMAR: =Pescade[ría
=Fish [shop

8 TEACHER:
[Pes-
[Fis-
((gives a questioning look to Omar who
laughs embarrassed))
Pescadera
Fish seller-female

[...]

9 TEACHER:
Zapatería <u>es la tienda</u>. él que arregla-
el señor-
**Shoe store <u>is the shop</u>. he who fixes-
the man-**

[((Inaudible - several students speaking
at the same time and the teacher speaking
over them))

10 TEACHER:
<u>ZAPATERO</u> y si es una señora?
<u>SHOE REPAIR MAN</u> and if it is a Mrs.?

11 STUDENTS:
Zapatera/Zapatería
Shoe Repair Woman/ Shoe store

((Responding chorally. Some of them produce
the correct form (zapatera), but some
others still make the same mistake
(zapatería))

12 TEACHER:
ZAPATE::RA
SHOE REPAIR WOMAN

13 RIM:
Yo también ten[go-
I also ha[ve-

14 TEACHER:
[Zapatería es <u>la tienda</u>
[Shoe store is <u>the shop</u>

Cómo se llama el que vende la fruta?
How is it called he who sells fruit?

[...]

((Nada writing on the board. Teacher has just dictated "Zapatero", but she gets stuck after writing "zap-"))

15 NADA: °Zapa-
              °Shoem-

16 TEACHER: ((Sounding out the syllables of the word in Spanish))
              Pa (1.1) Te (1.7) Ro (2.1)

(Nada writes them on the board)

Muy bien=
Very well=

=ahora
zapatera
**=now shoe repair woman
(or shoemaker/ shoe-seller-female)**

(.) Venga (1.0)
Come on

The lesson was organized somewhat inductively, by repeatedly engaging in the process of derivation with a list of words from the textbook. The narrow focus on vocabulary contrasts sharply with the rich communicative practices I described above. Moreover, the lack of scaffolding towards an eventual "discovery" of the underlying derivation rules, the drill-like nature of the task, and the lack of contextual anchoring for the long list of vocabulary (beyond those featured in this transcript, the lesson also included, e.g., arquitecto (architect), profesora (professor), cocinero (cook-chef), peluquera (hair-dresser), frutero (fruit-seller), panadera (baker), etc.), however, cancelled the benefits that have been associated with inductive grammar teaching. Indeed, as shown in the two drill sequences reproduced above, particularly in lines 9 through 14, some of the students still remain confused throughout the lesson as to which morpheme to use to derive the profession and which to use to derive the workplace. The lesson ends with individual students taking turns at the board for a public dictation featuring the activity vocabulary list (lines 15–16).

What struck me most about my observations in this program was the strong belief among the teachers that this kind of instruction was necessary to give immigrant students the technical literacy skills needed to succeed in their content-area classes. Central to this belief was the idea that allowing Moroccan

Arabic in the support classroom would be doing the children a disservice. Asking immigrant children to suspend their knowledge of one language to (supposedly) enhance the development of another, however, apart from being a testament to how subtractive schooling models have the power to endure often in the name of good intentions, deeply contradicts ethnographic evidence of immigrant children's syncretic linguistic practices, as examined above, and decades of research in bilingual language development (García & Wei, 2014). In the remainder of the chapter, I discuss additive pathways for schools to tackle academic language in ways that foster linguistic resilience by (1) positively acknowledging (and drawing from) immigrant children's sophisticated bilingual competencies, and (2) by disrupting the ideological trappings of monolingual language and literacy programs.

Drawing inspiration from Cultural Modeling pedagogies' strategy of explicitly cultivating students' metacognition, I argue that purposefully developing students metaknowledge of linguistic processes can be a useful entry point to navigate the tensions involved in making immigrant children's bilingual practices outside of school a central feature in literacy programs that seek to sustain additive learning. Indeed, previous literature has already discussed the importance of using *metalinguistic strategies* that help immigrant students make their tacit bilingual knowledge explicit. For example, Orellana and Reynolds (2008) have suggested ways of cultivating immigrant child language brokers' metalinguistic awareness of the metacommunicative strategies they routinely use when translating for adults, such as summarizing, retelling, or paraphrasing for quintessential school literacy tasks, such as summarizing a textbook passage in students' own words, or rhetorical style-shifting when writing for different audiences (Martínez et al., 2008).

Here, I draw attention to a metalinguistic knowledge that has received little attention to date, that pertaining to shared linguistic heritage or the similarities that immigrant (or other bilingual) children tacitly notice between languages in their linguistic repertoire. In this ethnographic case, it is well known that varieties of Arabic made important linguistic contributions to the development of modern Spanish. Historical linguists have documented Arabic influence into Spanish at the morpho-syntactic, semantic, and discourse levels (Penny, 2002). Even children as young as those in my study implicitly discern these connections much more than we usually realize. One afternoon, a group of girls came to do their homework in my apartment. As they ate the albaricoques (apricots) I offered as a snack, Wafiya said that in Morocco, there was also a fruit with that name (*albarquq*). My curiosity sparked, I asked the girls if they knew other Spanish words that sounded similar in Arabic. They did, of course! Although the technical name was unknown to them, they had even noticed a phenomenon by which Spanish incorporated Arabic vocabulary by *addition* to the already existing Latin lexicon, rather than by *replacement*. For example, Worda and Wafiya pretended to fight with each other about whether it was "cooler" to say *piscina* (swimming pool; Latin voice) or *alberca* (swimming pool; Arabic voice).

What are the possibilities of rigorously expanding on an exchange like this in schools: of systematically cultivating students' metalinguistic awareness about these historical connections? A good place to start would be to create spaces in the classroom for children to share the similarities that they have already noticed so that teachers can build on children's bilingual knowledge to enhance their awareness of the cultural, structural and formal properties of both languages. Once conversations like the ones I had with Worda and Wafiya start happening in schools, many different possibilities emerge. Let me mention a couple to show how teachers could approach this cultivation. At the formal structural level, and relating it to the last example I discussed, teachers could build on this conversation by explicitly teaching about how Spanish words that come from Arabic are recognizable by the morpheme a-/al-. Then, they could expand to other common morphemes and what they can tell us about the meanings of words, even words that students may have never encountered before, and about the types of text (on the colloquial-formality continuum) in which different kinds of word appear. After all, cultivating metalinguistic awareness of morphological knowledge about the origins and meanings of prefixes and suffixes is a strategy that is sometimes used in advanced placement courses to help students access "difficult" academic texts. Simultaneously, such lessons help disrupt the artificial ideological boundaries between Spanish and Arabic, as distinct national languages, by explicitly highlighting the amount of borrowings and other contact features between them. There is also great value in class discussions about language (and the kind of language that is valued in schools) that build on Worda and Wafiya's comparison of the *coolness* of using *alberca* versus *piscina*: what are the ideological basis of the children's comparison? How do the children's own ideas about this *coolness* intersect with present-day language ideologies about standard and academic language (with *piscina* being the standard word in academic settings, and *alberca* being widely used colloquially in the linguistic variety of southern Spain where the children live)? How do they intersect with historical language ideologies which justified giving deliberate preference to Latin-origin words (Penny, 2002)? These examples show the potential for how metalinguistic strategies can address both formal and ideological dimensions of language education, by putting children's bilingual knowledge at the center of the curriculum.

Implications for Teaching and Learning in Schools

One of the most pressing concerns of literacy educators I have known in Spain and the U.S. who work with immigrant children is that their students develop the formal linguistic knowledge and the technical skills that will allow them to master *academic literacy*, arguably the most critical building block of educational achievement. This is a concern that cannot be dismissed; after all, many educational scholars have powerfully argued that literacy is a civil right of the 21st century (Lee, 2008; Winn et al., 2011). But what linguistic variety/register counts as appropriate for *academic literacy*? Who is heard/seen as having or as being able to develop academic literacy? Are students allowed to show their linguistic and literacy competences, and if so, how? Current answers to these questions are laced with (racio-)linguistic ideologies that are suffused with moral and political interests about the nature of language, the relationship between orality and literacy (Bauman & Briggs, 2003), and the supposed language deficiency of certain racialized bodies (Rosa & Flores, 2017).

Because of this, giving immigrant students technical literacy skills alone, while essential, is not enough for additive schooling that truly seeks to achieve cultural and linguistic pluralist outcomes. Educators need to ensure that, in addition to providing these skills, they are also using their curricula to disrupt the ideological trappings of academic literacy instruction in schools, which are deeply steeped in deficit thinking about immigrant students as linguistically lacking, even languageless (Rosa, 2016), very often regardless of their actual empirically demonstrable multilingual competences, like those of the immigrant children I analyzed above. Building language and literacy curricula that simultaneously promote formal/technical literacy skills and provide critical perspectives on language and power is key for immigrant students to develop a longlasting sense of *linguistic resilience*; i.e., students' ability to withstand monolingual/monocultural hegemonic norms of educational achievement and to flourish and develop confidence in their linguistic abilities, despite the harmful messages conveyed by those norms.

A key ingredient in setting up the learning conditions for immigrant students to develop linguistic resilience is the cultivation of metalinguistic strategies in language and literacy classes. Here, I have emphasized in particular making explicitly visible for immigrant students their metalinguistic awareness of a shared linguistic heritage, especially in situations where the languages have a strong history of contact and influence (such as Spanish and Arabic). And because old colonial relationships are the basis for many contemporary migration patterns, it is likely that bilingualism patterns in many new immigrant communities will involve cases in which languages have indeed had a history of contact. Exploring these similarities not only allows students to develop grammatical technical skills relating to the morphology, syntax, and semantics of both languages (and not just of the dominant language at the expense of the non-dominant language); it also makes obvious something that language scholars have now understood for more than a century: the plural and hybrid historical influences that impinge on the development of any natural language.

Designing lessons that include attention to metalinguistic strategies, particularly (although not exclusively) those concerning shared linguistic heritage, can help educators accomplish several goals for additive learning and schooling: first, even in the most restrictive teaching environments where teachers may feel that they cannot make use of the bilingual instructional strategies that the translanguaging model has made available (García & Wei, 2014), this is one way to honor in the classroom the language practices displayed by immigrant children out of school. As my ethnographic examples demonstrate, the multiple languages in children's linguistic repertoire do not inhabit separate linguistic, social, and cognitive realms for the children, as they often do in many language and literacy classes for immigrant students. The role that validating immigrant students' full linguistic repertoire in the classroom can have in learning cannot be underestimated. Emphasizing shared linguistic heritage as a form of validation can be particularly important because it highlights points of continuity across time between the languages in immigrant students' repertoires. Building on continuities, rather than on home language-school language dichotomies, is crucial in developing a sociolinguistic and culturally responsive approach to curriculum and instruction.

Second, cultivating students metalinguistic and metapragmatic awareness about these historical-linguistic connections can enhance knowledge of cultural, structural and formal properties of the languages, and therefore give children the important technical/grammatical skills that teachers value while simultaneously decentering the teaching of literacy to immigrant children so that it does not reify Herderian hegemonic notions of languages as pure, discrete, and stable. In so doing, a curriculum that is mindful of these historical metalinguistic aspects of language development denaturalizes the cultural and ethnolinguistic ideological basis of so-called *national languages*. Furthermore, acknowledging the hybrid origins of languages can be a critical tool for educators to disrupt sociolinguistic inequalities in educational contexts and the pernicious and artificial ideological divisions between immigrant (also often labeled home/heritage/expressive) and national (also often labeled institutional/academic/mainstream) languages.

References

Alim, H. S. (2004). *You know my steez: An ethnographic and sociolinguistic study of style shifting in a black American speech community.* Durham, NC: Duke University Press.

Bauman, B. & Briggs, C. L. (2003). *Voices of modernity: Language ideologies and the politics of inequality.* Cambridge: Cambridge University Press.

Delpit, L. D. (1995). *Other people's children: Cultural conflict in the classroom.* New York: New Press.

Eksner, H. J. & Orellana, M. F. (2012). Shifting in the zone: Latina/o child language brokers and the co-construction of knowledge. *Ethos, 40*(2), 196–122.

García, O. & Wei, L. (2014). *Translanguaging: Language, bilingualism, and education.* New York: Palgrave Macmillan.

García-Sánchez, I. M. (2017). Friendship, participation, and multimodality in Moroccan immigrant girls' peer groups. In M. Theobald (Ed.) *Friendship and peer culture in multilingual settings* (1–33). Bingley: Emerald Books.

García-Sánchez I. M. (2014). *Language and Muslim immigrant childhoods: The politics of belonging.* Oxford: Blackwell-Wiley.

García-Sánchez, I. M. (2010). Serious games: Code-switching and identity in Moroccan immigrant girls' pretend play. *Pragmatics, 20*(4), 523–555.

García-Sánchez, I. M. (2005). More than just games: Language socialization in an immigrant children's peer group. *Texas Linguistic Forum, 49*, 61–71.

Goodwin, C. (2018). *Cooperative action. Learning in doing: Social, cognitive, and computational perspectives.* Cambridge: Cambridge University Press.

Guan, S.-S. A., Greenfield, P. M., Orellana, M. F. (2014). Translating into understanding: language brokering and prosocial development in emerging adults from immigrant families. *Journal of Adolescent Research, 29*(3), 331–355.

Gutierrez, K. & Rogoff, B. (2003). Cultural ways of learning: Individual traits or repertoires of practice. *Educational Researcher, 32*, 19–25.

Heath, S. B. (1983). *Ways with words: Language, life, and work in communities and classrooms.* Cambridge: Cambridge University Press.

Labov, W. (1972). *Language in the inner city: Studies in the Black vernacular.* Philadelphia, PA: University of Pennsylvania Press.

Lee, C. D. (2008). Revisiting playing in the dark: The hidden games of racialization in literacy studies and school reform. In S. Green (Ed.) *Literacy as a Civil Right* (151–168). New York: Peter Lang.

Lee, C. D. (2007). *Culture, literacy, and learning: Taking bloom in the midst of whirlwind.* New York: Teachers College Press.

Lee, C. D. (1997). Bridging home and school literacies: Models for culturally responsive teaching, a case for African American English. In J. Flood, S. B. Heath, & D. Lapp (Eds.) *Handbook of research on teaching literacy through the communicative and visual arts* (334–345). New York: Macmillan.

Martínez, R., Orellana, M.F., Pacheco, M., & Carbone, P. (2008). Found in translation: Connecting translating experiences to academic writing. *Language Arts, 85*(6), 421–431.

Moll, L. C. (1992). Funds of knowledge for teaching: Using a qualitative approach to connect homes and classrooms. *Theory into Practice, 31*(2), 132–141.

Orellana, M. F. (2009). *Translating childhoods: Immigrant youth, language and culture.* New Brunswick, NJ: Rutgers University Press.

Orellana, M. F. & Eksner J. H. (2006). Power in cultural modeling: Building on the bilingual language practices of immigrant youth in Germany and the United States. *National Reading Conference Yearbook, 55*, 224–234.

Orellana, M. F. & Reynolds, J. (2008). Cultural modeling: Leveraging bilingual skills for school paraphrasing tasks. *Reading Research Quarterly, 43*(1), 48–65.

Paris, D. & Alim, H. S. (Eds.) (2017). *Culturally sustaining pedagogies: Teaching and learning for justice in a changing world.* New York: Columbia University Teachers College Press.

Penny, R. (2002). *A history of the Spanish language,* 2nd edn. Cambridge: Cambridge University Press.

Philips, S. U. (2013). Method in anthropological discourse analysis: The comparison of units of interaction. *Journal of Linguistic Anthropology, 23*(1), 83–96.

Philips, S. U. (1983). *The invisible culture: Communication in classroom and community on the Warm Spring Indian Reservation.* Prospect Heights, IL: Waveland Press.

Rosa, J. D. (2016). Standardization, racialization, languagelessness: Raciolinguistic ideologies across communicative contexts. *Journal of Linguistic Anthropology, 26*(2), 162–183.

Rosa, J. D. & Flores, N. (2017). Do you hear what I hear?: Raciolinguistic ideologies and culturally sustaining pedagogies. In D. Paris & H. S. Alim (Eds.) *Culturally sustaining pedagogies: Teaching and learning for justice in a changing world* (175–206). New York: Columbia University Teachers College Press.

Scribner, S. & Cole, M. (1978). Literacy without schooling: Testing for intellectual effects. *Harvard Educational Review, 48,* 4.

Silverstein, M. (2003). Indexical order and the dialectics of sociolinguistic life. *Language and Communication, 23*(3–4), 193–229.

Street, B.V. (Ed.) (1993). *Cross-cultural approaches to literacy.* Cambridge: Cambridge University Press.

Winn, M.T., Behizadeh, N., Duncan, G., Fine, M. & Gadsden, V. (2011). The right to be literate: Literacy, education, and the school-to-prison pipeline. *Review of Research in Education, 35,* 147–173.

Zentella, A. C. (1997). *Growing up bilingual: Puerto Rican children in New York.* Oxford: Blackwell.

9

FINDING A WAY INTO STORYWORLDS: YOUTH CO-NARRATIONS OF CROSS-CULTURAL LIVES AS ANALOGUE FOR ACADEMIC LITERARY TALK

Patricia Enciso

We need stories—our own stories, family stories, historical, futuristic, fantastic stories and everyday stories as we shape who we are and who we might become (Anzaldúa, 1987; Bruner, 1986). And yet stories are not equally told, heard, or valued, especially in school settings. Despite increasing calls for including diverse literature and cross-cultural dialogue in education, youth have few opportunities to construct and navigate cultural "contact zones" (Pratt, 1991) through which they might reckon with the histories and meanings of one another's worlds and their shared futures.

In this chapter, I respond to the need for more diverse stories by describing a pedagogy of transcultural storytelling among non-dominant middle school youth, developed over a three-year ethnography of literary reading and weekly small group "story club" meetings. In an effort to foreground non-dominant youth voices and their storytelling, I turn to sociolinguistic theories of "voice" (Blommaert, 2005, 2008; Hymes, 1996) and "co-narration" with "small stories" (Georgakopoulou, 2006; Ochs & Capps, 2001) and apply these ideas to one storytelling episode in which youth used multiple forms of talk and interaction to describe street scenes involving police across four distinct real and imagined settings. Through my analysis of this storytelling event, I highlight the everyday expertise youth employed to create and cross into one another's worlds. I conclude by considering how youth's implicit knowledge of storytelling practices may be mobilized for new forms of transcultural literature study in the interest of their "contributions to collaborative practices of humanity" (Stetsenko, 2008, p. 489).

Reading and Telling Stories in Two Classrooms

In 2008, I began teaching and observing literature studies with youth and teachers in a middle school located in a large Midwestern metropolitan area where new immigrant and refugee families from Mexico, Central America, Cambodia, Kenya, Somalia, and Iraq had recently settled among intergenerational white urban Appalachian, Eastern European heritage, and African American families. I wondered how youth and teachers would navigate their multiple histories and perspectives, largely silenced in the official curriculum, as they introduced literature selections that acknowledged, but did not extend or elaborate on the multiplicity and complexity of non-dominant experiences. In particular, I wondered how youth's linguistic, narrative, and popular media repertoires, as well as their community cultural practices could be gathered and transformed into "cultural data sets" (Lee, 2007; see also Martinez, Montaño, and Rojo, this volume); i.e., familiar forms of talk and storytelling grounded in youth knowledge, that might serve as starting points for the forms of inquiry associated with insightful literature study (Enciso, Volz, Price-Dennis, & Durriyah, 2009) such as paying attention to details, questioning unusual descriptions or events, following a character's development, and hypothesizing about the meaning of figurative language (Lee, 2007; Rabinowitz, 1987). At the same time, I wanted to understand the forms of talk and interaction youth might create as they interpreted one another's worlds in face-to-face conversation, in much the same way that readers imaginatively cross into and question the distinct worlds created through literary works. Lee's (2007) research on cultural data sets was developed in a school with an almost exclusively Black population, where youth shared similar community spaces, linguistic repertoires, historical knowledge, and contemporary popular cultural references. I was interested in how cultural data sets for literature study might be gathered among a demographic of immigrant and non-immigrant peers. How might youth bring disparate and overlapping repertoires and resources to their reading experiences and how might their shared resources support an understanding of themselves as interdependent global peers?

Seeking Voice within Structural Misunderstanding

Classrooms can be hard places for non-dominant youth to talk about or tell their own stories. Time constraints alone mean that any attempt at storytelling will be partial. Non-dominant stories (and storytellers) are further subject to peer and adult interpretations, framed by media-based narratives and years of biased curricula that convert differences to deficits (Au, 2008; Noguera, 2003) or reduce culturally specific histories and details to stereotyped, single stories (Adichie, 2009). As Blommaert (2008) argues, non-dominant storytelling in school is vulnerable to exclusion due to "structural misunderstanding," that is, institutionalized forms of inequality that "systematically define what is unfamiliar as inferior" (p. 24). For example, immigrant youth in the sixth grade were automatically placed in an ELL language arts classroom in which English was taught at the expense of youth multilingual repertoires. Further, the separation between immigrant and non-immigrant youth meant that they had limited interactions with, let alone dialogue about their perspectives and experiences of immigration; yet such experiences were in the novels they were required to read in language arts classes.

After several discussions with the ELL teacher about observing in the classroom, I was invited to document youth interactions as they heard stories (on tape) and discussed central themes. Next door to the ELL classroom, a sixth/seventh grade teacher worked with a small group of students, all male, non-immigrant, of Appalachian, European, African American and Puerto Rican heritage, to support their language arts and social studies education as well as their emotional well-being. Both teachers and youth agreed to work together with me once a week in their side-by-side classrooms to read and talk about literature.

Over the first few months of observations in the ELL classroom, I documented the difficulty youth experienced in gaining recognition when they seemed to make a bid to tell a story. For example, when youth answered teacher-initiated questions with phrases like "One time ..." and "In Kenya ...", suggesting the beginnings of stories, their responses were perceived only as answers and thus revalued and addressed in the service of an academic function (e.g., correct or incorrect). In addition, I observed that youth stories and their related knowledge and repertoires were often ignored or misinterpreted as peers and their teacher heard only pieces of a story while other classroom interactions disrupted a full telling (Enciso, 2011).

To tell a story and be heard involves animating characters' actions, voices, and viewpoints, while staying attuned to the ways the telling entertains and persuades others of the story's reality and relevance. Sociolinguists recognize such tellings as interactive social achievements (Bauman & Briggs, 1997; Gumperz, 1982) reflecting the linguistic and semiotic resources of the storyteller as well as the situated, social knowledge and spaces that organize ideologies and relationships (c.f. Blommaert, 2005; Bucholtz & Hall, 2005). Within the constraints of structural inequality, tellers and listeners construct the context in which being heard might become possible. Wortham & Reyes (2015) have shown in their analyses of teacher and student dialogue in English classrooms that youth may answer teacher-initiated questions with a story-like response, yet their talk may be interpreted as off topic, incorrect, or confusing. In this view, storytelling, like any other form of representation of oneself among others, entails a social-political production of voice, described by Blommaert (2005) as an ongoing effort to "use language and other semiotic means in attempts ... to make [oneself] understood by others" (p. 427). The effort to be understood by others may be especially risky when the storyteller's social positioning is uncertain, and the story elements to be shared have no established, shared frame of reference (Enciso, 2011, 2017; Medina, 2010).

In both classes, youth seemed to enjoy following a story's plot and characters, but showed little interest in speculating about characters' viewpoints or relating their own experiences and knowledge to the author's created world. However, discussion was dominated in each class by one or two outspoken youth who consistently answered teachers' questions. Several youth also talked with some encouragement about their specific experiences, knowledge, and beliefs. Meanwhile, along the edges and outside of official classroom spaces, youth seemed to constantly tell, listen to, and view stories through face-to-face conversations and social media, using multiple languages and images to describe and comment on their own and others' local and global experiences. As Lee (2007) argues and sociocultural research has shown over and over again, youth expertise is often more fully expressed among peers outside school (c.f. Gutiérrez, 2008; Maira & Soep, 2005) or in classrooms where teacher-directed interactions are displaced by youth-centered inquiry (DeNicolo & Franquiz, 2006; Martínez-Roldan, 2003; Medina, 2010).

Story Club as a Forum for Youth Expertise

I needed to find a forum for youth to express and explore their knowledge and repertoires outside of the classroom. I proposed to the classroom teachers that we invite three or four youth from each class to meet once a week to become co-researchers who would tell, elaborate on, and evaluate texts and stories that might serve as useful data sets for their future literature study. Six youth, four from the ELL class (Sara, Habiba, Tucker, Tomás) and three from the adjacent class (Chris, Lee, and Paul), agreed to join story club meetings in the library at lunchtime. One additional youth (Aaqilah), from the ELL class, joined later sessions.

Sara, Habiba, and Aaqilah identified as Muslim, with different histories of migration and socialization in Islamic faith practices. All three girls arrived in the U.S. at about age six. They spoke English comfortably in conversation and often spoke together in Somali, while noting their understanding of and use of Swahili, Amharic, tribal languages, and conversational Arabic at home or in the company of peers or adults at school. They identified as transnational through their expressed knowledge of events and ongoing communications with family outside the U.S. Chris identified primarily as African American, while he also referenced family who were white and Puerto Rican. Tucker identified as Cambodian American and spoke English at school and Khmer at home. Tomás was born in the U.S. and was Mexican transnational, traveling to Mexico several times a year. His dominant home language was Spanish, but like many of the youth in story club, he was confident in spoken English, often using sophisticated vocabulary to express ideas.

In my interactions with youth, I was known to be a teacher and professor, a white Mexican-heritage middle-aged woman who liked books and reading and was interested in youth ideas and perspectives. One day a week, I assisted their teachers by reading and talking about a book with them, using visual and dramatic modes to support our dialogue (Enciso, 2011). By the time story club began in January 2009, we were familiar with one another, primarily through formal classroom interactions in the presence of their regular teacher. I wanted to construct a space with youth that followed their ways of talking about and interpreting one another's worlds.

Finding Our Way into Stories

Story club met one day a week in the school library during lunchtime, which meant that youth brought a school lunch to the group, marking the space as a more social gathering than an academically regulated place. Chris, Tucker, Paul, Tomás, Habiba, Sara and I met in mid-January, 2009, in the school library where we sat together around a small rectangular table. I planned to share several picture books to provide exemplars of storytelling topics and forms. I positioned myself as a listener, someone who was curious and interested in what everyone had to say. Generally, I occupied a liminal space between researcher and interested conversationalist. All sessions were audio- and videorecorded and later transcribed for analysis.

I opened our first session by asking everyone what they thought story club might be about. Their ideas included, "doing worksheets," "reading books," and "learning about other people" and "learning from their stories." I assured them we would not be filling in worksheets and it was not a book discussion club, but we would be telling and collecting stories of all kinds from everyday life, from stories we heard, or from any other source. Given my plan to work with youth on collecting stories and transcribing them in some way as texts for later study in their literature classes, I suggested that we look at the structures of stories together to help us tell our own stories. Using a series of panels from the graphic novel, *The arrival* (Tan, 2007), as an example, I asked them to think about how stories are told, in different sequences, with different viewpoints, and how we might find stories in our own lives to share with peers in language arts classes. I assumed, quite mistakenly, that everyone would share my interest in the *ways* stories are told. Not surprisingly, youth were far more drawn to the pleasure of telling and building on stories among friends. I persisted, however, in trying to emphasize story structures during the opening five to ten minutes of the initial story club sessions.

Seeing into One Another's Worlds

Ignoring my focus on story structures, Tomás pointed to an image of a fantastical animal figure in *The arrival* and asked about the size of its fish-like scales. I registered his comment as the beginning of a story about animals, a topic he had initiated in our one-on-one classroom conversations. His animal stories usually took place in Mexico and Texas, places familiar to him yet rarely engaged in the classroom as valued knowledge and experience. I wanted to hear about his connection with this image and I assumed his peers would also be interested.

I invited Tomás to tell us about his experiences with fish and he described going out with his father and uncles in a small boat in the Gulf of Mexico to fish for shrimp. With gentle prompting from me about the event (Did you fish at night? How many people were in the boat? What size were the shrimp? How did you cook them?), Tomás narrated and demonstrated how his father used a pole and line to catch large shrimp and brought them home to be grilled. In supporting Tomás's telling, I relied on our relationship, my awareness that he might be reticent to explain a complex and distant event to his peers, my genuine interest in the details of his story, and my desire to create a story structure that might be useful to other participants' ways of telling stories. While I asked questions of fact related to setting, characters, and actions, however, his peers interjected evaluative, intertextual, and interpersonal statements. Paul stated to no one in particular: "You shouldn't have to work for your food." Chris made an intertextual side comment, "The great white shark," as Paul looked across the table at Tomás and said he reminded him of someone he had just seen wrestling on television. As Blommaert (2005) argues, stories like Tomás's do not translate directly from one setting to another; such stories may include images familiar to others, but the place, events, and the experiences of traveling internationally presented new challenges in comprehension for difficult for his non-immigrant peers.

As I continued to casually turn pages in *The arrival*, I pointed to another surreal animal-like figure, which prompted youth to recall Sasquatch, the Loch Ness Monster, and el Chupacabra, and then briefly debate the possibilities that these creatures were fake, real, or legends. The topic of monsters shifted next to a bid from Sara to tell a story from Somalia. Although she initiated the story by engaging her peers with a familiar storytelling trope, she also managed potential skepticism by recognizing that she was moving a familial story into a space where it might not be "heard": "I have a story my dad told me that you might think is fake but it's actually real. Because there are people in Somalia that can control crocodiles." As Sara anticipated, Tucker interjected sarcastically: "Oh, really?" Sara continued, nodding, "They're supposed to be really ugly and there's this one [crocodile/man] who liked this beautiful girl ..." She explained that the old man threatened to kill the young woman unless her father agreed to let her ride [the crocodile] so she could be his bride. The father did as the old man asked and the beautiful young woman married the man.

As Sara completed her story, Tucker raised his hand, asking for the floor so he could describe "Arb," a traditional Cambodian female monster who appears as a floating head with entrails hanging from her neck and who eats sleeping children. In parallel with Tucker's tale of a dangerous female ghost figure, Tomás told part of the story of la Llorona as he chanted in her voice, "Mis hijos! Mis hijos!," which he translated for the group as "My babies! My babies!" and shared how afraid he felt when he heard this story. Chris then described how frightened he was by his grandma's story of a house out in the country where the children were eaten by a wild boar. Next, Habiba told a story set in Kenya, where dancing female djinn or spirits frightened the children and were chased by her father; and then Sara and Habiba told two more djinn tales that involved adults reciting stanzas from the Qur'an to defeat the spirits. Their compelling story bids became the subject of further storytelling over the next 15 sessions as youth questioned, contested, and confirmed a story's verifiability, details, and connections with other stories and media.

In the midst of storytelling, youth also commented directly on one another's identities. For example, in the first story club session, immediately following Sara and Habiba's brief stories of djinn and their father's reading from the Qur'an, Chris turned to me and then to Sara and said: "Can I ask a question? What's the Ko-ran?" Paul added, looking at Habiba: "Is this in Somalia?" Tucker addressed the whole group, informing them: "It's a holy book, like the bible. It's their bible." Chris responded again, looking at Sara: "Like the bible?" And Sara answered: "It's Islamic." Habiba and Sara were positioned by Chris and Paul as "other than Christian," and yet, with Tucker's explanation, they were not alone in their efforts to mobilize resources for responding to questions and remarks that might have become derogatory. In later sessions, Sara and Habiba also used their transnational knowledge to reverse Chris or Paul's implicit positioning of them as "other" by grilling them on their limited understanding of international monetary values, religious texts, and Islamic holidays (Enciso, 2016).

Rethinking Cultural Data Sets: From Texts to Small Stories and Co-narration

The first story club meeting established a pattern of storytelling for the next 15 sessions that began with greetings and news about school and home, a brief reminder by me of our previous storytelling, and then ten to 15 minutes of storytelling around a theme initiated by youth or a reference to previous meetings, along with questions and comments related to one another's stories and identities. Another round of storytelling would follow for ten minutes, or I would attempt to engage them in a review of their stories and their literary qualities. Although I persisted in asking youth to consider the relationship between our storytelling and classroom literature study, youth seemed to understand before I did, that these two settings were so different in tone and format that they could not be bridged by translating oral stories into textual prototypes for literary inquiry. As I talked with colleagues and read more widely about oral storytelling, I began to understand that our form (versus content) of storytelling was actually highly analogous to the most valued features of academic literary discussions: readers, like participants in informal storytelling, attend to and interrogate details, compare related experiences, reference and cross-reference the teller's description to uncover deeper significance, find and name significant personal and shared thematic threads, and generate hypothetical situations for analyzing and evaluating character/actors' actions and decisions.

During storytelling, youth also addressed one another's different perspectives and experiences while claiming their right to "tell their own story" and determine their own identities. From the standpoint of literary study, youth in story club were participants in a contact zone, authoring and interpreting worlds they valued. Our form of interactive storytelling is described by narrative and applied linguistic theorists as co-narration of small stories—and youth were experts in this practice.

Co-narration and Small Stories

One of the most accessible and widely studied forms of informal storytelling is "co-narration," first described by Ochs, Smith, and Taylor (1989) in their studies of dinnertime storytelling among family members who co-constructed daily events while questioning and elaborating on one another's descriptions and interpretations. Story club narratives fit Ochs and Capps' (2001) definition of co-narration, in which stories "tend to be temporally and causally nonlinear and oscillate back and forth between perspectives, which may conflict" (p. 6). Personal experience stories, embedded in dialogue, like those co-narrated in story club tend to "illustrate a point, make a comparison, support an argument, or otherwise elaborate a focus of concern" (Ochs & Capps, 2001, p. 37). Unlike storytelling that relies on a single-voiced teller's version of an event's chronology and perspectives, a co-narrated story moves across tellers' viewpoints. Co-narrations, as an everyday storytelling form, creates the possibility for envisioning and expanding participants' initial conception of the focal event.

Within the practices of co-narration, participants often tell small stories or single-voiced descriptions of events, with an expectation that others will share referents or add to the story as their conversation continues. Georgakopoulou (2007) describes small stories as part of a "trajectory of interactions" rather than "freestanding, finished and self-contained" (p. 40). As such, small stories constitute a familiar, taken for granted part of everyday interaction about the goings on and meanings youth ascribe to everyday life. Small stories may be initiated to entertain peers, through an opening line such as, Sara's "there are people in Somalia that can control crocodiles" or to assert authority and social positioning, as in her prelude: "I have a story my dad told me that you might think is fake but it's actually real." Her fuller telling was also preceded by

Tucker's evaluative statement, "Oh, really?," making her small story susceptible to further questioning among her peers. Small stories emerging through co-narration across a trajectory of interactions may be referenced and expanded on as a group builds an image of one another's worlds and perspectives on everyday life.

Making Connections: Transcultural and Literary Moves in Co-narrations with Small Stories

In my analysis, I was interested in how youth co-narrations and small stories involved the kind of moves described by Orellana (2015) as indicative of trans-culturality: "a movement beyond all borders that limit and constrain, into new uncharted territory" (p. xi). I was also interested in how their assertions, descriptions, questions, and evaluative comments reflected the kinds of move required of readers as they enter into unfamiliar story worlds. How did youth mobilize and transform their social, semiotic, and linguistic resources (voice) to create and sustain interest in one another's worlds? How might their expertise as storytellers become visible as a form of transcultural storytelling and reading? What risks in identity do youth take as they make their worlds visible to one another? How might youth experiences of storytelling support their under-standing of themselves in a pluralistic society? (See D'warte, this volume, for additional ways to center multilingualism, transculturalism, andtransnational experiences as resources for learning.

I selected the following episode as an illustration of our story club interactions because the topic was limited to only one session. Further, this relatively short epi-sode of only four minutes illustrates the relationship between youth everyday expertise as co-narrators and the transcultural moves that could be engaged during literary study. Drawing on narrative theory, I highlight four ways youth's everyday co-narration practices parallel the world-crossing demands of transcultural literary reading: narrative backgrounding (Minks, 2007), telling "small" second stories (Bamberg, 2011; deFina & Georgakopoulou, 2011), forming well-told stories (Hymes, 1996), and evaluating or comparing beliefs and practices (Bruner 1986; Lee 2007; Ochs & Capps 2001).

The focal co-narration episode occurred during the fifth story club session when youth were familiar with one another and had established a pattern of first greeting and then launching into a topic and co-narration. The episode was initiated by Tomás who had just returned from a brief trip to Mexico where he was walking in "la plaza" with his cousin and "almost got shot at by the Mexi-can police." I share this episode with caution because I do not want to suggest that Tomás's or other transnational youth's lives are centered in violence. His story was as surprising for him as it was for us. At the same time, readers in 2019 will also be aware of the many recent episodes in the U.S. when Black and brown children have been subject to violent policing in public spaces where they are supposed to be protected (Razza, 2018). I also ask, then, how youth position themselves and others in real and imagined global places where childhoods are policed and real and imagined lives are at stake.

Co-narrating La Plaza

As the storytelling episode began, Habiba and Sarah were already seated and talking about their math class and the detention the whole class had to serve that day. Tomás walked in with his lunch, followed by Chris and Tucker. As they settled in to eating their lunches, Tomás said he had been in Mexico and Habiba asked "Do you have a story for us?"

Tomás surprised us with a story opening that does exactly what a story is supposed to do: Create a break from the usual.

TOMÁS: I almost got shot at by the Mexican police.
ALL: (multiple voices) Awww. (laughter)
PAT: Oh. Tell us that story. That sounds good.
CHRIS: Rebels.
PAT: You almost got shot at by the Mexican police.
TOMÁS: In the plaza. At like one a. One a.m.
PAT: One a.m. in the plaza. Okay.
CHRIS: What in the heck were you doing in a plaza at one a.m.?

Many Mexican-heritage youth and adults know "la plaza" as a culturally specific lived place, where kids play, tease, and run around when it's cool at night. For Tomás, a familiar and unremarkable landscape was now open to question. He had to draw on his experiences and convert his linguistic resources into images that would make "la plaza" legible to his peers. His challenge was akin to authoring a culturally specific story world while anticipating the limits of readers' background knowledge.

Through our practice of co-narration Chris and Tucker openly voiced their uncertainty and need for clarity about Tomás's reasons for being in "la plaza" at one a.m.

CHRIS: What in the heck were you doing in a plaza at one a.m.?
TOMÁS: Walking arou:nd. Watching a ...
TUCKER: Isn't a plaza for shopping and stuff?
TOMÁS: (to Tucker). No:o.

Having walked in *zócalos* or *plazas* in Mexico, I was aware of how distinctive and unfamiliar they would be to youth who grew up in the U.S. Midwest. I asked Tomás to tell us a bit more about "la plaza."

PAT: (to Tomás) So explain la plaza. What is la plaza? In Mexico.

TOMÁS: It's somewhere, on the weekends, you get to chillin'.

CHRIS: Oh. You get to chill.

PAT: So is there anything like it in (our town) could you say? Is there anything like the plaza?

TOMÁS: Hum?

CHRIS: A park?

TOMÁS: Yeah. A park.

PAT: Like a park.

CHRIS: Da:ng.

TOMÁS: (xxx unclear) that one does not have swings in it.

PAT: Doesn't have what?

TOMÁS: Swings.

PAT: What does it have in it? What does the plaza have in it?

TOMÁS: It usually has uhm fishes in a po:nd.

(rising tone)

Tomás worked with the "park" frame to try to get us closer to the meaning of "la plaza."

He provided what narrative analysts call "narrative backgrounding" (Minks, 2007). Narrative backgrounding usually constitutes an explanation or break in storytelling, while it also contributes critical information related to the images, characters, events, and deeper worldview informing and framing a story. Narrative backgrounding may take different forms in literature, from extended descriptive prose to characters' brief asides or observations in texts; and, likewise, in co-narrations, as more elaborated explanations or, more often, responses to a series of questions. Minks (2007) argues that as children use narrative backgrounding in their storytelling, they not only establish their firsthand knowledge, but also identify a telling detail that may help them explain deeper cultural meanings with new audiences. In this sense, children hold considerable responsibility for building and interpreting images of place and time as they move into and across sociopolitical and imaginative borders.

Tomás helped us see that "la plaza" is and is not comparable to a Midwestern park. He described "la plaza" as a place to chill, swing, and observe "little fishes in a pond," all childhood pleasures that contrast sharply with his opening statement. He and I co-narrated "la plaza" so that its meaning in his story and life could be understood as more than a place where police shoot at kids. Tomás' effort to transpose a culturally valued place for an "outsider" audience is parallel to the efforts of non-dominant youth in literature discussions, whose experiences in global places have few accurate or deep points of reference through which to describe or interpret their implicit understanding of cultural distinctions.

Unstable Places, Unstable Positioning: Claiming My Own Story

Within our first few speaking turns, "la plaza," like global places in trans-cultural literature, became "an unstable stage for performing the meaning of a place" (de Certeau, 1984). "La plaza" was narrated as both placid and dangerous; like and unlike a playground or park. As de Certeau and other spatial theorists have argued, everyday public spaces are not static; they are remade by people who walk through and bring social life to bear on their intended orderliness. Place becomes an event, open to creative social practices (Massey, 1992). In both co-narration and literary interpretation, places hold deep cultural histories and meanings that may become more visible as characters/tellers/readers are positioned by and position themselves within a story world. Positioning oneself and others in public places, as suggested earlier, is a political-historical act of agency, vulnerable, for non-dominant youth, to state-sponsored policing.

Tomás and I continued to co-narrate his story until Chris initiated a position for himself *as Tomás*, who could challenge the police.

PAT: (laugh). Okay. So you're in the plaza at one a.m.
TOMÁS: Uh hmm.
PAT: What happened?
CHRIS: The police came up [like] =
TOMÁS: [The police]=
CHRIS: = "Hey! You get out of here!"
       And you was like, "No!"
       And they was like.
TOMÁS: No.

Tomás rejected Chris's positioning and telling and then told the story from his point of view, using impressive, implicit storytelling knowledge to convey the action and intensity of his experience:

The police said I was too little so I needed to go.
So, but my cousin was right next to me. So, and she got mad.
And then the police got mad at her.
And they started shooting at the wall.
And we started running.
And they started shooting at me and my cousin.
And they kept missing me.

Tomás held our attention with the linguistic features of a "well-told small story" (Georgakopoulou, 2006; Hymes, 1996). He used parallel action and sentence structures (e.g., shooting and missing), emotional markers (e.g., she got mad; police got mad at her), and repetitions (e.g., and then, and we, and they) to keep the action moving and his audience engaged. We all listened intently, trying to grasp what had happened in Tomás's world.

This moment of co-inhabiting Tomás's story place and time was followed immediately by an evaluation and inquiry into the rights of police in Mexico.

CHRIS: Wait! First of all, are they allowed to do that?
TOMÁS: I don't know.
SARA: Ye:ah.
TUCKER: They are in Mexico. I don't kno:w.
CHRIS: (Laughter)
TOMÁS: They don't care. They are now combined with the gangs. The Zetas.

Chris, Sara, and Tucker positioned themselves outside of the story and its specific place, as they asked about the reasonableness of the police actions Tomás described. Tucker recognized that he could not "know" what happens in Mexico, while Tomás briefly informed them that police, in collusion with gangs, are no longer accountable to rules or laws. This narrative backgrounding was not originally part of Tomás's storytelling, but through co-narration his story premise and story world expanded.

Next, Chris imagined himself in a Hollywood western or video game gunfight, to position himself in Tomás's world. Once again, Tomás refused Chris's actions in his world.

CHRIS: First of all, I would have shot back.
TOMÁS: No. (*rising tone*)

In the fast paced back and forth of co-narration, a teller's refusal to allow an "outsider" to take over the action may or may not be acknowledged. In transcultural literary reading, however, refusals such as Tomás's can be the subject of inquiry about whose story and whose knowledge may be aligned with colonizing narratives from film and television.

Following Chris and Tomás's brief exchange, Sara proposed a parallel street scene, set in Somalia, in which survival may depend on avoiding the police.

SARA: In Somalia, if the police comes to you,
      you gotta do what they say.
      Like before, when anybody sees the police,
      they will just go on their way and go home because they know
      they'll ask you for money
      and if you don't,
      they'll do something.

Narrative theorists would describe Sara's proposition as a *second story*, or telling, that follows in a chain of interactions, indicating acknowledgement of someone else's story (deFina & Georgakopoulou 2011). Second stories may indicate alignment with a speaker, even when the story content opposes the speaker's orientation. Overall, second stories point to a listener's real effort to understand what matters in the teller's story. In this case, although Sara implied her disagreement with Tomás' engagement with the police, she aligned with his positioning as someone whose stories and identities are also located outside the United States.

Opening Narrative Boundaries across Transcultural Places

De Certeau (1984) argues that stories about place flow and change with the people and interactions moving through them. In much the same way that Orellana (2015) describes transculturality as mobility beyond constraining borders "into new uncharted territory," places are created and recreated as "a mixing together of so many micro-stories" (p. 125). Transcultural literary reading among non-dominant youth will, likewise, entail multiple "micro-stories," viewpoints, and memories associated with the focal place. Indeed, transcultural literary discussions may be facilitated as co-narrations of place, focusing on readers' understanding of the story's setting in relation with their diverse histories, practices, and perspectives across places.

In the next segment, transcultural understanding seems to veer into uncharted territory as Tucker, Sara, Chris, Tomás, and I wonder about and *evaluate* one another's taken for granted knowledge of walking and chilling at night.

TUCKER: What are you doing at the plaza at one o'clock, in the morning?
TOMÁS: Walking around just chillin'.
PAT: Have you done that before?
SARA: Why?
TOMÁS: Yeah. A lot of times.
PAT: You have before?
CHRIS: In the morning?
TUCKER: Probably like 5 or 6 or 7, 8 or 9.
TOMÁS: You haven't?
CHRIS: (two-second pause before response) No:o!
TUCKER: But don't you think that is a bit too early?
TOMÁS: You mean late?
TUCKER: Don't you think you should be sleeping or something?
TOMÁS: Not over there.

Our movement into and across "la plaza" through co-narration allowed us to compare what it meant to be "from here" and "over there." We wondered about time (don't you think that is a bit too early?), cultural practices (Have you done that before? ... You haven't?) and the possibility of reframing action on the street (should you be sleeping or something?). Sara expressed a more pointed evaluation as she seemed to reference her earlier second story about police encounters in Somalia:

SARA: It is his fault.
He should have been listening to the police
if he knows that they can kill him.
Why would he disagree with them?

We did not pick up Sara's critique for further inquiry, but such evaluative statements are typical in co-narration and in transcultural literary reading as someone steps away from the world, taking a more distanced position to question a character's motives: Why did they do that? What were they thinking? Such questions may evoke dividing lines among youth or return them to the written narrative to examine the place, relationships, and histories that inform a character's decisions. Similarly, in co-narration, tellers find ways to circle back and ask more probing questions about one another's viewpoints and beliefs (Enciso, 2016). Often, however, there is no resolution or coherent final telling in co-narrations. In this sense, story club co-narration parallels the aims of transcultural literary reading: to generate possibilities across boundaries without the mandate to finalize or conquer.

As a global place, "la plaza" was out of reach for all but Tomás. As such, it became a landscape for the enunciation of specific cultural knowledge and ways of being in a public place that allowed him to build up a story of resistance and adventure. Sara located herself as transnational, along with Tomás, but drew on her knowledge of Somalia to highlight the unequal strength between children and police and to question—even discipline—Tomás and his cousin. Chris, who had only lived within the Midwest, mobilized his popular culture resources to voice his experiences in Tomas' street scene. Similarly, Tucker, whose Cambodian identity did not include transnational travel, located himself outside "la plaza" and in the familiar streets of his community where youth do not venture outside past dark. Together, these global peers had to consider the possibility that the norms and practices of their local and imagined street scenes could co-exist in the shared places of their school and community.

Youth Storytelling Expertise and the Potential for Equality in Transcultural Literary Rreading

In my description and analysis of story club co-narration, I highlighted youth's expertise with telling and interrogating small stories, partially told tales that become elaborated across multiple speaking turns and thereby form a focus for shared transcultural inquiry. In the brief "la plaza" episode, I foregrounded four features of talk in co-narration that may contribute to more equitable ways of hearing and supporting youth experiences, questions, and insights as they read and discuss transcultural literature: narrative backgrounding, second stories, well-told story features, and evaluation.

I also pointed to the ways "small stories" animate and destabilize a focal place so that youth begin to question their assumptions about their own and others' local practices. I argue that, collectively, these practices and features of co-narration with small stories constitute a form of youth everyday expertise that parallels the inquiry practices necessary for transcultural reading in contact zones.

In addition to making youth storytelling expertise visible, story club also became a liminal space, outside curricular demands, in which youth mediated topics and forms of narration. Youth constructed and critiqued their transcultural landscapes as they also shaped a liveable, enjoyable space for becoming global peers in an otherwise segregated, unequal community and school. In order to create a comparable space for storytelling in classrooms, teacher-directed narration will have to give way to youth-directed small-group co-narrations. I suggest that teachers begin facilitating and listening to storytelling outside the classroom, with the invitation to talk together about the stories they want to tell about their experiences or about tales they have been told, with the intention to bring selected stories back to the classroom.

In my experience as an adult co-narrator among youth, I initially showed pictures of everyday experiences and then listened as youth seemed eager to connect with and expand on their lives. For many youth, this kind of storytelling needs a bit of coaxing at first, in part because it usually happens outside school, with family and friends. As a co-narrator, I was also aware that I, too, was crossing into worlds that were unclear to me. I needed to remain uncertain and yet interested so that youth could hear my willingness to learn and be engaged, without an intention to take over the storytelling. My interest and comments, then, became oriented toward noticing our distinct perspectives and histories and how these shape tellings about our pasts and our positioning of one another in our shared futures.

References

Adichie, C. (2009). *The danger of a single story*. New York: TEDGlobal. Retrieved from http://www.ted.com/talks/chimamanda_adichie_the_danger_ofN_a_single_story.html

Anzaldúa, G. (1987). *Borderlands/la frontera: The new mestiza*. San Francisco, CA: Aunt Lute Books.

Au, W. (2008). *Unequal by design: High-stakes testing and the standardization of inequality*. New York: Routledge.

Bakhtin, M. M. (1981). *The dialogic imagination*. Austin, TX: University of Texas Press.

Bamberg, M. (2011). Who am I? Narration and its contribution to self and identity. *Theory & Psychology, 21*(1) 3–24.

Bauman, R. & Briggs, C. L. (1997). Poetics and performance as critical perspectives on language and social life. In R. K. Sawyer (Ed.) *Creativity in performance* (227–264). Norwood, NJ: Ablex.

Blommaert, J. (2008). Bernstein and poetics revisited: Voice globalization and education. *Discourse & Society, 19*(4) 425–451.

Blommaert, J. (2005) *Discourse: A critical introduction*. Cambridge: Cambridge University Press.

Bruner, J. (1986). *Actual minds, possible worlds*. Cambridge, MA: Harvard University Press.

Bucholtz, M. & Hall, K. (2005). Identity and interaction: A sociocultural linguistic approach. *Discourse Studies, 7*(4–5), 585–614.

De Certeau, M. (1984). *The practice of everyday life* (trans. S. Randall). Berkeley, CA: University of California-Berkeley Press.

De Fina, A. & Georgakopoulou, A. (2011). *Analyzing narrative: Discourse and sociolinguistic perspectives*. Cambridge: Cambridge University Press.

Dumas, M. J. & Nelson, J. D. (2016). (Re)imagining Black boyhood: Toward a critical framework for educational research. *Harvard Educational Review, 86*(1), 27–47.

Enciso, P. (2017). Stories lost and found: Mobilizing imagination in literacy research and practice. *Literacy Research and Practice Literacy Research: Theory, Method, and Practice, 66* (1), 29–52.

Enciso, P. (2011). Storytelling in critical literacy pedagogy: Removing the walls between immigrant and non-immigrant youth. *English Teaching: Practice and Critique, 10*(1), 21–40.

Enciso, P. (2004). Reading discrimination. In S. Greene & D. Abt-Perkins (Eds.) *Making race visible: Literacy research for cultural understanding* (149–177). New York: Teachers College Press.

Enciso, P., Volz, A., Price-Dennis, D., & Durriyah, T. (2010). Story club and configurations of literary insights among immigrant and non-immigrant youth. In R. Jiménez, D. Rowe, V. Risko, & M. Hundley (Eds.) *59th Yearbook of the National Reading Conference* (354–366). Oak Creek, WI: National Reading Conference.

Georgakopoulou, A. (2006). Thinking big with small stories in narrative and identity analysis. *Narrative Inquiry, 16*(1), 122–130.

Georgakopoulou, A. (2003). Plotting the "right place" and the "right time": Place and time as interactional resources in narratives. *Narrative Inquiry, 13*(2), 413–432.

Gumperz, J. J. (1982). *Discourse strategies*. New York: Cambridge University Press.

Gutiérrez, K. (2008). Developing a sociocritical literacy in the third space. *Reading Research Quarterly, 43*(2), 148–164.

Hymes, D. (1996). *Ethnography, linguistics, narrative inequality: Toward an understanding of voice*. New York: Taylor & Francis.

Juzwik, M. M. (2010). Negotiating moral stance in classroom discussion about literature: Entextualization and contextualization processes in a narrative spell. In P. Prior & J. Hengst (Eds.) *Exploring semiotic remediation as social practice* (77–106). London: Palgrave Macmillan.

Lee, C. (2007). *Culture, literacy, and learning: Blooming in the midst of the whirlwind*. New York: Teachers College Press.

Maira, S. & Soep, E. (Eds.) (2005). Youthscapes: The popular, the national, the global. Philadelphia, PA: University of Pennsylvania Press.

Martínez-Roldán, C. (2003). Building worlds and identities: A case study of the role of narratives in bilingual literature discussions. *Research in the teaching of English, 37*(10), 491–526.

Massey, D. (1992). Politics and space/time. *New Left Review, 196,* 65–84.

Minks, A. (2007). "Goblins like to tell stories": Miskitu childrens' narratives of spirit encounters. In M. Bamberg, A. De Fina, & D. Schiffrin (Eds.) *Selves and identities in narrative and discourse* (10–40). Philadelphia, PA: John Benjamins.

Noguera, P. (2003). *City schools and the American dream: Reclaiming the promise of public education.* New York: Teachers College Press.

Ochs, E. & Capps, L. (2001). *Living narrative: Creating lives in everyday storytelling.* Cambridge, MA: Harvard University Press.

Ochs, E., Smith, R., & Taylor, C. (1989). Detective stories at dinnertime: Problem-solving through co-narration. *Cultural Dynamics, 2,* 238–257.

Orellana, M. (2015). *Immigrant children in transcultural spaces: Language, learning, and love.* New York: Routledge.

Orellana, M. F. (2009). Translating childhoods: Immigrant youth, language, and culture. New Brunswick, NJ: Rutgers University Press.

Pratt, M. L. (1991). Arts of the contact zone. *Profession,* 33–40.

Rabinowitz, P. (1987). *Before reading: Narrative conventions and the politics of interpretation.* Ithaca, NY: Cornell University Press.

Razza, C. (2018). Ending the policing of Black bodies in public spaces requires not just a change of policy but a change of heart. https://www.theroot.com/ending-the-policing-of-black-bodies-in-public spaces-re-1825720407

Rosen, H. (1985). *Stories and meanings.* Sheffield: National Association for the Teaching of English.

Stetsenko, A. (2008). From relational ontology to transformative activist stance on development and learning: Expanding Vygotsky's (CHAT) project. *Cultural Studies in Science Education, 3*(2), 471–491.

Tan, S. (2007). *The arrival.* New York: Scholastic.

Vygotsky, L. S. (2004). Imagination and creativity in childhood. *Journal of Russian and East European Psychology, 42*(1), 7–97.

Wortham, S. & Reyes, A. (2015). *Discourse analysis beyond the speech event.* New York: Routledge.

10

WHERE EVERYDAY TRANSLANGUAGING MEETS ACADEMIC WRITING: EXPLORING TENSIONS AND GENERATIVE CONNECTIONS FOR BILINGUAL LATINA/O/X STUDENTS

Ramón Antonio Martínez, Leah Durán, and Michiko Hikida

In K-12 schools throughout the United States, bilingual Latina/o/x students often communicate by moving flexibly between English and Spanish in conversation—an everyday language practice that has been variously referred to as Spanish–English codeswitching or codemixing, Spanglish, and, more recently, translanguaging. In this chapter, we explore potentially fruitful connections between this everyday form of bilingualism and the kinds of writing valued in academic settings. Drawing on ethnographic data from our research in urban elementary and middle schools, we examine the everyday translanguaging in which bilingual Latina/o/x children and youth engage as they skillfully and creatively blur the linguistic boundaries between English and Spanish in their everyday talk. We highlight the bilingual skills that these students deploy in their everyday interactions, and we examine how these linguistic competencies overlap with specific skills highlighted in the Common Core State Standards for English Language Arts, including the composition of writing that is "appropriate to task, purpose, and audience." We argue that the skills already evident in the everyday translanguaging of bilingual Latina/o/x students constitute an untapped pedagogical resource that could potentially serve to support the teaching and learning of academic writing.

We then offer conceptually grounded practical approaches to leveraging students' linguistic competencies as resources for writing pedagogy across both monolingual and bilingual instructional contexts. Such approaches, we suggest, might help bilingual Latina/o/x students successfully meet and exceed existing standards, and they might also help educators begin to embrace more rigorous standards that are aligned with the communicative demands of our increasingly multilingual reality (see also D'warte, this volume). We conclude by situating our argument within a broader critique of monolingual approaches to schooling, in general, and to writing instruction, in particular. We argue that the monolingual ideologies undergirding current standards and instructional approaches discourage educators from recognizing bilingual Latina/o/x students' everyday linguistic competencies. As currently articulated, for example, the Common Core State Standards actually call for students to develop a more limited set of linguistic skills than those that many bilingual Latina/o/x students deploy in their everyday inter-actions in school. Indeed, this is an important tension that we address directly in this chapter. We suggest that bilingual Latina/o/x students' everyday linguistic competencies are more reflective of the kinds of communication skill necessary for success in an increasingly multilingual society, and we argue for expanding what counts as—and *who* counts *in*—academic writing. We focus specifically on translanguaging among bilingual Latina/o/x children and youth because these are the people from whom we have had the pleasure of learning in our ethnographic research, but we want to suggest that the broader principles described here likely apply to bi/multilingual children and youth in other communities.

Learning about Translanguaging

In our respective and collective ethnographic work in K-12 classrooms in California, Texas, Arizona, and Ohio, we have documented bilingual Latina/o/x students moving flexibly between English and Spanish in their everyday classroom interactions (Durán, 2016, 2017; Hikida, 2018; Martínez, 2009, 2010, 2013; Martínez, Durán, & Hikida, 2017). Consider the following example from a middle school in East Los Angeles, California: *Así le da de comer mi mom a mi nephew.* ("That's how my mom feeds my nephew.")

The alternation between Spanish and English in the excerpt above is an example of what linguists have historically called Spanish–English *codeswitching* or *codemixing*. More specifically, it is an example of *intra-sentential* codeswitching—or mixing languages within the sentence or phrase boundary. Gumperz (1982) defined codeswitching as "the juxtaposition within the same speech exchange of passages of speech belonging to two different grammatical systems or subsystems" (p. 59). Over the past five decades, scholarship on codeswitching has debunked the notion that it is a haphazard or deficient linguistic practice, framing it instead as a complex, systematic, and fundamentally normal expression of bilingualism (Zentella, 1997). Although research on codeswitching has included various combinations of languages, much of it has focused on Spanish–English codeswitching. Zentella's (1997) work, in particular, has helped to combat deficit perspectives that frame codeswitching among Latina/o/x youth as deviant and deficient, as she has highlighted some of the valuable social and communicative functions that codeswitching can serve in everyday conversation.

Some scholars studying codeswitching have suggested that bilingual speakers do not necessarily perceive themselves as mixing two separate languages, and that it might be more appropriate to characterize codeswitching as a dynamic bilingual *practice* than as the alternation of two separate *codes* (Álvarez-Cáccamo, 1998; García; 2009; Urciuoli, 1985). García (2009), in particular, has promoted this particular perspective, reviving the term *translanguaging* to refer to the ways in which bilingual speakers draw flexibly on their linguistic repertoires. For García, translanguaging is inclusive of—but not limited to—the practice that linguists have historically called codeswitching. Otheguy, García, & Reid (2015) define translanguaging as "the deployment of a speaker's full linguistic repertoire without regard for watchful adherence to the socially and politically defined boundaries of named (and usually national and state) languages" (p. 283). In essence, translanguaging is a broader umbrella category that includes codeswitching, but that also includes practices such as translating or interpreting (see Reynolds & Orellana, this volume), bilingual phenomena such as borrowing or loan words, or various other ways of drawing flexibly on one's full linguistic toolkit. The key distinction between codeswitching and translanguaging is conceptual. García (2009) notes that while codeswitching has generally been defined as the alternation or combination of two distinct codes, a translanguaging perspective begins with the premise that bilingual speakers who engage in so-called language mixing are simply drawing flexibly on a single linguistic repertoire. Despite scholarly disagreement about what to call this dynamic everyday form of bilingualism, and, at a more substantive level, how to conceptualize the linguistic faculties that enable it, there is near universal consensus that combining elements typically associated with two different languages is a normal, skillful, and intelligent form of bilingual communication.

We have sometimes used code-witching and translanguaging concurrently, framing the former as a specific form of the latter. In this chapter, however, we use the term translanguaging because a translanguaging perspective frames bilingual speakers' flexible linguistic practices as fundamentally normal. Of course, as Martínez and Martinez (forthcoming) note, "whether or not we need to choose a single term, and which term we should choose, are questions that cannot be answered without reference to the speakers themselves—to bilingual and bidialectal children and youth" (p. 28). None of the children or youth with whom we have worked in our respective or collective research has used either codeswitching or translanguaging to describe their everyday bilingualism. Many have used a term such as "Spanglish," but others have not favored a particular term at all. In fact, a popular perspective is reflected in the words of one middle school student from East Los Angeles who said: "I just call it talking." As this quote suggests, for many of the students with whom we have worked, this is a completely normal way of communicating, just as it is for much of the world's population. Indeed, in any language contact situation, it is typical for speakers to engage in some form of language mixing (see

García-Sánchez, this volume). In our own work, we have documented a seamlessness to this style of communication, and we have learned that the bilingual Latina/o/x students with whom we have worked do not always necessarily perceive themselves to be disrupting linguistic boundaries or mixing two distinct codes, and that even when they do perceive themselves do be doing so, they tend to see it as something fundamentally normal. We opt to use translanguaging in this chapter because it comes close to conveying the sentiment captured in the quote above—because it is oriented towards normalizing this everyday form of bilingual communication.

In our own work, we have documented the conversational functions that translanguaging served in a middle school English Language Arts classroom, including how it facilitated shifting voices for different audiences and communicating subtle nuances of meaning (Martínez, 2010); the language ideologies that these students articulated and embodied with respect to translanguaging (Martínez, 2013); their awareness of translanguaging (Martínez, 2014); how bilingual elementary school students co-constructed identities for themselves and their classmates by translanguaging in classroom interaction (Hikida, 2018; Martínez, Durán, & Hikida, 2017); and the kinds of translingual writing that bilingual students engaged in within the context of an English immersion classroom (Durán, 2017). In our view, bilingual Latina/o/x children and youth learn how to translanguage *by engaging in translanguaging*—and by doing so within meaningful bilingual contexts. Within these contexts, they often come to understand translanguaging as a fundamentally normal way of speaking even as they are simultaneously socialized to understand it as deviant and deficient (Martínez, 2013). Against the backdrop of dominant language ideologies, learning to translanguage can be seen as fundamentally counter-hegemonic—as what Patel (2016) describes as "the fugitive acts of learning" (p. 400) that occur within broader systems and structures of oppression.

Points of Pedagogical Leverage: Connecting Translanguaging with Academic Writing

One key insight that has emerged from our work is that the skills displayed in bilingual Latina/o/x students' everyday translanguaging overlap in striking ways with the kinds of academic writing that are valued in schools. This is important because dominant discourses about Latina/o/x children and youth often begin with the assumption that they lack the kinds of knowledge necessary for academic success. It is assumed, for example, that whatever these students are doing with language and literacy outside of school must necessarily be divergent from or even antithetical to learning in school. In contrast to this deficit-oriented assumption, Carol Lee (2007) has demonstrated that "cultural displays of knowledge rooted in everyday experiences of ethnic groups and other communities of practice generally viewed as unrelated to schooling can be scaffolded in service of domain-specific learning" (p. 18). Because we have often documented bilingual Latina/o/x students shifting voices for different audiences through their everyday translanguaging, we have explored connections between this skillful use of language and relevant content area standards. Although this certainly is not the only skillful use of language that we have observed or the only connection to relevant standards that might be made, it is one that has emerged as salient for us. In particular, these students' audience awareness overlaps with the skills highlighted in the Common Core State Standards (CCSS) for English Language Arts. For example, the Writing Standards for Sixth Grade call for students to:

> *Produce clear and coherent writing in which the development, organization, and style are appropriate to task, purpose, and **audience**.*
>
> (CCSS.ELA-LITERACY.W.6.4)

This particular standard invokes the skill of audience awareness, which also featured quite prominently on the California statewide language arts standards that prefigured CCSS. In other words, audience awareness is not a new idea in the world of language arts standards.

As we mentioned above, students' ability to shift voices for different audiences presupposes a high degree of audience awareness. For example, as Leah has documented elsewhere (Durán, 2016), one first-grade student in Texas, Yamilet, wrote two invitations to a class project showcase. One, to her mother, was written primarily in Spanish (see Figure 10.1): *Querida mamá, puedes venir a mi proyecto? Por favor que voy a cantar y bailar. Mami, por favor ven. Mami. please te lo ruego, por favor. Hice un proyecto de un perro. Mamá, por favor, please.*

While primarily in Spanish, the invitation in Figure 10.1 also makes use of repetition for emphasis across languages: both "please" and *por favor*. The other invitation (see Figure 10.2), written to a cousin close to her age, was primarily in English: "Dear Kevin, Can you come to my show? We are gonna dance and show my project. Kevin please Kevin!"

These two invitations each show a high degree of sensitivity to their readers. Yamilet varied languages, likely because of the different linguistic preferences of her mother and cousin. She also showed variation in register. For her mother, she used the more formal-sounding *Te lo ruego* ("I beg of you"), and for her young cousin, a more casual, "We are gonna dance and show my project." Finally, across both invitations, she used the rhetorical techniques of persuasive writing: establishing key background information (that the event featured her class project, that the reader was invited to the event) and polite emotional appeals (*por favor, please!*). While the CCSS emphasize fact-based argumentative writing over persuasive skill, Texas state language arts standards call for students to develop exactly this kind of persuasive writing ability by the time they reach high school:

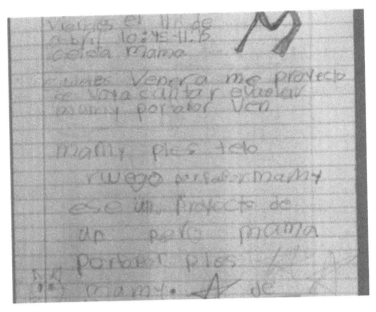

FIGURE 10.1   Yamilet's invitation to her mother

FIGURE 10.2   Yamilet's invitation to her cousin

> *Students write persuasive texts to influence the attitudes or actions of a specific audience on specific issues.*
>
> (Writing/Persuasive Texts E (16))

Whether the focus is on fact-based argumentative writing or more persuasive writing, attention to audience is consistently emphasized across content area standards. We say that we want students to develop audience awareness in states, such as California, that have adopted CCSS, as well as in states, such as

Texas, that have not. Our work with bilingual Latina/o/x children and youth has allowed us to highlight how they display such awareness in their everyday speaking and writing.

These students' audience awareness is also sometimes reflected in their *meta-pragmatic commentary* (i.e., their talk about how they use language). For example, Brianne, a sixth grader at a middle school in East Los Angeles, once explained why she engaged in translanguaging with her classmates by saying, "You know two languages and … like, and they understand you, too, so, like, why just put it to waste?" (Martínez, 2013, p. 285). Brianne's explanation reveals how she thinks about communicating with interlocutors who share her bilingual competence. She speaks both English and Spanish, and her classmates are similarly bilingual, so why *wouldn't* they draw flexibly on both languages in their conversations? Why would it make sense for them to limit themselves to a subset of their linguistic resources? More to the point, why do schools demand that they do so (Martínez, 2018), essentially letting those resources go to waste? Ramón has argued that schools insist that bilingual Latina/o/x students "limit themselves to a narrower range of linguistic tools than they have at their disposal" and "assume that a more limited display of their linguistic repertoires is a better sign of language proficiency" (Martínez, 2018, p. 517) because of monoglossic language ideologies that essentially erase bilingual audiences. In contrast to these monoglossic perspectives, Brianne's quote above suggests an awareness of bilingual audiences—even a privileging and normalizing of those audiences.

We should also emphasize that the audience awareness that we have documented is not limited to students' awareness of those who share their bilingual repertoires. Some students with whom we have worked reported switching to one language or another when they perceived that their interlocutors did *not* necessarily share their linguistic competence. Zulema, a middle school student in east Los Angeles, reported that she never codeswitched with a Filipina student in her class because that student "doesn't really understand Spanish." Pancho, one of Zulema's classmates, similarly noted that he usually avoided mixing languages around students "who don't know Spanish." In some cases, students reported switching to a classmate's dominant language to help facilitate communication, a pattern that we have documented in our analyses of classroom interaction across different settings (Hikida & Martínez, 2019; Martínez, Durán, & Hikida, 2017). In contrast, some students also reported switching to another language to conceal what they were saying from those present. Victor, for example, shared that he sometimes spoke "Spanglish" around monolingual people whom he did *not* want to understand him. As these examples of metapragmatic commentary reveal, students displayed a nuanced and sophisticated awareness of the communicative abilities and needs of different audiences.

In previous work, Ramón has argued that the skills reflected in children's everyday translanguaging could potentially be used as resources for cultivating academic literacy (Martínez, 2009, 2010, 2018). In particular, he has focused on bilingual students' ability to shift voices for different audiences and to communicate subtle shades or nuances of meaning. Drawing on Carol Lee's (2007) Cultural Modeling framework, as well as on the work of Marjorie Faulstich Orellana, and other scholars who build on this tradition (Martínez et al., 2008; Orellana & Reynolds, 2008), we argue that bilingual Latina/o/x students' everyday translanguaging constitutes an untapped pedagogical resource that could potentially serve to support the teaching and learning of academic writing. By documenting examples of students' translanguaging and using these examples as what Lee (2007) calls "cultural datasets," teachers can help students cultivate metalinguistic awareness by calling attention to the audience awareness already evident in their everyday use of language. Video and/or audiorecordings of students' translingual talk or even informal notes could be used as cultural datasets (see also Martinez, Montaño, & Rojo, this volume). These artifacts could then be transcribed, which would serve the purpose of making students' skillful translanguaging visible to teachers and to students themselves. Through a series of *metalinguistic conversations* (Martínez, 2010), teachers could help students further identify and examine the specific nature of these skills. The next step would involve providing structured opportunities for students to practice applying these same skills to academic tasks, texts, and genres.

Opportunities to identify, apply, and cultivate this kind of skillful academic writing do not need to emerge only from an analysis of student talk. On the contrary, student writing itself might also serve as an organic cultural data set on which to build subsequent instruction. Teachers can identify examples of students' spontaneous translingual writing, which can then be examined with an eye towards identifying skillful uses of language. Of course, a more deliberate approach to noticing and building on students' translanguaging could also be generative. For example, Leah has illustrated how a writing curriculum that is audience-focused can promote flexible and dynamic forms of bilingualism and biliteracy even in restrictive language policy contexts (Durán, 2016, 2017). The following curricular artifact illustrates one way that this might look. Figure 10.3 shows an excerpt from a "language chart" (Roser et al., 1992) that was used in an English immersion classroom where the teacher was open to incorporating and building on students' bilingual competencies (Durán, 2016, 2017). In this particular classroom, the teacher shared a series of children's books with the class, and then used the language chart to invite students to notice what aspects of the author's craft they might be able to try out in their own work.

This excerpt records one day in a weeklong study of four bilingual books by author Carmen Tafolla. In the far left column, the teacher has photocopied the cover of each book read. After reading the book out loud, she invited students to describe what they noticed about the book, what connections they made to their own lives, and what techniques they might try out in their own writing. She then recorded students' contributions on the language chart, aiming to

ook Titles	What we noticed	Connections	Things to try in our own writing
	-pueden hacer bigotes ( )	shared a paleta de Sandía con su mamá.	a book about paletas
	-La niña le dio un pedacito al perrito ( )	got a paleta from her vecinos Paletería (truck).	-write bilingual books (words in English and Spanish)
	-You can paint your tongue blue and scare your brother ( )	buy paletas que te pica at the store with his mom.	
	-The man with the cart went down the hill. ( )	had a banana paleta.	
	-The girl shared with the woman vendiendo frutas. ( )	had a paleta de limón from a truck	

FIGURE 10.3 Language chart

accurately represent what children said in their own words. In response to the first book, children made a number of contributions, in English ("You can paint your tongue blue and scare your brother"), in Spanish (*La niña le dio un pedacito al perrito*) and in both (*The girl shared with the woman vendiendo frutas*). All of the responses in which students made connections to their own lives could be characterized as translingual (e.g., *M. got a paleta from her vecino's paletería*). Perhaps most critically, students noted the connection between what the author did with language in her books and what they, too, could do in their own composition: write bilingually. The transcription of their talk into the language chart provided not only a record of their learning, but also a bridge between what they already did in oral language and what they might do as writers. The very techniques that they noted in Tafolla's writing (writing about *paletas*, writing using words in Spanish and English) were ones that many students did indeed explore as writers throughout the remainder of the school year. Because the teacher's overall writing curriculum was explicitly audience-focused, students thought and talked a great deal about the use of these strategies for specific audiences, many of which were bilingual.

Building on these insights, we argue that making real bilingual audiences central to writing instruction could generate meaningful and authentic opportunities for bilingual Latina/o/x students to draw on and apply their skillful audience awareness. For example, teachers can invite students to write for various groups of people, including those closest to them, such as family, friends, neighbors, and classmates. These important people in children's lives can serve as authentic audiences as children write across multiple genres and for multiple purposes. For example, as Leah has demonstrated in her work, teachers can engage students in writing stories, letters, invitations, flyers, family message journals, public service announcements, and poetry—all with these real (and often bilingual) audiences in mind (Durán, 2016, 2017). And regardless of whether or not any given audience is bilingual, teachers can guide students in thinking out loud about the choices they make and the techniques they use in their writing. If a particular piece of writing is intended for students' parents, for example, teachers might begin that writing unit by asking students to brainstorm, share, and discuss their parents' linguistic backgrounds and how they themselves use language to communicate with their parents. If a student's parents were bilingual, such discussions might lead that student to write only in Spanish, only in English, or in a combination of the two. If that student's parents were monolingual Spanish speakers, that student might decide to avoid using any English—or they might decide to introduce some new English vocabulary to their parents in a way that made it accessible and comprehensible. The point is that any such decisions would be deeply informed by ongoing classroom discussions and activities, as teachers made space for students to think carefully about writing in relation to audience. Again, any written artifacts generated as part of such curricula could subsequently serve as texts for students to revisit and analyze with an eye towards identifying these and other skills. Whether through building on what students are doing in their translingual speech or in their translingual writing, clear connections can be made that help leverage their existing skills to help them meet relevant literacy standards.

Expanding what Counts as—and Who counts in—Academic Writing

What we have learned ethnographically about the everyday translanguaging of bilingual Latina/o/x children and youth leads us to suggest that educators, researchers, and policymakers should expand what counts as academic writing. In our view, the monolingual ideologies undergirding current writing standards and instructional approaches discourage educators from recognizing bilingual Latina/o/x students' everyday linguistic competencies. If we look closely at these ideologies, we can identify three key assumptions: (1) that monolingualism is normal and that bilingualism is a deviation from that norm; (2) that bilingualism itself can be explained in monolingual terms; and (3) that the primary or only audience worth communicating with is a monolingual one. The first assumption is one that we have addressed in previous work (Martínez, 2013), and it relates closely to the second assumption, which manifests itself in policies and practices of *language separation* (Martínez, Hikida, & Durán, 2015). If monolingualism is normal, then it makes sense that we can understand bilingualism in monolingual terms—according to a monolingual logic. From a monoglossic perspective, bilinguals are simply two monolinguals in one, so it makes sense that we should demand language separation as evidence of bilingual competence. These monoglossic ideologies get inscribed in restrictive "English-only" language policies that forbid bilingual instruction (Martínez, 2013), but also in dual language policies that designate different times, activities, settings, and sometimes even different teachers for each language (Martínez, 2017). In addition, such ideologies get enacted across monolingual and bilingual instructional settings in teacher's moment-to-moment interactional moves to discourage students' translanguaging (Martínez, Hikida, & Durán, 2015).

Here we want to briefly address the third assumption—that the only audience worth communicating with is a monolingual one. This assumption is implicit in any and all writing standards and instructional approaches that exclude languages other than English, including the CCSS, which focus exclusively on writing in English. These monolingual writing standards and pedagogies prepare bilingual Latina/o/x students to write with a single audience in mind—monolingual English speakers. By only preparing students to communicate with monolingual English speakers, we send students the powerful message that this is the only audience that matters—that these are the only people worth communicating with (Martínez, 2017). Even in dual-language settings, which arguably prepare students to communicate with speakers of other languages, the focus is still on monolingual communication. In Spanish–English dual-language classrooms, for example, Spanish becomes the medium of communication for Spanish-speaking audiences, while English is the medium for English-speaking audiences. What gets lost in this equation is the fact that many Latina/o/x students speak *both* languages, that they sometimes disrupt the supposed boundaries between the two, that they might actually want to communicate with others who are similarly bilingual, and that they might want to do so in ways that are reflective of this shared bilingual competence. When we do not invite bilingual Latina/o/x students to write with a bilingual Latina/o/x audience in mind, we signal to them that these people—people like them—are not worth communicating with (Martínez, 2017).

Expanding what counts as academic writing, then, should also necessarily involve expanding *who* counts *in* academic writing. If we value bilingual Latina/o/x students and we want them to write for real audiences that matter to them, then we need to prepare them to communicate outside of the narrowly defined boundaries of monolingual academic language. Preparing these students to engage with multiple audiences prepares them to value multiple communities—multiple groups of human beings—beyond those that are implicit and unmarked in normative monolingual standards and instructional approaches. Brianne's comment above about being bilingual and, therefore, being able to engage with other bilinguals who "understand you, too" reflects the fact that many bilingual Latina/o/x students already think about and engage with bilingual audiences in their everyday lives. If we follow their lead, we can begin to recognize, privilege, and normalize these audiences, and we can begin to reimagine "academic" language as inclusive of more than just English and as exclusive of the strict separation of languages (see also García-Sánchez, this volume).

Monoglossic Repair: Why we Need an Expanded Definition of Academic Writing

There are many reasons why we need to expand what counts as academic writing—and who counts in academic writing—including the fact that bi/multi/translingual composing is more reflective of the kinds of linguistic and rhetorical competency that are necessary in an increasingly multilingual society. However, one particular reason that we want to emphasize here is that bilingual kids often *internalize* the notion that "academic" writing is (or should be) monolingual—written in a single language. Even in bilingual settings, where structures, processes, and perspectives arguably converge to support the "minority" language in various ways, "academic" language is still framed as monolingual, and this idea still seems to shape how bilingual kids write.

As one example, consider the case of Alex, a second-grade student in a Spanish–English dual-language classroom in Los Angeles. Alex is the U.S.-born child of Mexican immigrants, and he has grown up speaking both Spanish and English. A truly amazing simultaneous bilingual, Alex would often combine Spanish and English in his speech in ways that displayed tremendous linguistic dexterity. He would also sometimes combine the two languages in his writing. As the bulk of his writing instruction was in Spanish during second grade, this often took the form of inserting single English words or phrases into otherwise Spanish sentences or paragraphs. One place that he did such writing was in his *Libre Escritura* ("Free Writing") notebook, which is featured in Figure 10.4.

In Figure 10.4, we see two adjacent pages from Alex's "Free Writing" notebook, which were written over two consecutive days in May. On the first day, Alex produced the draft on page 146, in which he tells the story of taking a test to earn a white belt in his karate class. He then proceeded to edit and revise that draft on page 147 the following day. The photo in Figure 10.4 was taken on the second day, during the revision process, but before Alex had finished the revised version. What this juxtaposition of the two different versions illustrates is how Alex changed his composition from one day to the next.

In Figure 10.5, we see a close-up view of Alex's original draft, which we might classify as an example of *translingual* composing.

As Figure 10.5 reveals, Alex's original draft includes the sentence *vino el profesor y iso el test para sinta blanca* [sic], which translates as "the teacher came and gave the test for white belt" in English. Alex's use of the English word "test" in this otherwise Spanish text is reflective of his translingual composing practices. Of course, "test" is also an English borrowing or loan word that has been fairly accepted and commonly used in many dialects of Spanish in both Latin America and Spain for decades now. In fact, it is so well incorporated into Spanish that it appears as a word in most dictionaries of the Spanish language, including the dictionary of the Real Academia Española. What is important to note, however, is that Alex repairs—or corrects—this instance of translingualism when he edits

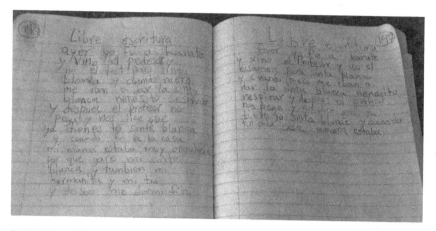

FIGURE 10.4 Monoglossic repair

and revises his draft the very next day. As seen in Figure 10.6, Alex replaces the word "test" with an approximation of the conventional Spanish translation, *examen*, which he renders as "ecsamen." Apparently, Alex understood "test" to be only an English word and not an acceptable Spanish word.

When Ramón noticed the discrepancy between the two versions of the text, he sat down with Alex and asked him why he had changed the word "test" to "ecsamen" in the final version. Alex's response was: *Porque así se dice en español.* ("Because that's how you say it in Spanish.") That Alex would use editing and revision time as an opportunity to eliminate English from his composition suggests the influence of monoglossic language ideologies. To correct or improve his draft meant, in this case, making it monolingual. And, in fact, he made it more "monolingual" than a monolingual Spanish speaker might have, enacting purist ideologies and policing linguistic boundaries in his own writing more than the Real Academia Española has done with respect to this particular loan word in its official dictionary.

As is common in the emergent writing of second graders, both versions of Alex's composition contain a fair bit of *invented spelling*—approximations of conventional or standardized orthography that reflect a student's developing understanding of sound–symbol relationships. Of course, masterful literacy teachers recognize such approximations as evidence of what kids *do* know rather than simply as proof of what they don't yet know. Such teachers, for example, would likely notice that Alex's spelling of "ecsamen" contains graphic representations of all of the sounds present in the conventional pronunciation of the word *examen* (and they might even notice that it almost perfectly mirrors the phonetic transcription of the word using the International Phonetic Alphabet). In this case, however, it is important to point out that

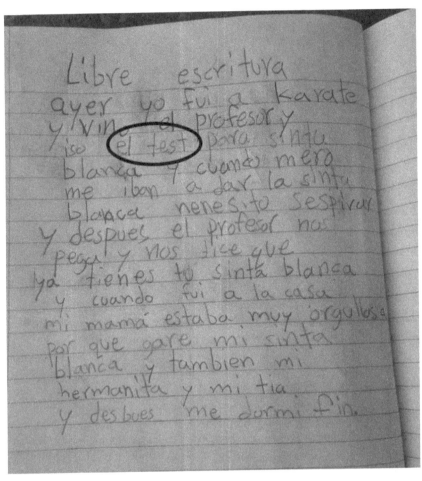

FIGURE 10.5 Original (translingual) draft

Alex used the *conventional* spelling for the word "test" and only used an invented spelling when he substituted the Spanish translation. Somewhat iron-ically, then, the first (translingual) version was actually more conventional orthographically than the revised (monolingual) version. And if the use of orthographic conventions is part of what we mean when we say "academic language," then we might even invoke that logic to argue that the first version was more "academic." From this perspective, Alex essentially traded a more "academic" translingual version for a less "academic" monolingual version— and all with the goal of making his writing more like the kind of writing that kids are expected to produce in schools. It was Alex's effort to make his

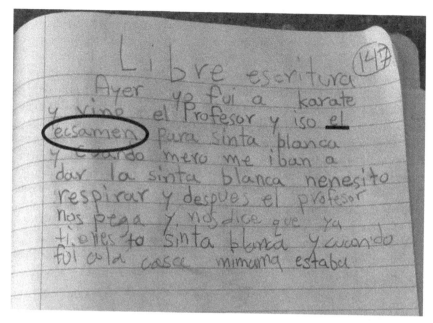

FIGURE 10.6 Revised (monolingual) version

composition more conventional—more "academic"—that ultimately resulted in this monolingual revision.

All of this is to say that bilingual Latina/o/x kids quickly come to understand that monolingual writing is expected of them and that it is the kind of writing that is most valued in schools, and their understandings of these expectations and values can profoundly shape the writing that they produce in academic settings. Of course, this need not be the case. Attention to audience should lead to more than just monolingual writing. Indeed, audience awareness should sometimes necessitate writing in more than one language—and even across those languages. As we mentioned above, preparing bilingual Latina/o/x students to communicate with bilingual audiences prepares them to value bilingual human beings.

Embracing a Translanguaging Perspective

Considering our data, it is worth emphasizing the usefulness of a translanguaging perspective for allowing us to focus on what seems meaningful in the context of our analysis. This conceptual lens offers an alternative to categorizing the things that children say as belonging to one language or another—a process which can sometimes be ambiguous and subjective. For example, in looking at the language chart mentioned earlier, perhaps the word *paleta* in the sentence "X had a banana paleta" is an example of codeswitching, or perhaps it is better described as a loan word that refers to a specific kind of popsicle. Similarly, Alex's use of "test" in his journal entry might be understood as a lexical switch to English or as an established loan word in Spanish. Rather than belabor these distinctions, we can look at these respective utterances as belonging to translingual contexts in which many linguistic resources were useful. This approach seems to better fit the ways in which the children we know often talked about language: sometimes they talked about English or Spanish, but sometimes that distinction did not seem important. In our view, "it is neither necessary nor desirable to disentangle—semantically or conceptually—the supposedly distinct hybrid language practices in which students engage" (Martínez, 2009, p. 26). A translanguaging perspective allows us to talk and think more flexibly about the dynamic, flexible, and fundamentally normal ways in which bilingual Latina/o/x students draw on their translingual repertoires in their everyday interactions, and about the possibilities for understanding and engaging with these translanguaging practices in academic settings.

Conclusion

There is a supremely skillful attention to *audience* displayed in the everyday translanguaging of many of the bilingual Latina/o/x students with whom we have worked, and this audience awareness might serve as a generative point of pedagogical leverage for the teaching and learning of academic writing. A Cultural Modeling approach to identifying and building on skills such as these could help bilingual Latina/o/x students and their teachers recognize how their everyday use of language overlaps with the kinds of writing valued in schools. By making cultural data sets the objects of analysis, we argue, teachers can work with students to help provide structured opportunities for identifying, analyzing, applying, and extending related writing skills. In our view, this would be an important contribution to *translanguaging pedagogies* (García, Johnson, & Seltzer, 2017), as well as a very concrete way of engaging in *culturally sustaining pedagogy* (Paris, 2012). Teachers would be leveraging bilingual students' linguistic competencies and expanding their linguistic repertoires, of course, but they would also necessarily be sustaining what these children and youth already know and do that typically gets erased and/or marginalized in school.

We also want to emphasize that ours is an alternative framing of bilingual Latina/o/x children and youth—an alternative mode of perceiving them. The normative tendency is for society to view bilingual Latina/o/x students as doing *less than* what is expected—less than the standard, so to speak. These students are systematically represented as deficient or "at risk." What we want to suggest is that these children and youth are often doing *more than* what is expected—that they're going **beyond** *the standard.* There may be specific features or conventions that they haven't yet mastered or that they haven't demonstrated in their writing, but even those particular features overlap with things they're already doing. And any efforts to help these students move towards mastery should build directly on what they're already doing (Martínez, 2018).

Our point in emphasizing that bilingual Latina/o/x children and youth are doing more than the standard is not only to highlight how they are already meeting existing ELA writing standards (although this is a central piece of our argument), but also to push educators, policymakers, and researchers to see beyond those standards—to expand what counts as academic writing and who counts in academic writing. We need to create and sustain pedagogical spaces that encourage bilingual Latina/o/x children and youth to think and write outside monolingual perspectives—to write for audiences that matter to them (including bilingual audiences) and to do so in ways that make sense to them (including by blending Spanish and English in their writing). By following the lead of bilingual Latina/o/x student authors, we have the exciting opportunity to reimagine who academic writers are, how they might write, and for whom they might do so. In short, we have the opportunity to begin reinventing "academic" writing itself.

References

Álvarez-Cáccamo, C. (1998). From 'switching code' to 'code-switching': Towards a reconceptualisation of communicative codes. In P. Auer (Ed.) *Code-switching in conversation: Language, interaction and identity* (29–48). New York: Routledge.

Durán, L. (2016). Revisiting family message journals: Audience and biliteracy development in a first-grade ESL classroom. *Language Arts, 93*(5), 354–365.

Durán, L. (2017). Audience and young bilingual writers: Building on strengths. *Journal of Literacy Research, 49*(1), 92–114.

García, O. (2009). Bilingual education in the 21st century: A global perspective. Malden, MA: Wiley/Blackwell.

García, O., Johnson, S. I., & Seltzer, K. (2017). The translanguaging classroom: Leveraging student bilingualism for learning. Philadelphia, PA: Caslon.

Gumperz, J. J. (1982). Conversational code-switching. In J. J. Gumperz (Ed.) *Discourse strategies* (59–99). Cambridge: Cambridge University Press.

Hikida, M. (2018). Holding space for literate identity co-construction. *Journal of Literacy Research, 50*(2), 217–238.

Hikida, M. & Martínez, R. A. (2019). Languaging, race, and (dis)ability: Discerning structure and agency in classroom interaction. In R. Beach and D. Bloome (Eds.) *Languaging relations across social worlds: Retheorizing the teaching and learning of literacy and the language arts* (69–90). Routledge.

Lee, C. D. (2007). *Culture, literacy, and learning: Taking bloom in the midst of the whirlwind.* New York: Teachers College Press.

Martínez, R. A. (2018). Beyond the English learner label: Recognizing the richness of bi/multilingual students' linguistic repertoires. *The Reading Teacher, 71*(5), 515–522.

Martínez, R. A. (2017). Dual language education and the erasure of Chicanx, Latinx, and indigenous Mexican children: A call to re-imagine (and imagine beyond) bilingualism. *Texas Education Review*, 5(1), 81–92.

Martínez, R. A. (2014). "Do they even know that they do it?": Exploring awareness of Spanish–English code-switching in a sixth-grade English language arts classroom. *Bilingual Research Journal*, 37(2), 195–210.

Martínez, R. A. (2013). Reading the world in Spanglish: Hybrid language practices and ideological contestation in a sixth-grade English language arts classroom. *Linguistics and Education*, 3(24), 276–288.

Martínez, R. A. (2010). "Spanglish" as literacy tool: Toward an understanding of the potential role of Spanish–English code-switching in the development of academic literacy. *Research in the Teaching of English*, 45(2), 124–149.

Martínez, R. A. (2009). *Spanglish is spoken here: Making sense of Spanish-English code-switching and language ideologies in a sixth-grade English language arts classroom*. Unpublished doctoral dissertation, University of California, Los Angeles.

Martínez, R. A., Durán, L., & Hikida, M. (2017). Becoming "Spanish learners": Identity and interaction among multilingual children in a Spanish–English dual language program. *International Multilingual Research Journal*, 11(3), 167–183.

Martínez, R. A., Hikida, M., & Durán, L. (2015). Unpacking ideologies of linguistic purism: How dual language teachers make sense of everyday ranslanguaging. *International Multilingual Research Journal*, 9(1), 26–42.

Martínez, R. A. & Martinez, D. C. (forthcoming). Chicanx and Latinx students' linguistic repertoires: Moving beyond essentialist and prescriptivist perspectives. In J. MacSwan & C. Faltis (Eds.) *Critical perspectives on codeswitching in classroom settings: Language practices for multilingual teaching and learning*. New York: Routledge.

Martínez, R. A., Orellana, M. F., Pacheco, M., & Carbone, P. (2008). Found in translation: Connecting translating experiences to academic writing. *Language Arts*, 85(6), 421–431.

Orellana, M. F. & Reynolds, J. (2008). Cultural modeling: Leveraging bilingual skills for school paraphrasing tasks. *Reading Research Quarterly*, 43(1), 48–65.

Otheguy, R., García, O., & Reid, W. (2015). Clarifying translanguaging and deconstructing named languages: A perspective from linguistics. *Applied Linguistics Review*, 6(3), 281–307.

Paris, D. (2012). Culturally sustaining pedagogy: A needed change in stance, terminology, and practice. *Educational Researcher*, 41(3), 93–97.

Patel, L. (2016). Pedagogies of resistance and survivance: Learning as marronage. *Equity & Excellence in Education*, 49(4), 397–401.

Roser, N. L., Hoffman, J. V., Labbo, L. D., & Farest, C. (1992). Language charts: A record of story time talk. *Language Arts*, 69(1), 44–52.

Urciuoli, B. (1985). Bilingualism as code and bilingualism as practice. *Anthropological Linguistics*, 27(4), 363–386.

Zentella, A. C. (1997). *Growing up bilingual: Puerto Rican children in New York*. Oxford: Blackwell.

11

TRANSLITERACY PRACTICES BY YOUTH IN NEW IMMIGRANT COMMUNITIES

Jennifer F. Reynolds and Marjorie Faulstich Orellana

Introduction

On the tape that we gave her to record herself, as part of a study of the work that the children of immigrants do as translators/interpreters or "language brokers," ten-year-old Estela can be heard reading *The Night Before Christmas* to her five-year-old sister:

1   That (.) was the night before, Christmas,
2   esa era la Navidad, la noche después, de na–, de,
3   después de Navi– *(exhales)* antes de Navidad.
4   When all?, when all through the house
5   Tee was the night before Christmas
6   when all the houses,
7   when all the houses
8   Ok. *(exhales softly)*,
9   Tee was the night before Christmas,
10   Te es la,
11   la noche de,
12   de *(exhales softly)*,
13   antes de Navidad.
14   Digo, después de la Navidad
15   When all through the ni–,
16   the house.
17   Cuando todo,
18   eh, adentro de la casa.
19   Not a creature was st– stirring.

20   Ni siquiera un animal estaba, staring,
21   em, mirando.
22   Not even a mouse,
23   ni siquiera un ratón.

As may be evident in this phrase-by-phrase transcript, Estela perseverated in an effort to achieve a precise translation of the text. These 23 lines of transcript represent her reading of just the first two lines of the text (which as they appeared in the original poem in the *Troy Sentinel* newspaper in 1823 in New York, are: "Twas the night before Christmas, when all thro' the house, not a creature was stirring, not even a mouse"). Rather than reading a longer passage and summarizing it, or using the pictures to tell the story, as did some of the children in our study, Estela translated phrase by phrase, first reading the English passage aloud before working laboriously to identify what she assumed to be equivalent words in Spanish. Listening to her, we were struck by just how intent she seemed to be on delivering a "flawless" translation, and we wondered what lessons could be taken for classroom instruction from a closer look at how she managed the challenges of this text in this everyday, home-based "family literacy" practice (Orellana et al., 2003).

In this chapter, we situate this focused analysis of one home translation/reading event in relation to what we have learned from a wider examination of the work that the children of immigrants do when they use their knowledge of two languages to speak, read, write, listen, and do things for others on a wide range of tasks, set in varied relationships and contexts, with a variety of written texts. We note that these home literacy practices conform closely with the kinds of literacies that schools hope their students will engage in and thus there is much to learn from considering how children engage in such practices at home. In fact, storybook reading has long been the method early institutionalized and venerated as the best means to enculturate all of America's youth into societal expectations about literacy (Heath, 1983). It matters little that teaching training philosophies have switched from autonomous to ideological models that either presume that literacy is a neutral and technical skill that is an important precursor to the acquisition of advanced social and cognitive skills or one that is culturally and contextually variable, as it is a social practice replete with tacit assumptions about what are valued forms of knowledge and ways reading and interpreting what we call "texts."

Zooming in on the strategies that she used in reading *The Night Before Christmas* to her sister, we will show how Estela drew on her personal repertoire of language in order to make meaning of this text for herself and then render it in Spanish for her sister. We then take a closer look at how Estela's approach to reading this text both aligned with and diverged from typical school and disciplinary reading practices, considering what her attempts to provide a verbatim translation reveal about her understandings of reading, and about the constraints imposed by particular text types and language forms. This also provides insight into how children's translingual capacities—voiced aloud in acts of translation— may reveal their understanding of texts written in English. We use this analysis to suggest some specific ways that teachers could draw connections between home and school ways of reading—using home biliteracy practices like the translation of storybooks as a bridge to support academic literacies, *as well as vice versa* (i.e., how teachers could better support and sustain home language practices). And so the detailed unpacking of a specific example that highlights the skills of an "exceptional" child language broker may help to reveal how entrenched autonomous models of literacy are across disciplinary literacy practices, such that they reinforce each other and surface in this particularly rich example. By exposing the underlying ideological assumptions in a transdisciplinary text, together with a broader discussion of the actual variability and flexibility of language and literacy practice enacted by child language brokers, we aim to enable educators to imagine what it would mean to support *all* bilingual children's reading skills by leveraging their language and literacy brokering experiences for the expansion of their literate competencies—not just those of "exceptional" translators like Estela.

Language and Literacy Brokering

We define language brokering as the many ways in which people use their knowledge of two or more languages (including varieties of a single "national" language) to speak, read, write, listen and do things for others. This work is generally done by the children of immigrants because they have skills and knowledge that adults may not—including the ability to speak English without a marked accent, to read and write in English, and to draw on bicultural understandings. All of these are essential for meeting the demands of everyday life in immigrant communities, and immigrant youth are routinely called on to leverage their linguistic, cultural, social, and pragmatic knowledge in order to help their families navigate life in a new land. These language and literacy brokering practices are ubiquitous, normative, and integrated into many everyday household tasks, and they are consequential for learning and development, including of the kinds of things that schools value. But they are rarely recognized or built on in school.

The practice of language brokering was barely recognized by researchers or educators until the 1990s, when educational researchers Jeff McQuillan and Lucy Tse (1995) first surveyed young adults about their experiences and the impact it had on their educational trajectories. From there, study of the practice was taken up by developmental psychologists, who mostly focused on implications for youths' emotional and psychological development, rather than the skills they garnered from this work. (See, for example, Chao, 2006; Love & Buriel, 2007; Weisskirch, 2017).

Over the last two decades, attention to the phenomenon has burgeoned, and there has been a shift from viewing the practice as problematic, to considering what children may learn from this work. Researchers have named the metalinguistic competencies that brokering cultivates (Malakoff & Hakuta, 1991) and its relation to school success (Acoach & Webb, 2004; Buriel et al., 1998). (See Orellana & Guan, 2015 and Weisskirch, 2017 for a fuller survey of the literature.) A study by Dorner, Orellana, and Li-Grining (2007) revealed that children who have considerable experience mediating exchanges between speakers or different languages scored higher than their peers on standardized tests of reading and math, even when controlling for other differences. A study by Guan, Greenfield, and Orellana (2014) showed that young adults who grew up brokering for others scored higher than their peers on measures of transcultural perspective taking (the capacity to see from different culturally inflected points of view).

Our own qualitative work has concentrated on documenting what language and literacy brokering actually looks like, in varied contexts, situations, relationships, and activities, as well as just how children and their families negotiate these situations. We have catalogued an immense range of tasks and texts that the children in our study named (Orellana et al., 2003; Orellana, Dorner, & Pulido 2003), and we have analyzed in close detail the strategies they used as they pooled their knowledge and skills to get these jobs done. Often, this work was done in collaboration with others (parents and siblings) and offered tremendous opportunities for learning about language, literacy and culture. (See Eksner & Orellana, 2012 and Orellana, Martínez, Lee, & Montaño, 2012 for an examination of the supports parents provide to their children; see Reynolds & Orellana, 2014 for the metalinguistic awareness youth display as they reflect on their translation experiences; see García-Sánchez, this volume for elaboration on both similarities and differences between home language brokering relationships and the relationships that proscribe literacy practices in school.) Among other things, we have considered the particular demands of brokering in parent–teacher conferences (García-Sánchez, Orellana, & Hopkins, 2011; Reynolds, Orellana, & García-Sánchez, 2015); medical encounters (Martínez et al., 2017); and in public spaces where immigrants are overtly racialized (Reynolds & Orellana, 2009).

We have also given specific attention to the demands of literacy brokering: the oral interpretation of written texts. We identified the wide variety of genres and types of text that children tackled in this form of "homework" (Orellana, 2009): legal documents (jury summons, unemployment and welfare applications), religious course materials, school information (informational letters and flyers, field trip permission slips and other forms, parents' ESL homework and report cards), financial forms (bank statements, credit card applications, mortgage and insurance information), storybooks, greeting cards, product labels, instruction manuals, newspapers, personal records, song lyrics, ads, receipts, and more. These materials addressed diverse subject matter from many domains (financial, medical, legal, religious, educational, recreational, commercial) and served distinct purposes (to inform, entertain, secure goods or rights, perform rituals), set in particular relationships and activity settings. This is an under-recognized form of family literacy (Álvarez, 2014; Orellana et al., 2003; Perry, 2014; Reyes, 2012); children encounter an immense amount of words through their language brokering experiences and recognizing this is important given the resurgence of deficit ideas about immigrant families as is evident in recent discussions about presumed "word gaps" (Hart & Risley, 1995; see also Avineri et al., 2015). In one of our first publications exploring Cultural Modeling we featured work that child language brokers performed and how it could be best leveraged within public school settings (Orellana & Reynolds, 2008). Through ethnographic observations conducted in schools from two different districts, combined with a writing task and interviews with youth themselves, we revealed the tendency for educators to orient to words, and not to see other kinds of linguistic skill that youth bring to school, and other ways of connecting them to academic literacies. See other chapters of this volume for examples that move beyond vocabulary (Ek, Enciso, Pacheco and Morales, García-Sánchez, all this volume). Such supports include interpreting different kinds of cross-disciplinary text and using children's growing bilingual capabilities to do so even when the most obvious strategies might involve metalinguistic analyses of word cognates, word and other forms of speech play.

Reading Strategies and Approaches to Interpretation

Given the wide range of texts that children are asked to broker for others, the varied purposes for doing so, and the variable skills, experiences, and competencies that different children bring to this practice, it should come as no surprise that children in our study adopted diverse strategies to parse the texts and explain them to others. Sometimes children read line by line, as Estela did in her reading of *The Night Before Christmas*, and rendered short translations as they went. Sometimes they read an entire text silently, then summarized its meaning or paraphrased it. They made decisions about which concepts or details needed to be explicated and which might be skipped altogether. Their own approaches varied over time, as well as across contexts, situations, and tasks. For example, when we initially observed nine-year-old María reading a letter that was sent home from her school, she parsed it line by line, as Estela did. But four years later we watched María tackle a similar letter; she read it silently and then summarized it in Spanish for her mother. Many of the older youth in our studies seemed quite conscious of the strategies they adopted, and were able to articulate them for us. At the same time, virtually all of the participants in our study *displayed* greater competence than they seemed aware of, and were more likely to name their limitations than their abilities.

Among the children that we followed over a period of several years, Estela was exceptional in terms of the breadth, depth, and care that she gave to her language brokering work. The oldest of three girls, (aged five and one at the time of this reading, when Estela herself was 11), Estela was considered the "right hand" of her family, and was in many ways a prototypical language broker, one who shouldered many responsibilities for her newly immigrant parents. She appeared delighted to take the audiorecorder that we offered her, to record her translation work whenever she chose, and produced numerous examples for us. In addition to her recording of *The Night Before Christmas*, Estela taped herself reading *Big Dog, Little Dog, The Three Little Pigs*, an insurance letter concerning a car crash, and several letters from school. She also recorded herself helping her father to fill out an application for credit (see Reynolds & Orellana, 2009), and we recorded her in her own parent–teacher conference (see Orellana, 2009; see also García Sánchez & Orellana, 2006). We also recorded another youth in our study, Junior, reading storybooks aloud for his siblings in addition to mediating his own parent–teacher conferences. In the recordings of his storybook readings, Junior did not vocalize personal asides about interpretive decisions as he was making them, although he did provide line-by-line translations of the text, as did Estela. This demonstrates that both children were aware of school based storybook reading aloud practices and were appropriating them for their out-of-school sibling care. They both enacted the expectation that teachers read aloud, line by line, without inviting audience participation or discussion until after the story is completed. However, Estela's practices of verbalizing her metalinguistic asides during the act of reading, interpreting, and translating the text provide an intimate lens into the complex interpretive processes that other children also engaged in—the things children do as they read, if they are given the opportunity to work through texts without having their reading processes tightly controlled or delimited Teachers might support reading growth by noticing the strategies youth already enact as they draw on their linguistic and cultural toolkits to process and produce different texts. They can enhance and further modeling such strategies, making reading *processes* more visible for all.

The Process of Literacy Brokering Articulated

In this section, we examine more of Estela's reading of *The Night Before Christmas* and pay attention to how she verbalized those understandings. We do this to show what is possible for skilled and practiced language brokers, which will lead to our discussion of how those skills could be built on in school. At the same time, we use our analyses to reveal some of the underlying assumptions about reading and translation that seemed to drive Estela's attempts at verbatim translation and her careful separation of Spanish and English, and that may, in fact, get in the way of a more natural, authentic, and engaged approach to translation and to reading—the ways of reading that Estela displayed when she was brokering for her family in everyday circumstances without worrying about "performing" her skills for the researchers or enacting the prototypical school-valued way of reading stories. We suspect that these ideas about reading and translation were largely cultivated in school, and thus suggest that teachers can play an important role in helping students develop flexible literacy strategies that will serve them in their home language brokering work, rather than having school literacies *impede* on the flexibility that youth need to manage myriad tasks that are involved in language brokering.

As in the opening vignette, Estela frequently monitored her translations, striving for more precision or detail. For example, she first translated "before Christmas" as *después de Navidad* ("after Christmas") and then self-repaired to *antes de Navidad* ("before Christmas") (lines 1–3). This precision corrected for meaning. At times, however, her drive for precision led to problematic translations, as was the case when she first correctly translated the contracted "'Twas" as *Era*, but then focused too narrowly on the stylized font with its large capital letter "T," and self-repaired her reading to utter the letter "t," which she then translated into Spanish as the letter "t" as well. This resulted in her reading on line 5: "Tee was the night before Christmas."

Unlike some of the youth we observed, Estela skipped very little, and what she skipped was usually non-central to meaning. Her performance revealed only a few, generally minor, transformations of meaning. For example, when she first read "stirring" (line 19), she used English phonology. Then, however, in proceeding with the Spanish translation, she corrected to the English "staring," presumably because she was trying to make sense of the actions of the mouse. The verb "to stir," used as a gerund ("stirring") would be an infrequent vocabulary term for most readers, and a challenging one for emerging bilinguals. The verb "to stare" is still somewhat specialized, but certainly more common. Estela clearly knew the word "staring," and could use it appropriately. So she reinterpreted "stir" as "stare" and rendered her interpretation as *mirando* ("looking").

Across texts, and even within her reading of this one story, Estela displayed versatility in her approach to translation. She provided both "close" translations *and* explanations of concepts/terms, occasionally adding information to make things more explicit. Her explanations about the texts were to the point and highly comprehensible, and she displayed an excellent command of both Spanish and English vocabulary. For example, she knew that an appropriate translation for "chubby" would be *gordito*. (This appeared later in her translation of the story.) She deployed a variety of strategies to tackle words that she did not know, both in English and Spanish. For example, when she did not know the meaning of the English word "kerchief" she used context cues and the illustrations to guess *pijama de dormir*" as in "pajamas for sleeping." She also used sound effects to dramatize action, as in the sound of reindeer hooves "pawing and prancing" on the roof, which she rendered as *chakachaka*. In performing her translations, she often displayed her thought processes; this thinking aloud revealed her tacit understanding of how to translate. While she occasionally resorted to a "best guess" interpretation, she usually signaled her awareness that it was indeed a guess (for example, by adding "or something like that").

Remarkably, Estela managed to retain many of the poetic aspects of the texts she read, including some of the rhyme, repetition, and parallel structures (e.g., "Now dash away, dash away, dash away all" becomes *Ahora vámonos, ahora vámonos, vá:monos ya todos*). This clearly was challenging with a text like *The Night Before Christmas*, which was written entirely in anapestic tetrameter, a form of poetic meter that Dr. Seuss also used. This poetic form exploits the structural properties of English where syllable length varies. Specifically, anapestic tetrameter has four feet in a line of verse with each foot having two unstressed syllables before a *stressed* syllable: "$Twas_1$ the_1 $night_1$, be_2fore_2 $Christ_2mas_3$ and_3 all_3 $through_4$ the_4 $house_4$." Spanish, however is a syllable-timed language, which means that each syllable is the same length and so the same rhythmic effects cannot be achieved in the same way given the different underlying linguistic structures. Despite these structural differences in the two languages, Estela performed lively oral Spanish translations and read with expression, much as a good teacher or storyteller would, in order to entertain her very young sister, when she sometimes became distracted or disengaged.

Let's see how Estela contended with the next two lines of verse from the original text and then juxtapose it with how she read, interpreted, and translated each passage. In doing this, our aim is to unpack the complex and at times unconscious choices involved in this kind of reading/translation work, in addition to the more conscious ones that Estela verbalized as she makes sense of the text.

> Lines from original text
> The stockings were hung by the chimney with care,
> In hopes that St. Nicholas soon would be there;
>
> **Excerpt of Estela's storybook translation for her sister**
>
> **Estela**: The stockings were hung by the chimney.
>> Las,
>> Las medias estaban colgadas en la chimenea.
>> Por la chimenea.
>> With care. *Con, con:, con:*
>
> **Sister**: *caca*
> **Estela**: *con::, con::, con cuidado.*

Here, Estela focused on producing a reading of the text as a piece of *prose* and not a piece of poetry. She quickly and accurately read it using English phonology. Her processing of these English sentences as prose, moreover favored "referential transparency." That is, she reduced the multiple functions of language to a singular function—that of referring—which was then given primacy. Her sister, however, seemed oriented to the poetic functions of language, which enable a playful modality. When Estela searched out loud for the best equivalent of the English "care," uttering *con con con* ("with, with, with"), the sister took this as an invitation to help out and engaged playfully by supplying the Spanish word, *caca*, which is a term from a Spanish baby-talk resister meaning "poop." *Care~con~caca*—all play with consonance, repeating the phoneme/k/which exists in both English and Spanish. Given that the referent is recognizable as preschool "potty time" vocabulary, her sister is playing with meaning, too.

From a Cultural Modeling perspective, Estela and her sister took on a particular literary challenge in this translation excerpt, not unlike what expert translators do. Literary scholars strive to balance the poetics and semantics of texts, following the artistic traditions engendered in the genres being translated. Their aim is not only to help readers understand what is denoted in the text (i.e., the literal meaning), but also what is connoted (i.e., the conveyed/implied meanings). Legal approaches to translation and interpretation, contrariwise, tend to privilege literal meanings at the expense of all others. We see this tension between literal and poetic in Estela's work, even as she also attended to affective dimensions of the storybook reading itself. That is, given that the sister was as oriented to Estela as she was the story, her use of *caca* was affective—connecting to playful feelings associated with sibling relationships. The affective dimensions of language as text are also often treated secondarily in verbatim translation. Estela in reading this text aloud did not lose the affective dimensions of storybook reading as a social act, and one often used in nurturing exchanges, even though her driving concern for accurate, correct reference dominated.

Additional evidence supporting our contention that Estela was striving for verbatim translation is that she carefully tracked and reproduced English syntax, even in Spanish when another word order might be appropriate. This choice, to retain parallel syntax, which was probably influenced both by the English word order, moreover revealed that she had to make some tacit semantic choices triggered by the verb in bold.

> The stockings **were**   hung   by   the chimney   with care.
> *Las medias* **estaban** *colgadas por*   *la   chimenea con   cuidado.*

In English "to be" is the infinitive form of what linguistics call a copular verb. It is used to combine a sentence subject with its predicate. Spanish, however, has two different forms of "to be." Each form specializes to indicate different semantic and grammatical information. *Ser*, for example, may be used to describe an enduring or essential quality of a person or thing, to denote a person's profession, to indicate relationships between people, to indicate possession, and to indicate the time. *Estar* is used to denote temporary conditions of a person or thing, to denote location and is used as an auxiliary verb in conjunction with verb stems inflected with *-ando* (for verbs ending in *-ar*) or *-iendo* (for verbs ending in either *-ir* or *-er*) to indicate continuous action. Estela chose the appropriate *estar* form of "to be," conjugated using the past imperfect tense, denoting the temporary condition and location of the stockings. Had she chosen the other verb (*ser*) in combination with the inflected verb *colgar*, the sense would have been entirely different—and incorrect for this sentence—meaning someone who is a distracted, habitually forgetful person.

Estela could have also made a different choice in translating this sentence to emphasize the manner ("with care") in which the stocking had been hung. This is something that the passive construction in English achieves. Had she decided to emphasize the manner, then she might have selected the Spanish reflexive verb form, *colgarse*, which obscures the agent of the action. This translation would have then been, *Y con cuidado se habían colgado las medias en la chimenea* ("And with care they were hung, the stockings on the chimney"). And one final observation that supports our contention that she was privileging accuracy in pursuit of verbatim translation happened when she self-repaired *en la chimenea* ("on the chimney") for *por la chimenea* ("by the chimney").

While Estela was concerned with finding equivalent forms, she seemed attentive to selecting the ones most comprehensible to her audience. Consider her rendering of line two:

> In hopes that Saint Nicholas soon will, would be there.
> Con esperanzas que Santa Claus va llegar.

Here she first read "will," but self-repaired to "would." This retained the original tense/aspect form in English. However, in Spanish, she changed to present tense and in so doing selected the most common verbal phrase to indicate future action in Spanish *va a llegar* (going + verb (= to arrive)). Arguably, this made the action feel even more immediate, building up to the anticipation of St. Nicholas' arrival.

Finally, rather than retain the equivalent saint's name in English and archaic Spanish *San Nicolás*, Estela selected the fully incorporated modern loan word into Spanish, "Santa Claus." As this tradition of celebrating St. Nick did not exist in Mexico, where arranging posadas to enact the story of Mary and Joseph seeking shelter before the birth of baby Jesus is more common, the referent used to refer to him as Santa Claus reflects regional histories of cultural borrowing. The combined impact of this reading thus builds excitement and anticipation into the arrival of a kind figure that would be familiar to Mexican children, even though it may not be the cultural tradition that their families actually practice at home. It moreover reflects the bicultural experiences these children are forming in school. In other words, Estela did an excellent job at cultural translation as well in the choices she made during linguistic translation as she accurately read the English text as a piece of storybook prose.

We have used our close analysis of Estela's reading to show the sophisticated translanguaging skills she deployed as she read and interpreted this English storybook for her sister. We have shown how masterfully she balanced translating both the meaning and the aesthetics of the text, how carefully she chose her words and phrasing, how she attended to the audience in her dramatic enactment of a poetic text as storybook prose, and how the linguistic resources in her emerging bilingual repertoire were more often a help than a hindrance in the interpretation of a complex text. As we have noted, Estela was in some ways exceptional in these abilities, but all of the youth that we observed displayed these same kinds of competency, in different degrees, as they tackled different kinds of translation task. *Thus our first point is that teachers might recognize these competencies and help youth to apply this same kind of linguistic dexterity to school literacy tasks.*

At the same time, we want to go further, and suggest how school notions of literacy may actually *constrain* some of the dexterity that youth garner from their language brokering work. This points to a second important role that teachers could play in supporting home language practices like this one, rather than transmuting authentic family relationships and naturalistic discursive practices into school-like ones. (See Kibler et al., under review, for a different view of how family members sometimes work together to read and discuss texts, drawing on their translingual repertoires, when they are *not* enacting school-like literacy practices.)

As we suggested above, Estela's tacit orientation to the translation of this text seems shaped by the "autonomous" literacy (Street, 1984) and language separation models that predominate in schools, as well as by ideologies about language and translation. That is, she seemed to believe that a "flawless" translation stays very, very close to the words themselves, rather than focusing on larger textual units of meaning as well as they the social and affective meanings inherent in literacy practices. The linguist John Haviland (2003, p. 767) has argued that the prevailing ideologies of translation assume "referential transparency" (that meanings are inherent and transparent in words) and "verbatim theory." This assumes that translation is a matter of simply proceeding by finding equivalent words and sentence structures (and that such equivalency is possible or always desirable). As we have amply demonstrated above, it is not, and by only attending to the different disciplinary literate practices and how those differentially shape taking from texts, are we able to see just how complex the interpretive processes are. We owe a special thanks to Estela who made her decision-making process audible as she treated these occasions to practice and hone both her English reading and her translation skills, parsing the words as she performed her skills for us (which further suggests that she saw this focus on word precision as primary).

Leveling Home and School Literacies and Building Mutual Support Systems

What can we learn from this close analysis of Estela's reading of a single text—as well as from our more general understanding of the diverse kinds of text that immigrant children regularly read and interpret for their families in their lives outside of school—that will serve the work of teaching and learning in school? Put another way, how might school literacy instruction recognize, sustain, support, and expand the kinds of skill that Estela and other language brokers deploy and develop through their home literacy brokering work? How might this instruction both facilitate the acquisition of valued school literacy skills *and* support children's home translation work—both *leveraging* and *leveling* home and school literacy practices, and bridging between them?

It should be evident that home language and literacy brokering practices like the ones we discussed and illustrated here have direct relevance for the kinds of literacy skill that are valued and fostered in school. Indeed, these practices map onto each other much more closely and directly than do some of the other everyday cultural practices that are reported in other chapters of this book. Family literacy brokering requires that children read for meaning, with accuracy, and to explain their understanding to others. It involves reading and responding to many varied kinds of text, including ones that would be considered beyond their grade level in school. Families have clear *purposes* for reading and responding to these texts; they *matter* for their lives.

As noted above and in prior work (Orellana & Reynolds, 2008), our first suggestion for teachers is simply to recognize that these practices are ubiquitous in immigrant communities, and to acknowledge, validate, and value them. The importance of this move cannot be underscored enough. Most of the youth that we spoke with said they *never* talked about their language-brokering work in school. They were surprised that we were interested in something they saw as a normal, mostly unremarkable part of their everyday experiences. While they knew that some things were harder than others to translate, they did not fully grasp the complexity of the work they did, the sophistication of the strategies they deployed, or the power of their own language skills. Translating was "just something you do to help your family." Thus teachers can play an important role in helping youth to see the value of their work. (However, we would caution teachers not to go overboard in this; treating the practice as an important, and skillful, but *normal*, part of everyday life is better than exoticizing or fetishizing it.)

Giving children opportunities to talk about texts they have translated at home (as well as other forms of language brokering) is an easy way for teachers to learn about the translation work that your students do. The teachers we worked with had some general understanding that some children did this work, but very little knowledge about the specifics: the actual texts their students translated, the purposes of the translations, and the challenges they encountered therein. Teachers could invite students to bring in texts they translated at home—perhaps even giving extra credit for this "homework" (Orellana, 2009). The first step to building on what children do at home is to learn about what exactly they do, by asking youth to share their experiences.

That sharing in itself is valuable—and not just as a way for teachers to learn about students' experiences. Creating space for conversation about language-brokering experiences will allow youth to share their knowledge, skills and experiences *with one another* in culturally sustaining ways (Alim & Paris, 2017). Most of the young people in our study did not realize that other kids did these things; they had never talked about brokering with their peers. They never had the opportunity to learn from the diverse strategies they deployed, to consider other ways of approaching similar tasks, or sharing in both the joy and frustration of this work. In our focus group interactions with the youth, where they had free rein to discuss and dramatize their experiences, we saw how much they gained from discussing their experiences and learning from each other. They even joyfully transferred their translating skills to pleasurable and playful forms of translingual speech play in peer group interactions (Reynolds & Orellana, 2014). Schools can play an important role in supporting out-of-school literacies by simply creating space for this kind of exchange.

Teachers can further support language brokers by helping them to see the complexities of the work, and the skills that they already are deploying, while enabling youth to draw from their entire linguistic repertoires. This is where we hope our close analysis of Estela's reading is helpful. As we have tried to show, Estela put many school-valued literacy skills to good work in her translation of this text. She deployed a wide range of literary strategies. What might help her most would be the opportunity to consider just where, when, how and why she might choose from among her linguistic and literate toolkit for different kinds of reading and translation task. Teachers can help students to consider the effectiveness of different kinds of reading and translation strategy, for different kinds of text, audience, or purpose. When is it important to focus on individual words and retain close translations of them? What do these close translations reveal about similarities and structural differences within and across codes and how might they be discussed to explicitly foster children's metalinguistic knowledge? When is it more helpful to summarize, extrapolate, modify, or adapt? And when is it ok—or even valuable—to take poetic license? Thinking aloud about these things will help immigrant youth in their work of literacy brokering even as it supports their more general growth as readers, writers, and critical consumers and producers of words and texts.

When teachers build on language-brokering practices by creating space for bilingual youth to draw on their full linguistic repertoires as they make sense of English texts, they build on a longstanding tradition with outstanding results in heritage language schools in the United Kingdom. Educator Cen Williams in the 1990s explicitly promoted the use of translation in pedagogic practice to deepen Welsh and English native-speaking youths' comprehension and processing skills in both languages to achieve effective communication skills in listening and speaking as well as reading and writing (Lewis, Jones, & Baker, 2012). This is what has come to be termed "translanguaging." (See Ek, Martínez et al., this volume.)

While the home language can be a tool for sense making and processing of difficult texts, as we have demonstrated, the press for literal translation can also constrain other kinds of meaning making beyond the quest of achieving referential transparency, as we also detailed above. Teachers are thus in a position to prompt students to also consider the poetic structuring of texts, and other textual and social constraints. We can remind children how different texts are deployed rhetorically for building affective social ties and can be pleasurable—as the story-club space that Pat Enciso (this volume) created also did. We can model *enjoyable, imperfect* reading processes, rather than emphasizing "accuracy" at all costs. We can honor and make it okay to do what Estela does: to talk as she goes along, thinking aloud, revisiting words and ideas, playing with both poetics and pragmatics of language. Once again, we can help students to adopt *flexible* literacy strategies, ones that are appropriate for particular texts, audiences, purposes, and situations. And perhaps sometimes, we should just "get out of the way," giving our students time and space to work through texts in their own way, choosing for themselves particular strategies and approaches. We can listen as they read in order to notice the choices students make, and reflect that to them at other times, rather than interrupting them in our efforts to "help" (and implicitly teaching them that our role is that of monitor of correctness).

Summary and Conclusion

In this chapter, we have examined in close detail the strategies that one language broker deployed as she read and translated stories for her sister. We considered how Estela's approach to reading this text both aligned with and diverged from typical school and disciplinary reading practices, and what her attempts to provide a verbatim translation of this text revealed about her literate understandings. We suggested some specific ways that teachers could draw connections between these home and school reading practices, with the aim of *expanding* their repertoires of linguistic practice and being able to deploy them flexibly and appropriately for different tasks, texts, relationships, and purposes.

Language-brokering practices are rich sources of everyday learning for immigrant youth and ones that directly bridge "school" and "every day" ways with words. By recognizing, naming, and making evident those connections, teachers can support children in doing work that enhances their families' well-being even as it contributes to their own academic growth and development. Indeed, acknowledging the wide variety of texts that language brokers grapple with in the contexts of their everyday lives, and the many strategies they adopt in these authentic and purposeful literacies, may help to broaden the overly narrow conceptions of texts and ways of reading and using texts that predominate in school.

References

Acoach, C. L. & Webb, L. M. (2004). The influence of language brokering on Hispanic teenagers' acculturation, academic performance, and nonverbal decoding skills: A preliminary study. *Howard Journal of Communications, 15*(1), 1–19.

Alim, H. S. & Paris, D. (2017). What is culturally sustaining pedagogy and why does it matter? In H. S. Alim & D. Paris, (Eds.) *Culturally sustaining pedagogies: Teaching and learning for justice in a changing world*. New York: Teachers College Press.

Álvarez, S. (2014). Translanguaging tareas: Emergent bilingual youth as language brokers for homework in immigrant families. *Language Arts, 91*(5): 326–339.

Avineri, N., Johnson, E., Brice-Heath, S., McCarty, T., Ochs, E., Kremer-Sadlik, T., Paris, D. (2015). Invited forum: Bridging the "language gap." *Journal of Linguistic Anthropology, 25*(1), 66–86.

Buriel, R., Perez, W., De Ment, T. L., Chavez, D. V., & Moran, V. R. (1998). The relationship of language brokering to academic performance, biculturalism, and self-efficacy among Latino adolescents. *Hispanic Journal of Behavioral Sciences, 20*(3), 283–297.

Chao, R. K. (2006). The prevalence and consequences of adolescents' language brokering for their immigrant parents. In M. H. Bornstein & L. R. Cote (Eds.) *Acculturation and parent–child relationships: Measurement and development* (271–296). Mahwah, NJ: Lawrence Erlbaum Associates.

Dorner, L., Orellana, M. F., & Li-Grining, C. P. (2007). "I helped my mom," and it helped me: Translating the skills of language brokers into improved standardized test scores. *American Journal of Education, 113*, 451–478.

Eksner, J. & Orellana, M. F. (2012). Shifting in the zone: Latina/o child language brokers and the co-construction of knowledge. *Ethos, 40*(2), 196–220.

García Sánchez, I. & Orellana, M. F. (2006). The construction of moral and social identities in immigrant children's narratives-in-translation. *Linguistics and Education, 17*(3), 209–239.

García-Sánchez, I. M., Orellana, M. F., & Hopkins, M. (2011). Facilitating intercultural communication in parent-teacher conferences: Lessons from child translators. *Multicultural Perspectives, 13*(3), 148–154.

Guan, S. A., Greenfield, P. M., & Orellana, M. F. (2014). Translating into understanding: Language brokering and prosocial development in emerging adults from immigrant families. *Journal of Adolescent Research, 29*(3), 331–355.

Hart, B. & Risley, T. (1995). *Meaningful differences in everyday experience of young American children*. Baltimore, MD: Paul H. Brookes.

Haviland, J. B. (2003). Ideologies of language: Reflections on language and U.S. law. *American Anthropologist, 105*, 764–774.

Heath, S. B. (1983). *Ways with words: Language, life, and work in communities and classrooms*. Cambridge: Cambridge University Press.

Kibler, A. K., Palacios, N., Paulick, J. H., & Hill, T. (under review). Languaging with siblings: Dynamic apprenticeships into and beyond reading fluency in Mexican and Honduran immigrant homes.

Lewis, G., Jones, B., & Baker, C. (2012). Translanguaging: Origins and development from school to street and beyond. *Educational Research and Evaluation, 18*(7), 641–654.

Love, J. A. & Buriel, R. (2007). Language brokering, autonomy, parent-child bonding, biculturalism, and depression: A study of Mexican American adolescents from immigrant families. *Hispanic Journal of Behavioral Sciences, 29*(4), 472–491.

Malakoff, M. & Hakuta, K. (1991). Translation skill and metalinguistic awareness in bilinguals. In E. Bialystok (Ed.) *Language processing in bilingual children* (141–166). Cambridge, MA: Cambridge University Press.

Martínez, K., Orellana, M. F., Murillo, M. A., & Rodriguez, M. A. (2017). Health insurance, from a child language broker's perspective. *International Migration, 55*(5), 31–43.

McQuillan, J. & Tse, L. (1995). Child language brokering in linguistic minority communities: Effects on cultural interaction, cognition and literacy. *Language and Education, 9*(3), 195–215.

Orellana, M. F. (2009). *Translating childhoods: Immigrant youth, language, and culture.* New Brunswick, NJ: Rutgers University Press.

Orellana, M. F., Dorner, L., & Pulido, L. (2003). Accessing assets: Immigrant youth as family interpreters. *Social Problems, 50*(5), 505–524.

Orellana, M. F. & Guan, S. A., (2015). Immigrant family settlement processes and the work of child language brokers: Implications for child development. In C. Suarez-Orozco, M. Abo-Zena, & A. K. Marks (Eds.) *The development of children of immigration* (184–199). New York: New York University Press.

Orellana, M. F., Martinez, D., Lee, C.H. & Montaño, E. (2012). Language as a tool in diverse forms of learning. *Linguistics and Education, 23*, 373–387.

Orellana, M. F. & Reynolds, J. F. (2008). Cultural modeling: Leveraging bilingual skills for school paraphrasing tasks. *Reading Research Quarterly, 43*(1), 48–65.

Orellana, M. F., Reynolds, J., Dorner, L., & Meza, M. (2003). In other words: Translating or "*para*-phrasing" as a family literacy practice in immigrant households. *Reading Research Quarterly, 38*(1), 12–34.

Perry, A. (2014). "Mama, sign this note": Young refugee children's brokering of literacy practices. *Language Arts, 91*(5), 313–325.

Reyes, I. (2012). Biliteracy among children and youth. *Reading Research Quarterly, 47*(3), 303–327.

Reynolds, J. F. & Orellana, M. F. (2014). Translanguaging within enactments of quotidian interpreter-mediated interactions. *Journal of Linguistic Anthropology, 24*(3), 315–338.

Reynolds, J. F. & Orellana, M. F. (2009). New immigrant youth interpreting in white public space. *American Anthropologist, 111*(2), 211–223.

Reynolds, J. F., Orellana, M. F., & García-Sánchez, I. (2015). In the service of surveillance: Immigrant child language brokers in parent-teacher conferences. *Langage et Société, 3* (153), 91–108.

Street, B. V. (1984). *Literacy in theory and practice.* New York: Cambridge University Press.

Weisskirch, R. S. (2017). *Language brokering in immigrant families: Theories and contexts.* New York: Taylor & Francis.

12

EXPLORING, THINKING, AND LEARNING ABOUT LANGUAGES AND LITERACIES WITH YOUNG PEOPLE IN SUPER-DIVERSE AUSTRALIAN CLASSROOMS

Jacqueline D'warte

The global movement of people has significantly changed the cultural and linguistic landscape in almost every country. Australia has become one of the most "super-diverse" (Vertovec, 2007) nations in the world. In addition to the 2.8% of Australians who are Aboriginal and Torres Strait Islander peoples, "Australians" come from over 200 countries, identify with over 300 different ancestries, and speak more than 300 languages; and 21% of people speak a language besides English at home. Approximately 49% of Australians were either born overseas or have at least one overseas-born parent, a proportion higher than the United Kingdom, Canada, New Zealand and the United States (Australian Bureau of Statistics, 2016). Australian cities, urban and peri-urban neighborhoods are becoming multilingual environments. Written language within neighborhoods continues to document the presence of a wide variety of linguistically identifiable groups of people; these linguistic landscapes (Blommaert, 2010) reflect the continuing social change taking place in Australia. This changing landscape has important implications for Australia's equitable schooling project.

Like many countries in the global north, equity discourses in Australia continue to be coopted and reframed. Australia has seen a clear shift away from an examination of the broad and complex interplays between the social, economic, and educational factors that compound disadvantage and marginalization, to a reframing of equity as *quality* (Riddle, 2018). This equity as quality context has been used to justify Australia's national assessment program and to relegate difference to a problem fixed by further commitment to standardized English curriculum and assessment practices. Current policies and practices actively ignore the complex interplay between social, cultural, economic, and educational disadvantages and this continues to create challenges for many young people. This is played out for non-dominant groups and those from immigrant and refugee backgrounds with focused attention to what is perceived as limited or lacking in their knowledge of the language and literacies practices most valued in school. Students' linguistic strengths and the resources that are abundant in their communities (Cox, 2015; French, 2015) are ignored and arguably compounds inequality for these groups. A focus on young people's expertise has the potential to make educators and students, partners in learning and can create conditions that begin to shift the cultures of power (Delpit, 1988) that work to exclude.

This chapter presents ethnographic research undertaken with teachers and students in schools in Western Sydney, one of the most socioeconomically, linguistically, and culturally diverse regions in Australia (Australian Bureau of Statistics, 2016). It uses data from three super-diverse classrooms within a larger study (D'warte, 2018, forthcoming) that engaged elementary and middle school students and teachers as co-researchers, investigating the mobility of students and the school communities' cultural, linguistic and communicative resources. Attention is given to how research was undertaken *with* children as co-researchers and informants (Bucholtz et al., 2014) engaged in tasks framed as research and the ways teachers and students learned *about and with* each other. Discussion centers on how positioning young people as *knowledge producers rather than knowledge consumers* deepened both teachers' and students' understandings and awareness of student languages and dialects and the plurilingual practices they used to navigate their multilingual worlds. Analysis suggests this work engaged teachers and students as partners in learning that went beyond celebrations of cultural and linguistic difference to enhance and reimagine classroom teaching and learning.

Changing Linguistic and Cultural Landscapes

Complex 21st Century Classrooms

Although unevenly distributed, many Australian classrooms include young people who speak many different languages and dialects of English. While between and within group practices and experiences are diverse, these young people draw on multiple ways of learning and understanding and are increasingly mobile and connected across time and space (Pennycook, 2010). However, monocultural, monolingual, perspectives frame conceptualizations of language and literacy in curriculum, pedagogy and assessment in the Australian education system (Eisenchlas, Schalley, & Guillemin, 2015) and therefore ignore this diverse educational landscape.

Many educators suggest that the lived and evolving reality of contemporary Australian classrooms demands a re-examination of current curriculum, pedagogies and assessment practices. Current practices do not place cultural and linguistic flexibility at the center of teaching and learning and therefore hinder rather than facilitate equitable schooling. These conditions offer little opportunity for young people to recognize the "repertoires of linguistic practice" (Gutiérrez

& Rogoff, 2003) they bring to school, and instead lead them to internalize deficit views of their own skills. Despite a large body of educational research that reveals the ways classroom practices and experiences privilege dominant groups (Gorski, 2011) finding ways to counter this by providing productive, meaningful learning opportunities for those whose practices and experiences are less valued within classrooms continues to prove challenging for many educators in super-diverse contexts.

Calls for the critical review and redesign of current educational policy and practice are being echoed by educators around the world. A rethinking of pedagogical theory and practice is realized in the conceptualization of *culturally sustaining pedagogies* (Paris and Alim, 2017). This conceptualization builds on the ground-breaking work of other social justice orientated scholars (for example, Delpit, 1988; Ladson-Billings, 1994; Lee, 1995; Moll & Gonzalez, 1994; Nieto, 1992). Paris and Alim (2017) contend that pedagogical theory and practice must center on the dynamic and evolving nature of languages, literacies, race/ethnicity, cultural practices, and ways of knowing of young people in 21st century classrooms. They scholars call on educators to consider ways to engage themselves and their students in the critical examination of the intersections between these dimensions. This critical examination goes some way to ensuring new pedagogies can indeed become culturally sustaining.

Situated and Dynamic Repertoires

Diverse and Dynamic Practices

In the current global era, across disciplines, scholarship has focused considerable attention on people's linguistic and communicative practices and the linguistic consequences of widespread mobility. Global shifts have problematized the act of classifying languages and speakers; the notion that language is a bounded entity is now challenged by idea that language is a practice and the study of actual languages now encompasses the study of the actual *practices* of people. Language research reveals that language practices are complex and interrelated; they do not transpire in a linear way or function separately but emerge from one linguistic system (García & Wei, 2014). *The linguistic repertoire* of an individual speaker is dynamic, characterized by the language varieties they acquire, know and use within their communities; the "linguistic repertoire" is a conceptualization that has much resonance in educational scholarship.

Educators have learned that the *linguistic repertoires of young people* encompass complex linguistic, communicative and semiotic resources (Blommaert, 2010). Languages can be used separately or together for different purposes in different places and spaces with different people and myriad communicative practices result in plurilingual repertoires (Moore & Gajo, 2009). García (2009) defines bilinguals as individuals who have communicative skills, oral and/or written with various degrees proficiency in two or more languages. In the Australian context, this includes young people who are first-language speakers of Aboriginal English (AE), a non-standard dialect that differs from standard Australian English in morphology, syntax and semantics (Eades, 2013). Super-diverse classrooms comprise young people who are bidialectic/bilingual and plurilingual.

Ethnographic educational research continues to offer evidence of young people using both/all their languages (and varieties of those languages) to communicate and make meaning outside the classroom in rich and complex ways (Cox, 2015; D'warte, 2016; Orellana, 2016; García-Sánchez, this volume). Young people may have a variable and sometimes fragmentary grasp of a plurality of differentially shared styles, registers and genres that may be picked up and/or partially forgotten as they move through their lives. It is unrealistic to expect teachers to master all students' languages or have a comprehensive knowledge of their students' full linguistic repertoires. However, understanding, validating and enhancing the many and varied linguistic interactions and relationships young bilingual/plurilingual people have with multilingual others (García & Wei, 2014), in different contexts, when they are the locus and actor of contact (Marshall & Moore, 2016), offers many learning opportunities for teachers and students.

Reframing Everyday Practices

Rapidly changing accountability and assessment contexts can negatively shape both teachers' and students' views of students' linguistic and cultural resources, especially when success is measured by standardized English tests. New challenges are posed by a crowded curriculum and teaching standards that can hinder rather than support teachers' capacities to respond to linguistic and cultural diversity (Lucas & Villegas, 2013). However, a pluralist present and future is slowly changing the educational context. Paris and Alim (2017) see the valorization of language as a central component of culturally sustaining pedagogy.

Over the last three decades, deficit perspectives have been challenged by conceptual notions that reframe everyday practices as assets; these include for example, "Cultural Modelling" (Lee, 2007), "language as resource" (Ruiz, 1984), "funds of knowledge," (Moll et al., 1992) and "community cultural wealth" (Yosso, 2005). These orientations are underpinned by the assumption that the language and literacy practices of young people developed outside school, in their homes and varying community contexts, are tools that mediate learning and development in school. Research reveals that enabling access to the full breadth of students' language practices can be a vital resource for further language development (e.g., Cummins & Early, 2011; García & Wei, 2014). New thinking calls on educators to reframe understandings of assets pedagogies and the ways they are taken up in school. Instead of being tools that can be used to validate dominant norms and valued knowledges, they can be tools to problematize and disrupt them.

Linguistically relevant pedagogies (Lucas & Villegas, 2013), culturally sustaining pedagogies (Paris & Alim, 2017), and new classroom pedagogies for language teaching and learning such as "translanguaging" (García, 2014) seek to not only take up but extend the practices of bilingual, dialectical, and multilingual young people. Encompassing a holistic view, they center on the linkages between languages and across languages and include using the standard academic languages required in school. Super-diverse classrooms comprise young people with diverse histories, languages, and trajectories and in this new world, local diversity and global connectedness co-exist; young people reshape and recontextualize global materials in their local communities (Lam, 2006). This reshaping and recontextualization can also be central to teaching and learning.

Learning that goes beyond the naming of dominant languages and the presentation of static notions of culture, to instead critically examine and interrogate everyday practices and experiences is crucial. Designing and developing innovative, multimodal language learning experiences that place cultural and linguistic flexibility at the center of teaching and learning can enhance curriculum and address issues of identity, agency, and power in the production of knowledge. Disrupting rather than sustaining the monolingual classroom domain can potentially extend outside the classroom and work to further acknowledge and enhance the skills, knowledges, and ways of being that are essential for life in the present and future. The remainder of the chapter details in-school, ethnographic research that builds on the research and thinking presented in this opening discussion.

Engaging Teachers and Students in Exploring, Thinking, and Learning about Language and Literacies

In this chapter, I present a research project, combining linguistic ethnography (Rampton, Maybin, & Roberts, 2014) with design research (Edelson, 2002) undertaken in classrooms with teachers and students over an 18-month period. I focus on a subset of the larger study, analyzing data from three classrooms, in three urban schools and suggest this work could be adapted by teachers for their own pedagogical practice. Data were collected from weekly or bi-weekly interventions and observations of between 40–90 minutes during the English language arts block and, in some cases, math, history and geography lessons, across school terms. Observations, field notes, and audiorecorded lesson segments captured student to student and student to teacher and researcher interactions. The corpus of data also included students' work samples, language maps (D'warte, 2014), and audiorecorded interviews with teachers, students, and caregivers.

The participating schools had high enrollments of children from refugee and migrant backgrounds with a significant proportion of students classified as English as an additional language/dialect (EAL/D) learners; between 76–99% of the school population were identified as being from language backgrounds other than English (LBOTE). The three classes, two year 5 classes and one year 3–6 class of students newly arrived to Australia, comprised children aged eight to 12 years old, who spoke many different languages and dialects of English. Between nine and 17 languages were spoken across the three classes. Arabic was spoken by the largest number of students, followed by Hindi, Vietnamese, Greek, Mandarin, and Samoan. Teachers were positioned as classroom researchers investigating students' language and literacy practices, experiences and learning and documenting practices and strategies that offered opportunities to learn about and with students.

Positioning Young People as Knowledge Producers

This study began with the teachers, students, and me discussing the nature of research. Attention was given to who does research, how and why it was done, and for what purposes. Common across the three classrooms was considerable interest in my role as an educational researcher and the kind of research undertaken in universities; questions about what classrooms looked like, how often teachers went to class, and how much homework was assigned, were frequent. Discussion then turned to the in-class project, communicated as an investigation of how and in what ways young people in Western Sydney were reading, writing, talking, listening, and viewing in one or more languages inside and outside school.

In each class, young people learned they would be part of a larger group of classroom researchers and that the project aimed to support their teachers and others learning to be teachers, to understand more about their experiences and the language skills and understandings they possessed. We shared the view that this research may help teachers to make lessons better and more interesting for them and we invited them to join us as co-researchers in exploring these hypotheses. We further suggested that, as experts of their own lives, they would be active participants in their teachers' learning and as researchers of their own practices, they might also learn more about themselves and their own communities, and the skills and expertise they possessed. We communicated our desire to learn *with them and from them* and to help us consider how, if at all, home languages and practices could become a part of classroom learning and perhaps change what we do in classrooms. Analysis of introductory classroom visits reveals that, in almost all cases, young people seemed surprised that teachers wanted to learn more about them. While happy to be knowledge producers for teachers, they were equally skeptical about whether this would be taken up in classrooms. Most often they were curious about how this would happen and why this research mattered; this is reflected in the classroom exchange between students, researcher and teacher below. These introductory sessions offered us further opportunity for reflexivity, particularly in relation to effecting change in school practices. Please note all names used in this chapter are pseudonyms.

TITO: Will you tell teachers what we do and what we think?

JACQUI: Well, yes, what do you think about this? Is this a good idea? I hope you will be sharing your findings and thoughts with them rather than me. I will share what we have learned with people learning to be teachers. Or perhaps you can do that. I will invite you to the university to meet people learning to be teachers.

CLASS: Students talking to each other.

TOBY: I guess if it makes teachers better it's good. How do you know they will listen?

JACQUI: That is a great question T. I guess you and the other classes can help us answer that question? Miss Orlo what do you think?

MS ORLO: I guess that is why we are doing this project, so we can listen to you and learn from you.

JACQUI: What do you want teachers to know about you? What do you think they will want to know or what do you want to should share with them?

[Students talk to one another]

WATT: How much homework we do.

ROMAN: How much gaming.

TOBY: How much internet fun stuff.

ALI: We can't learn them our language.

USEF: Teachers know we speak other languages but we don't use our languages in school.

EMAN: They can know us better.

JACQUI: Would you like to use your languages in school and learn each other's languages? Have a talk at your tables. I will ask each table.

[Jacqui calls on each table]

TABLE 1: Yeah.

TABLE 2: No we need English.

TABLE 3: Fun, maybe.

TABLE 4: Mahi, Toby, Benny can't write in their language.

TABLE 5: Nah, we can't hide.

RINA: We don't know each other's languages.

KENZI: We won't understand each other.

HAMAD: My parents want me to learn English only.

ZADI: We need to get better at English.

ROMAN: Will we learn each other's languages? That's too many languages, too hard.

MAHMOOD: We just do it, we don't think about it?

JACQUI: We are going to ask you all to think and talk about these things with us by being researchers. We will find out if teachers get to know you better and if you got to use your languages in school?

TITO: I want teachers to know more about our languages.

FERHAN: I want my friends to know my language.

AMELIA: They can know me.

MAHMOOD: It would be so fun.

USEF: So teachers might be better teachers?

SOLOMON: Will we learn more?

JACQUI: They are great research questions Solomon and Usef. I will write them down so we can make sure to try and answer them.

While students were asked to be participants in this research, in reality they had little choice and were directed by teachers. Research suggests that strong teacher–student relationships shape the way young people think and act in school (Hamre & Pianta, 2003). Positioning students as experts and possible knowledge producers offered them some agency in the ongoing work. We were generally interested in hearing from students but were well aware of the limitations imposed by dominant classroom norms. As communicated by Tito, Toby, and others across the three classrooms, teachers might listen, but would they actually hear what was communicated? Teachers' reassurances did little to quell this view as the project began, and evident power dimensions in the classroom prompted these young people to consider the impact their views may have on individual relationships and learning.

Opening sequences across the three classrooms offered some insight into what students saw as valued in schools, such as homework, as detailed above, and conversely what was not: for example, gaming and using the internet, as communicated by Roman and Toby. A common view was that teachers knew they spoke languages other than English and this was unimportant or rarely discussed, as expressed by Usef. These young people were skeptical about the value or importance of using home languages given the opportunity. They had no experience of using home languages in school, and conceiving of how this might happen was problematic for everyone. Across classrooms, data reveal a general agreement that teachers could know them better, if they knew more about their languages. The following comment from Amin in a second Year 5 class reflects the common sentiment: *Teachers ask us what we speak but that's all, we don't talk about it again.*

Many young people communicated the challenges they faced in learning English and writing in English. They felt this work might take the focus off English and suggested their parents would be unhappy. Opening transcripts reveal an awareness of the importance and value of English, as communicated by Zadi, and that the focus should be on getting better at English. Using home languages in the classroom presumably would not assist in this endeavor. English was, of course, privileged and dominant ideologies that dismissed the value of home languages for learning within classrooms were foregrounded. Foundational knowledge was not seen as fundamental to learning and linguistic difference was positioned as deficit.

Deepening Understanding and Awareness

We hoped to move beyond identifying the linguistic practices of young people, and merely *labelling* them as *assets*. Many scholars have elucidated how this does not challenge discourses that marginalize the practices of non-dominant youth (Lee, 2007; Orellana, 2016; Paris & Alim, 2017). However, within the larger schooling project young people's linguistic practices often go unrecognized; influenced by broader school and district practices and policies that frame them as deficits. Carol Lee (2017) suggests we must also support students in feeling efficacious and seeing the relevance of learning. Equally important is facilitating dialogue and metacognition; we hoped to do this by engaging young people in an exploration and interrogation of their own linguistic knowledge and skill.

Each class was engaged in substantive conversations about the multimodal ways in which people communicate, and prompted to think about the ways languages, technology, signs and symbols, and embodied practices such as gesture, body language, dance, music, art and film, make meaning and facilitate communication between people. In two classes, this was done with prompts placed in the center of a piece of A4 paper, and students responded in groups. Young people were also tasked with observing, listening, talking, and recording the practices and languages used within the school. Asked to pay keen attention to their ongoing communication, two classes kept language diaries and each week discussed their findings. For young people still learning English, support was provided by advanced same-language partners, older students, community and parent volunteers, or bilingual teacher's aides. This offered an opportunity for students and the school community to call on their full linguistic repertoire.

Each class turned the focus on themselves by developing specific interview questions to ask each other about the ways they were reading, writing, talking, listening, and viewing in one or more languages in myriad places and spaces inside and outside of school (e.g., individual languages spoken and learned, multimodal activity, e.g., translating, texting, Skyping). Using audiorecording devices they interviewed one another in groups of four or five. In a series of teacher-scaffolded lessons, each group collected, collated, and presented their own group data (e.g., using graphs, tables) to the class, all data were combined to create a whole class data set. Each class data set was the catalyst for ongoing discussion and additional learning.

In one class, discussion about languages and language varieties included, for example, using Arabic to study the Koran and the similarities or differences between Arabic words in Somalia, Egypt, Saudi Arabia, and or Iraq. In another, students learned that almost everyone was born in the Middle East, yet spoke ten languages or dialects of Arabic. Two-thirds of these young people learned languages other than English on Saturday in after school programs and communicated in multiple languages and multiple modes in local and global environments. Their linguistic practices were directed by a range of purposes and interests, including, but not limited to, speaking with grandparents and family members in online environments, translating regularly for family members and friends in multiple places and spaces, studying the Koran, cultivating friendships, gaming, listening to and downloading music, and audio-visual viewing of all kinds. Home languages were most often spoken at shops, at community events and in multiple online environments, but not in their classroom, at school events, or outside their immediate neighborhood. Several discussions centered on parents' desire for young people to continue to learn home languages in after-school language programs; many young people expressed conflicting feelings about this, often expressing the view that English learning was most important and this could only be realized by abandoning home language learning. Classes were encouraged to share their developing understandings and to reflect on their findings. Representative comments below are from two classes who were asked to share one thing they had learned at the end of the term of work.

I loved being a researcher, it made me think.
I think being bilingual is like lifting weights, heavy weights, one on each arm and you get stronger and stronger.
I learned I am normal.
I learned I sometimes mix up languages but it's not bad.
I learned how much my parents like me talking about this.
I am not good at English or Vietnamese.
I think about formal and informal and the way it changes every day.
I learned about Arabic and Hindi and different writing and sounds.
I learned more words to help my writing more and about accents and adjectives in my language.
Not everyone wants me to speak Chinese but I borrowed more Chinese books.
I learned about classical Arabic and other ways we do language.
Language is not about where you come from, it is about who you are.
It helped me teach people about my language, its important because people can know you better, I felt happy and not so lonely.
The more we know each other's languages, the less wars we will have.
I got to hear other languages and respect about other languages and if you respect people you feel safe.

These comments suggest the plural and dynamic nature of students' linguistic and cultural practices and identities were beginning to be foregrounded. An interrogation of normal and an examination of multilingual practices in urban settings revealed that monolingualism was abnormal. Often these young people came to view their own skills and understandings in new ways, realizing for example that code switching was not bad and that being bilingual was an incredible skill. These understandings were not present at the start of the study. Alternatively a few came to view their abilities as limited; these students lacked confidence in employing their full linguistic repertoire. Metapragmatic awareness about their multilingual realities and how they used plurilingual practices to navigate those realities were paramount as students made linguistic comparisons, examined changes in register, and engaged in discussions about translating and language brokering in local and global spaces. They honed their skills as linguistic ethnographers in investigating individual phonological and graphological processes, vocabulary, grammar, punctuation, and aspects of orthography as realized in multiple languages.

Identity and respect were also foregrounded in ongoing discussions. Amina's comment about war focuses on the importance of sharing languages, and their capacity to deepen understandings that could go some way to disrupting con-flicts—something she had a clear knowledge of from her experience of coming to Australia as young refugee. Ideas about safety, intercultural understanding, and belonging were increasingly linked to language. Across classes, students showed interest and engagement in this work. Both oral and written reflections from these three classes revealed strong evidence of student enthusiasm and increasing self-esteem and confidence.

Teachers reported increased understandings of what their students knew and could do. This included not only the range of language and dialect these young people employed in their everyday worlds, but the sophistication of their prac-tices and competencies particularly in relation to translating for families. (See García-Sánchez, Reynolds & Orellana, this volume, for exploration of the skills involved in translating.) They were surprised by the sophisticated insights young people offered about what they were learning and the ways they continued to share their language practices. They were delighted by how engaged students were and what they perceived to be an increase in the complexity of the work students produced and the ways this could be applied across the curriculum as reported by these teachers:

> They were excited about being researchers and this easily became the subject of math, science, and even history lessons.
>
> Lessons were better and more interesting. Almost all my students said the work was hard but they enjoyed it. This was the case for writing particu-larly, from writing very little to writing great descriptions, arguments, and persuasive essays that meant something to them.
>
> Well, they got excited and started writing about themselves and it became more complex because they knew it would be shared in our group discussions, it was important.
>
> I finally thought yes, we can encourage home language use, if they could write in home languages they were excited, even if they couldn't

they wanted to learn more, asking parents and consulting bilingual dictionaries.

I have come to see the benefit of trying to find out and include their home languages and practices. Learning has been meaningful for all of us: me, the parents, and the kids. It's become an integral part of what we do in the classroom now. It's not something I did before, I didn't think about it. It has changed our class culture.

Plurilingual Practices and In-school Learning

As Lee (2017) suggests this work was supporting young people in feeling efficacious and enthusiastic and seeing the relevance of learning through the tasks they were assigned. We were also keen to move beyond celebrations of language to the facilitation of dialogue and metacognition in this exploration of multilingual knowledge and skill. Using A4 paper and a range of coloring materials young people made *language maps* (D'warte, 2014). Maps entailed drawing and labelling the ways they were reading, writing, talking, listening, and viewing with different people in different places in their everyday worlds. Mapping offered young people who were still learning English, in particular, an alternative way to share their information. It also offered teachers additional information about their students' practices and the ways in which home and school were navigated. Multimodal material and activity featured prominently and revealed students' individual experiences and increasing understandings of register dimensions as expressed in these comments:

> My friends and I learned more about our language and we talked about what we do; we change it up all the time.
>
> It (mapping) gets you to draw and talk about your language and it feels kind of interesting because it feels like that people want to know about how you and your language and stuff. It made me think about what I do and how I can think about this more when I have to do English work.

Maps were taken home and shared with parents; students audiorecorded themselves talking about them. Evidence reveals that maps became a catalyst for ongoing conversations about language and learning between students, parents, and teachers. It prompted the writing of persuasive essays about the importance of multilingualism and the problem of linguistic supremacy. The strong relationship between language and identity was foregrounded and this prompted teachers to begin to consider how to include and use more multilingual material in their curricula. Teachers made explicit connections between the communicative purposes and experiences young people detailed in the research findings and the formal requirements of the school-based syllabus directed tasks, in ways not unlike the authors of the chapters of this book suggest. While teachers used students experiences to expand English word banks containing adjectives and adverbs for descriptions and modal verbs for persuasive essays, they also developed multilingual word banks with the help of parents, school community members, and online bilingual resources and they began to employ translanguaging practices (García, 2014; see also Martínez et al., this volume).

This included writing multilingual texts and in two classes the inclusion of a bilingual reading program that involved parents and bilingual teachers in reading books in Korean, Tamil, Spanish, German, Hindi, and Chinese (see Naqvi et al. 2012). In one class, students were particularly captivated by a Hindi bilingual reading session, and with the support of a Hindi-speaking parent, the class wrote bilingual comics in English and Hindi. In a second class, students embarked on individual studies of languages across the world, researching the frequency of languages spoken and the places in which they were spoken in the world. This included, for example, research about Spanish, Arabic, and Urdu, and prompted rich discussions about migration and linguistic supremacy in Australia. In a third class, a bilingual book writing project was initiated. Parents, community members and teachers, and first-language partners in younger and older grades composed bilingual stories in multiple languages that were shared across the school. This task contributed to the purchase of additional bilingual books for the school library and the take-up of this program in other classes not originally involved in this project.

The dynamic *linguistic landscape* (Sayer, 2010) offered an additional teaching and learning space for focusing on multilingual and multimodal texts and meaning making. Supported by teacher aides and parent volunteers and using a blank street grid and mobile devices, such as tablets and digital cameras, students walked along the street observing and cataloguing language, images, signs and symbols along the street. Mapping revealed much about the linguistic landscape of the neighborhood: 14 languages were heard and eight of these could be identified by students. Somali was spoken by women in a hairdressing salon. English was the dominant written language, while some signs were written in Arabic and less frequently Chinese, but few people were heard speaking English. Discussing the ways languages and dialects were used locally led to discussions about the value of different languages and the place of English in Australia; discussion centered on whether street signs could or should be written in the communities' languages.

The linguistic landscape revealed much about the neighborhood and how practices and relationships were organized for their families and for different groups of people. Analyzing how the neighborhood had continued to grow and change revealed how the area historically was an important market place for Aboriginal people. Employing their full linguistic repertoire, young people interviewed parents, family members, friends, and cousins, asking about their knowledge and perceptions of the neighborhood. Applying their research skills, and math, geography, and history knowledge, they created audio-visual presentations and invited Elders, residents and families to a presentation of this work at the school assembly.

Learning About and With Young People

In all classes, teachers learned of young people's practices, and identities that they otherwise had no knowledge of. Before the project, teachers had been unaware of the range of languages spoken not only by students but by the wider school community. In two classes, teachers learned that several young people were Aboriginal. Discussion and critical reflection led to the interrogation and disruption of abstract or fixed versions of the linguistic and culturally situated practices of communities. Young people's transcultural and translingual competencies were foregrounded in lessons examining how language and literacies worked and shifted across and around practices, communities and countries and worked to achieve a widening range of purposes for a variety of audiences. Researching language and places in young people's local and global world generated authentic tasks that addressed valued school based outcomes across domains. The classroom and neighborhood became a rich, hybrid place in which to promote learning and thinking as well as for reflecting on identity, place, immigration, and belonging. Mathematical skills were employed in collecting and gathering data and in constructing, interpreting, and evaluating data displays that showcased linguistic, digital, and material worlds. Young people produced complex written texts such as persuasive essays and information reports that detailed the geography of places and the ways people interacted within their immediate environment.

These classes engaged in critical conversations about language and identity and for young people from immigrant and refugee communities in these classrooms, learning moved away from typically focusing on what was limited or lacking. Attention was paid to the positioning of young people as knowledge producers. Evidence suggests a noticeable shift occurred in the positioning of the teacher and I as the sole knowledge producers. Young people's initial ambivalence also began to shift in the foregrounding of their plural and dynamic practices and identities as outlined in these comments:

> I shared that language isn't just about speaking. It's about where people came from and it is their culture and a part of someone.
> I think every class should do this; it was awesome, I felt nervous and embarrassed at first, but I could answer all the questions and I used my language. I felt proud.
> J and Miss N were interested in our languages Miss N didn't know I translated. At first I hated doing the language diaries but it got fun and I talked about words and language stuff with my big brother and father and I always had something to talk about.

This work does not replace bilingual programs. In most mainstream classes, languages other than English are not central to curriculum work and they are not counted as measures of mainstream success. In many mainstream classes, students' foundation knowledges, skills, and experiences go unrecognized. In these classrooms, young people with diverse histories, languages, and trajectories came together as a learning community and this offered the potential for collective meaning making. However, more work needs to be done in drawing on the mobility of students and communities cultural, linguistic, and communicative resources. Many young people believed the class focus on languages other than English was temporary as realized in the following young people's comments:

> Yes teachers listened and I used my languages a bit in my writing, I like listening to my friends' languages, but we need to learn English better.
> We won't do it again I don't think, we did it just because we were researching.
> I can't use Vietnamese very well. I only need it at home, so it's not in the test so it doesn't matter.

Restrictive language polices subordinating the use of languages other than Australian English can cause young people to feel alienated from their teachers and from the classroom content they need to learn to feel successful. Academic benefits are associated with increased engagement and the use of languages can promote a deeper understanding of material. Enabling young people to present complex representations of who they are, and what they know and can do can is a first step in disrupting persistent and persuasive educational marginalization. Our goal of engaging young people as active participants in their teachers' learning and the promise that they might learn more about themselves, their communities and expertise they possessed needs more dedicated work.

The idea that home languages and practices could become a part of classroom learning and perhaps change what we do in classrooms needs much further consideration and attention. Young people were right to be skeptical about whether the knowledge they shared would be taken up in classrooms. There was a positive and significant change in individual classrooms in the take-up of translanguaging practices and the inclusion of multilingual material and literacies. However, in one school, policy mandated that English was the only language to be used in the playground. Students were put on detention if they used home languages at play; this playground surveillance sends a clear message about the value of English and the place of other languages in this setting. Disrupting rather than sustaining the monolingual classroom domain is crucial. The future is multilingual and multicultural and perpetuating and fostering a pluralist present and future (Paris & Alim, 2017) requires more dedicated work.

References

Australian Bureau of Statistic (2016). Cultural diversity: Who we are now. Retrieved from http://www.abs.gov.au/ausstats/abs@.nsf/Latestproducts/2024.0Main%20Features22016

Blommaert, J. (2010). *The sociolinguistics of globalization*. Cambridge: Cambridge University Press.

Bucholtz, M., Lopez, A., Mojarro, A., Skapoulli, E., VanderStouwe, C., & Warner-García, S. (2014). Sociolinguistic justice in the schools: Students researchers as linguistic experts. *Language and Linguistics Compass, 8*(4), 144–157.

Cummins, J. & Early, M. (Eds.) (2011). *Identity texts: The collaborative construction of power in multilingual schools*. Stoke-on-Trent: Trentham.

Cox, R. (2015). What language are you?' A glimpse into multilingual childhoods. *English in Australia, 50*(1), 49–54.

Delpit, L. D. (1988). The silenced dialogue: Power and pedagogy in educating other people's children. *Harvard Educational Review, 58*(3), 280–299.

D'warte, J. (forthcoming). Report: Enhancing English learning: Building on linguistic and cultural repertoires in 3 school settings. Sydney: Department of Education and Western Sydney University.

D'warte, J. (2018). Recognizing and leveraging the bilingual meaning making potential of young people aged 6-8 years old in one Australian classroom. *Journal of Early Childhood Literacy*, 1–31.

D'warte, J. (2016). Students as linguistic ethnographers: Super-diversity in the classroom context. In D. R. Cole & C. Woodrow (Eds). *Super dimensions in globalisation and education* (19–35). Amsterdam: Springer.

D'warte, J. (2014). Exploring linguistic repertoires: Multiple language use and multimodal activity in five classrooms. *Australian Journal of Language and Literacy, 37*(1), 21–30.

Eades, D. (2013). *Aboriginal ways of using English*. Canberra: Aboriginal Studies Press.

Edelson, D. C. (2002). Design research: What we learn when we engage in design. *The Journal of the Learning Sciences, 11*(1), 105–121.

Eisenchlas, S., Schalley, A., & Guillemin, D. (2015). Multilingualism and literacy—attitudes and policies. *International Journal of Multilingualism, 12*(2), 151–161.

French, M. (2016). Students' multilingual resources and policy-in-action: An Australian case study. *Language and Education, 30*(4), 298–316.

García, O. (2014). Multilingualism and language education. In Cl. Leung & B. V. Street (Eds.) *The Routledge companion to English studies* (84–99). New York: Routledge.

García, O. (2009) *Bilingual education in the 21st century: A global perspective*. Oxford: Wiley-Blackwell.

García, O. & Wei, L. (2014). *Translanguaging: Language, bilingualism and education*. New York: Palgrave Macmillan.

Gorski, P. C. (2011). Unlearning deficit ideology and the scornful gaze: Thoughts on authenticating the class discourse in education. *Counterpoints, 402*, 152–173.

Gutiérrez, K. & Rogoff, B. (2003). Cultural ways of learning: Individual traits or repertoires of practice. *Educational Researcher, 32* (5), 19–25.

Hamre, B. K. & Pianta, R. (2003). Early teacher–child relationships and the trajectory of children's school outcomes through eighth grade. *Childhood Development, 72*(2), 625–638.

Ladson-Billings, G. (1995). Toward a theory of culturally relevant pedagogy. *American Educational Research Journal, 32*(3), 465–491.

Ladson-Billings, G. (1994). *The dreamkeepers.* San Francisco: Jossey-Bass Publishing Co.

Lam, W. S. E. (2006). Culture and learning in the context of globalization: Research directions. *Review of Research in Education, 30*(1), 213–237.

Lee, D. C. (2017). An ecological framework for enacting culturally sustain pedagogy. In D. Paris & S. Alim, *Culturally sustaining pedagogies. Teaching and learning for justice in a changing world* (261–273). New York: Teachers College Press.

Lee, C. D. (2007) *Culture, literacy, and learning: Blooming in the midst of the whirlwind.* Amsterdam/New York: Teachers College Press.

Lee, C. D. (1995). A culturally based cognitive apprenticeship: Teaching African American high school students' skills in literary interpretation. *Reading Research Quarterly, 30,* 608–630.

Lucas, T. & Villegas, A. M. (2013). Preparing linguistically responsive teachers: Laying the foundation in pre-service teacher education. *Theory into Practice, 52*(2), 98–109.

Luke, A. (2011). Generalizing across borders: Policy and the limits of educational science. *Educational Researcher, 40,* 367–377.

Marshall, S. & Moore, D. (2016) Plurilingualism amid the panoply of lingualisms: Addressing critiques and misconceptions in education. *International Journal of Multilingualism, 15*(1), 19–34.

Moll, L., Amanti, C., Neff, D., & Gonzalez, N. (1992). Funds of knowledge for teaching: Using a qualitative approach to connect homes and classroom. *Theory Into Practice, 31* (2), 132–141.

Moll, L. C. & Gonzalez, N. E. (1994). Lessons from research with language-minority children. *Journal of Reading Behavior, 26*(4), 439–456.

Moore, D. & Gajo, L. (2009). French voices on plurilingualism and pluriculturalism: Theory, significance and perspectives. *International Journal of Multilingualism, 6*(2), 137–153.

Naqvi, R. (n.d.). *Dual language books project.* Retrieved from http://www.rahatnaqvi.ca/wordpress/

Naqvi, R., Thorne, K., Pfitscher, C., & McKeough, A. (2012). Dual language books as an emergent literacy resource: Culturally and linguistically responsive teaching and learning. *Journal of Early Childhood Literacy, 13*(4), 501–528.

Nieto, S. (1992). *Affirming diversity: The sociopolitical context of multicultural education.* New York: Longman.

Orellana, M. F. (2016). *Immigrant children in transcultural spaces: Language, learning, and love.* New York: Routledge.

Paris, D. (2012). Culturally sustaining pedagogy: A needed change in stance, terminology, and practice. *Educational Researcher, 41*(3), 93–97.

Paris, D. & Alim, S. (2017). *Culturally lsustaining pedagogies. Teaching and Learning for justice in a changing world.* New York: Teachers College Press.

Pennycook, A. (2010). *Language as a local practice.* London: Routledge.

Rampton, B., Maybin, J., & Roberts, C. (2014). Methodological foundations in linguistic ethnography. *Working Papers in Urban Language and Literacies* (Paper 125). London: King's College.

Riddle, S. (2018). Resisting educational inequity and the "bracketing out" of disadvantage in contemporary schooling. In S. Gannon, R. Hattam, & W. Sawyer (Eds.) *Resisting educational inequality* (17–30). New York: Routledge.

Ruiz, R. (1984). Orientations in language planning. *Bilingual Research Journal, 8*(2), 15–34.

Sayer, P. (2010). Using the linguistic landscape as a pedagogical resource. *ELT Journal, 64*(2), 143–154.

Vertovec, S. (2007). Super-diversity and its implications. *Ethnic and Racial Studies, 30*(6), 1024–1054.

Yosso, T. J. (2005). Whose culture has capital? A critical race theory discussion of community cultural wealth. *Race, Ethnicity and Education, 8*(1), 69–91.

13

LEVERAGING YOUTH CULTURAL DATA SETS FOR TEACHER LEARNING

Danny C. Martinez, Elizabeth Montaño, and Javier Rojo

At Willow High School (WHS),[1] an urban school in Los Angeles, Danny (the first author) conducted ethnographic research on Black and Latinx youth communication in English language arts (ELA) classrooms during the 2010–2011 academic year. The chatter of youth speaking to one another was regularly audible at WHS, in hallways, in outside gathering spaces, and, most important to this study, inside classrooms. Youth spoke about a range of topics: commiserating about assignments, debating conflicts among peers, debriefing parties, or discussing current events in the news. During that academic year, Danny documented youth using a range of communicative practices including Black languages, Spanish/English codeswitching, style shifting, and the use of mainstream varieties of English and Spanish to engage in meaning making with their peers and their teachers. While we have argued that Black and Latinx youth practices are evidence of their linguistic dexterity (Martinez & Montaño, 2016; Orellana et al., 2012), many youth perceived their practices as unremarkable, with several reporting that they wanted to learn how to "talk right." Youths' deficit rationales (Martínez, 2010) were shared with teachers who too often stigmatized and marked Black and Latinx youth as deficient.

Fast forward to the 2016–2018 academic years at Northern California High School (NCHS), a suburban school located in a racially and ethnically diverse community nestled between the Bay Area and Sacramento Capital region of California. At NCHS, our research team observed two ELA classrooms over two academic years, documenting how teachers treated the communicative practices of non-dominant youth as useful for learning. We began research at

---

1 Place names and the youth participant names are pseudonyms.

NCHS by collaborating with two teachers, Mr. Michelson and Mr. Alcordo, who were identified by their administrators as strong teachers seeking to do more with the linguistic diversity of youth they were experiencing in their classrooms. Both teachers were curious how their participation in research might strengthen their pedagogical practices. After a few months of observation, it was clear that NCHS youth, like the youth in the school Danny studied in Los Angeles, displayed a range of communicative practices, most of which highlighted the linguistic flexibility found throughout the community. However, like similar schools across the United States with large numbers of non-dominant youth, many teachers and leaders believed the communicative practices of youth needed to be fixed.

In this chapter, we share how our team was inspired by Carol Lee's (2007) *Cultural Modeling* tradition: specifically, her notion of youth cultural data sets as tools for non-dominant student learning. We extend her work to consider how youth cultural data sets can also facilitate teachers' exploration and learning about leveraging the communicative repertoires of Black and Latinx youth in schools in respectful and humanizing ways. We believe teachers must engage in learning experiences that allow them to reflect on what they are counting as language in their classrooms, and how their views about youth communication can become either affordances or constraints for non-dominant youths' full participation in content area learning.

Black and Latinx Languages in Society and Schools

Decades of research have now provided rich documentation of the languaging practices that Black (Alim, 2004; Goodwin, 1990; Smitherman, 2000), Latinx (Martínez, 2010; Orellana, 2009; Zentella, 1997; Ek, Martínez et al., Pacheco & Morales, Reynolds & Orellana, all this volume), Asian (Reyes & Lo, 2009), and Indigenous (McCarty, Romero-Little, & Zepeda, 2006) communities deploy as part of their communicative repertoires (Rymes, 2010). The multiple and varied communicative practices of non-dominant communities are often textured by the mixing and meshing of languages and the use of languages considered dialects and/or varieties, all of which are deployed by individuals to communicate meaningful messages with others. In school settings, the attitudes and beliefs toward non-dominant language (and their speakers) often conflict with research about language. One major belief is that standard or academic varieties of English are precursors for learning in schools (Franquiz & de la luz Reyes, 2000).

In an effort to disrupt the hegemony of English (Shannon, 1995), and patterns of teachers dismissing the communicative repertoires of non-dominant youth, scholars have argued for rethinking and reorganizing how language is treated in schools. It is often believed that racially and ethnically minoritized youth do not possess the appropriate linguistic skills to perform well on academic tasks in schools. While not all minoritized youth are speakers of "non-standard" languages, these groups are treated as needing to be fixed (Gutiérrez, Morales, & Martinez, 2009).

We look toward Lee's (2007) notion of Cultural Modeling as a framework that highlights the ingenuity of Black language and literacy practices. Rather than do away with the communicative practices of Black youth (as many curricular programs attempt), the Cultural Modeling framework treats these practices as powerful resources steeped in cultural ways of being, ripe for mapping onto subject specific domains. For example, Lee (2007) discusses mapping the Black language practice of *signifying* onto literary reasoning in the ELA learning context for Black youth.

Lee (2007) further argues that "Cultural Modeling is a framework for the design of learning environments that examines what youth know from everyday settings to support specific subject matter learning" (p. 15). Applied to minoritized communities, a Cultural Modeling framework treats diversity as a resource (Cole, 1996; Moll, 2000), leveraging cultural and communicative practices as part of everyday classroom learning. An important part of Cultural Modeling is that teachers must make clear to youth how their everyday knowledge and practices are useful for content area learning. This must be done explicitly by teachers who take youth tacit knowledge and provide language to name these phenomena. Lee (2007) reports how Black youth in her classes were experts at signifying; however, they had never heard of the term signifying, or many other terms used to describe their discursive prowess.

Here we draw on the Cultural Modeling framework to highlight for teachers how Black and Latinx youth engage in a range of communicative practices that are important to consider as pedagogical strengths. While the research presented here does not take up all the tenets of Lee's Cultural Modeling framework, we are interested in how the everyday experiences of minoritized youth in classrooms, ethnographically captured through fieldnotes, audio- and videorecordings, can serve as cultural data sets for teacher learning. Lee (2007) states that cultural data sets "represent practices and knowledge that schools not only devalue, but which schools have historically viewed as detrimental to academic progress" (p. 58). In our more recent research at NCHS, we were interested in teachers' thinking about and reflecting on youth classroom practices that may be viewed as either valuable or unfavorable for learning. While we observed NCHS participating teachers treating language more expansively than Danny found at WHS, there were still questions about what to do within everyday moment-to-moment interactions. Therefore, exploring youth data sets within classrooms was a welcomed and generative use of data that could mediate discussions among teachers.

Finally, we were interested in the ways that the Cultural Modeling framework treated the everyday tacit knowledge of youth, particularly historically marginalized youth. Lee (2007) argues that youth cultural knowledge must be leveraged in ways that are synonymous with subject-specific domains. In the Cultural Modeling tradition cultural data sets are crucial for understanding youth experiences, as well as their cultural and communicative practices. In this chapter, we are using data that represents youth cultural and linguistic practices within classrooms as generative tools for teacher learning experiences.

Leveraging Communicative Repertoires for Classroom Learning

Readers may note that we use the term "leveraging" in this chapter. In language and literacy research, leveraging often means to *build on, draw on,* or *use* the cultural and communicative practices of children and youth in classrooms as resources for learning. However, researchers vary with respect to the purpose of leveraging these practices: some see the goal as simply getting students to the seemingly more prestigious language practices that are valued in school (Martinez, Morales, & Aldana, 2017). We have argued for a more transformative definition of leveraging where the home and community languages of non-dominant children and youth are supported, privileged, and used dynamically in classrooms via spoken and written texts provided by teachers (Martinez et al., 2017). We also believe that these communicative texts should be familiar to youth, used by them within everyday communicative activities. This notion of leveraging is particularly important as it forefronts and makes clear how historically non-dominant children and youth are treated as intellectually inferior based on flawed myths about that their language practices. While leveraging students' communicative practices has been an ongoing call for teachers of linguistically diverse youth, this is not an easy task.

When we bring the idea of "leveraging" to classrooms, we are asking teachers to view and treat the communicative resources that children and youth already possess as powerful and useful for learning. In some cases, this has meant that teachers use the home communicative practices of students to access "academic" and "standard" varieties of English. However, we want to step back to consider what this means for non-dominant children, youth, and families in our schools. From our perspective, leveraging the "less desirable" communicative practices of non-dominant children and youth to access "better" language does not translate into a productive approach to instruction. Rather than making clear to linguistically diverse youth that their home and community languages are worthwhile for learning, it marks these practices as inferior. Unfortunately, some scholars and practitioners have taken this approach to leveraging.

Instead, we want to think about ways to move leveraging in the direction of "leveling" (Zisselsberger, 2016), that is, raising the prestige and status of the communicative practices of non-dominant children and youth to be on par with those considered "powerful" language and literacy practices. This move is central for non-dominant students to begin understanding and making sense of how their home and community practices are powerful, important and lucrative in our increasingly diverse society where individuals don't speak in one "standard" or "academic" way across their everyday practices (Alim & Smitherman, 2012; see also Martínez et al., this volume).

We know from the research that non-dominant children and youth enter classrooms with rich cultural funds of knowledge learned from their families and communities (Moll et al., 1992), robust literacy practices (Gutiérrez, 2008; Lee, 2007; Orellana & Reynolds, 2008), and expansive communicative repertoires (Alim, 2004; Martínez, 2010; Orellana et al., 2012; Paris, 2011; Zentella, 1997). We also know that human communication is imperative to learning (Cole, 1996) and human development (Rogoff, 2003) across the lifespan. For teachers, this is a reminder that students must have opportunities to speak to one another in classrooms to fully internalize ideas and concepts they are expected to know. It is also critical that teachers remember that the home and community languages of youth should not be stigmatized in classrooms. In fact, these languages should be utilized in meaningful ways to encourage learning.

Many pre- and in-service teachers we speak with *want* to leverage the home and community language and literacy practice of their students, but often feel discouraged by too few examples of what this looks like and larger demands to provide students with access to standard or academic varieties of English. It is also not always clear just *how* leveraging home and community languages will encourage disciplinary competencies. To mitigate these concerns, we focus on how to *notice* moments in classroom interactions where leveraging youth communicative repertoires takes place, or not. We show how we used audio and video recordings captured in diverse ELA classrooms from previous research at WHS with teachers in at NCHS.

We were inspired to create this kind of space for teacher learning after consulting the work of math education scholars who discussed videos of classroom instruction with teachers in "video club" working group meetings. During video clubs teachers watched themselves and their colleagues deliver instruction (Sherin & Han, 2004). After viewing, teachers and researchers participated in focused conversations about instruction and student learning. Sherin and Han (2004) report positive outcomes for teachers whose attention shifted from discussing what *teachers* were doing in the video clips to what students were *learning*. Teachers began shifting their instruction based on video club conversations in order to enhance student learning. We draw on this important work to consider how ELA teachers respond to viewing and listening to clips, or youth cultural data sets, of student talk in ELA classrooms. We feature one meeting of teachers that we called the Leveraging Language Working Group (LLWG) where NCHS teachers explored youth cultural data sets from WHS to reflect and discuss what they might do given the tensions explored in the video clips presented.

The Importance of Teacher Learning and Reflection

Too often professional development experiences are treated as activities for teacher learning. However, during professional development little time and effort is given to measure teacher learning. Also missing are opportunities for teachers to reflect on their own teaching practices, or those of their peers, or other actual teachers in practice (Borko, 2004; Kennedy, 2016). From our own experiences as teachers and researchers within schools, we know that PD opportunities often feel forced and decontextualized from the realities of teaching (see Kennedy, 2016, for supporting arguments). In thinking about larger policies and what we know about human learning, we sought to provide teachers with learning steeped in real classroom experiences. By providing our participating teachers with access to video clips of actual ELA teachers, we created opportunities to reflect on their own teaching practices, imagine moves they might make in similar circumstances, and shift practices they *notice* as problematic based on their own reflections, and those of their peers.

Below we highlight youth cultural data sets from two Latino students and their interactions with their Latina teacher at WHS in Los Angeles. Given the lack of attention to actual data of classroom interactions in PD for teachers, this work seeks to provide teachers with time to engage in the intellectual work of teaching by being in conversation and debate around teaching practices. Our ultimate goal in the larger project is to document teacher changes over time as they engage in varied practices to support the leveraging of students' communicative repertoires. *For this paper we ask, how can data sets for classroom interactions generated from Black and Latina/o/x youth's talk support teacher learning?*

Northern California High School

The Leveraging Language Working Group took place at Northern California High School (NCHS), a suburban school nestled between the San Francisco Bay Area and the Sacramento Capital area. NCHS is touted as one of the most diverse high schools in the state of California with racial and ethnic groups demographics that consist of 29.7% Black, 27.3% Latinx, and 24.9% Filipino. This was followed by 6% white, 3% Asian, 2% Pacific Islander, less than 1% Native American, and 2% of youth who identify as mixed race. While the diversity of this school is often celebrated, community members, educators, and politicians recognize the great injustices affecting the educational lives of NCHS youth. NCHS appears to be a well-funded school sitting at the base of several rolling hills surrounded by multilevel single-family homes on hilltops, but we quickly learned that the views that the teachers enjoy differs from the reality that many youth experience. Many of the youth who attend NCHS travel from surrounding lower income neighborhoods. Few of the youth who actually live in the neighborhood surrounding the school attend NCHS. This context is important given the larger narratives about youth who attend NCHS, most of whom are Black, Latinx, and Filipino, youth who are often racialized by their skin color and communicative practices.

Our Teachers

Mr. Michelson, who identified as white, was a first-year teacher at the time of our study. Mr. Alcordo, who identified as Filipino, was in his fourth year as a teacher during the study. Both volunteered as participants in the larger project because they wanted to learn more ways of supporting their linguistically diverse youth and they were interested in being a part of the research team based on their own teaching. Both exhibited a keen awareness of the diversity in their students' communicative practices and wanted to consider how to use these practices more productively in their instruction. Based on our own observations, we believe Mr. Michelson and Mr. Alcordo engaged in practices that *expanded* what counted as language in their classrooms. They regularly leveraged the communicative practices of youth, yet they still exhibited practices that could be refined.

Leveraging Language Working Group

This LLWG was organized by the research team and with Mr. Michelson and Mr. Alcordo who then invited other teachers in their department. In total, we had five teachers who sat in a U shape facing a screen where an LCD projector was set up to display video clips, and audio speakers to listen to the interactions. Danny facilitated the working group, Elizabeth took notes, and while Javier was absent from the interaction, he provided fieldnotes from prior observations along with transcripts from the interaction.

The working group meeting was held during a lunch period in Mr. Michelson's classroom. During our meeting we introduced teachers to data sets by explaining to them that each of these pieces of data came from actual classrooms. We wanted to know from these participants: "What would you do if this was your classroom?" For some clips, we stopped at certain points where we wanted teachers to discuss what they would do, We would then follow up by playing the entire clip to see if their reactions lined up, or not, with the actual interaction. We would then ask: "How do you feel about the teacher's response?" "How might have you responded?" With these questions we sought to have teachers 1) consider the importance of moment-to-moment decision making, 2) understand the repercussions of such moment-to-moment discursive decisions that teachers make in their uptake of youth voices, and 3) reflect and reimagine the possibilities of leveraging youth voices in their own classrooms.

Generating Youth Cultural Data Sets for Teacher Learning

In the Cultural Modeling tradition, the research team observed and wrote fieldnotes about teaching interactions with attention to the cultural and communicative practices of youth at NCHS, and their teachers, within two ELA classrooms during the 2016–2017 academic year. We found that Black, Latinx, Filipino and other youth at NCHS displayed a range of communicative skills that were often described as "slang," "dialects," or "youth language" by youth and their teachers. The communicative practices were similar to those documented by Martinez (2017) and Paris (2011) where Black languages were prominent across racial and ethnic groups, code- and style shifting regularly deployed, and linguistic dexterity normalized within youth groups. We also found that both teachers, in varying ways, leveraged the diverse cultural and communicative practices of youth in their teaching by using text (written and digital) that featured non-dominant discourse practices, and often taking up the "language of students" themselves during instructional practices. These practices run counter to practices documented by Danny in previous research. Therefore, based on observations of Mr. Michelson and Mr. Alcordo, we argue that both teachers have expansive notions of what *counts* as language for learning in the ELA learning context.

After classrooms observations, teachers often reported not feeling confident about something they said during class, how they addressed certain youth contributions, or general uneasiness with an instructional decision. Many of these moments of uncertainty were related to tensions felt by teachers when youth language intersected with expectations within the ELA learning context (e.g., that youth would use academic or standard varieties of English in order to display proficiency). After consultation with the whole research team, we believed the youth cultural data sets from WHS could help mediate conversation and reflection experienced by our participating teachers.

WHS Cultural Data Sets

The data presented during the LLWG at NCHS come from Danny's ethnographic research documenting Black and Latinx youth communication at WHS during the 2010–2011 academic year. The clip shared with NCHS teachers explores Ms. Luz's classroom when she was speaking to her entire class. The clip also highlights two Latino youth in her class. While we do believe that youth cultural data sets from the NCHS contexts could have provided more meaningful conversations because teachers were familiar with the teacher, students, and even instructional plans, the WHS youth cultural data sets provided a foundation for engaging in conversation. We hope that data from WHS presented in this chapter can illuminate ways that youth cultural data sets can become generative for teachers.

Cultural Data Sets for Teacher Learning

In the following section, we highlight reactions to one cultural data set from WHS that represents a moment where youth were asked to respond to a known answer question, a question that may be considered to have a single "appropriate" answer. For example, the following question asked by a teacher would have fixed "known" answer: What are the names of the dueling families in Romeo and Juliet? The known answer would be the Capulets and the Montagues. When a student's answer deviates from the known answer question, a disruption occurs and teachers can evaluate the response as incorrect. While known answer questions are fairly typical in classroom instruction, researchers have found these questions to be less productive than open-ended questions since they simply require students to regurgitate facts rather than to discuss, debate, or interpret information (Rymes, 2010). Below, we will first highlight both participating teachers responding to a cultural data set from the WHS data corpus.

"He Was Shanked"

We wanted to know how teachers might respond when presented with youth communication that deviated from standard or academic varieties privileged in the ELA classroom. The following transcript highlights Ms. Luz's tenth grade ELA classroom at WHS after reading Act III, scene I of *Julius Caesar*, the scene where Brutus gathers his men to assassinate Caesar. In the transcript below, Ms. Luz asked her students to consider what Caesar might be thinking, and what he would say to his attackers. This clip also highlights a known answer question being deployed by Ms. Luz. Last, we believe this clip demonstrates how youth communication can have a powerful role in discussions about literature, if teachers are receptive. As we played the clip to NCHS teachers we stopped the audio after line 9, and line 20, and asked teachers what they might do if they were the teacher in the interaction.

Classroom Data Set 1A: He was shanked!

1.	Ms. Luz:	Ce-sar trus:te:d (0.5) Bru:tus:
2.		And in fact?
3.		When he's stabbed?
4.		By all these men~right?
5.		He's jumped right?
6.	Jordy:	He was:[
7.	Ms. Luz:	[And he's stabbed by all these men?
8.		[Girls: shh:
9.	Jordy:	[he was sh:anked
		(Break in audio for LLWG)

In the first nine lines, Ms. Luz began reviewing the act and scene where Caesar was assassinated. We stopped the clip after Jordy exclaimed "he was sh: anked" in line 9. We then asked teachers to reflect on what they heard in this clip and to consider what *they* would do next if they were the teacher.

Teachers immediately laughed and endorsed Jordy's utterance in line 9, with Mr. Alcordo stating, "Caesar *was* shanked." In their alignment with Jordy, teachers focused on the accuracy of the word "shanked" to describe how Julius Caesar was assassinated. Mr. Michelson was the first to state that Jordy's utterance should be treated as a contribution to the ongoing discussion, pointing to the specific connotation of the term "shanked" and why Jordy used this term. He stated:

> I think that even shanked also comes with a different connotation, it comes with context. So someone being shanked can be a different thing than someone being stabbed. There's a whole picture painted with the idea of shanked … it adds to the reading that this student was doing.

Here, Mr. Michelson is making sense of how Jordy's utterance provides context to the scene in which Caesar was attacked. He is also acknowledging that "shanked" can mean something similar to, yet different from, stabbed. While he does not explain what these differences are, his colleagues nod in agreement. Mr. Michelson continues: "There's a whole picture painted with the idea of shanked," arguing that "shanked" captures and adds to the dramatic assassination of Julius Caesar. Finally, Mr. Michelson ends his initial statement by recognizing that Jordy is engaging in a "reading" of *Julius Caesar*. In fact, all participants agreed that Jordy's reading of the scene was rich, and potentially an anchor for youth to connect based on scenes from films.

Mr. Alcordo added to this line of thinking by distinguishing how Jordy's contribution of "shanked" is a much more colorful explanation for the action. He explained that saying "shanked" paints "a whole picture" of the event, echoing Mr. Michelson's statement. Interestingly, Mr. Alcordo adds to the conversation by arguing that the use of the word "shanked" connotes that the actions of Brutus and his allies were, "pre-meditated … yeah so it adds to the reading that the student is doing. So yeah, he was [shanked]." Here, there is agency granted to Jordy for producing a reading that not only sets a colorful and dramatic scene, but also complicates his three-word contribution by saturating its meaning.

After these contributions, both teachers began to take up one of the initial questions: What would you do if you were the teacher? First, they both agreed on acknowledging Jordy for his contribution. Mr. Michelson shared that he would make sure to highlight "shanked" for the entire class through various "in the moment" activities like adding "shanked" to a word wall, asking other students to define the word, asking Jordy to find the origins of the word through a quick online search, or creating a larger activity where students rewrite this scene using updated language. Mr. Alcordo agreed with this list of activities and simply noted how perhaps he would not spend so much time on this, but he would definitely acknowledge the contribution without stigmatizing the use of the word as "non-standard" or "not academic English." Ultimately, for Mr. Michelson and Mr. Alcordo, "shanked" made sense, contextually and instructionally. We argue that the expansive understanding of language that we had already observed permitted Mr. Alcordo and Mr. Michelson to imagine an interaction where the word "shank" could mediate the understanding of a literary text.

"I'm from the Projects"

After conversation about transcript 1A ended, teachers wanted to know how Ms. Luz responded to Jordy. Prior to beginning this clip we provided teachers with context about the WHS, particularly that the school was surrounded by three housing projects, one of which shared a gate with WHS.

Classroom Data Set 1B: I'm from the projects

10.	Ms L:	(2.0) Alright so when he's stabbed by all these men?
11.		Isn't it a fact that
12.		He only reacts to his best friend?
13.		The last guy to stab 'em?
14.		The rest he's more in sho:ck
15.		And just like trying to control his pain:
16.		°Or bleeding~or ~something.
17.		But when his best friend stabbed him?
18.		what does he say to him.
19.	Henry:	I'm from the project[s.
20.	Miguel:	[°Et tu Brute
21.	Class:	((laughter))
		((Break in audio for LLWG))
22.	Ms L:	He does not say I'm from the projects Henry?

After hearing the clip, both teachers reported being disappointed that Jordy's comment was ignored. Both Mr. Michelson and Mr. Alcordo believed there was a missed opportunity to build on Jordy's contribution, and, more explicitly, the language he and other youth could bring into the classroom to make discussions more engaging, colorful, and meaningful. Mr. Alcordo believed that Ms. Luz overlooked an opportunity to use "the kids' momentum to get them more involved" in further discussion, particularly to move away from simply answering questions, his own critique of her use of a known-answer-question. Mr. Michelson, however, did reflect on his feelings of disappointment and looked closer at the previous transcript 1A. He articulated his understanding that Ms. Luz had only a "split" second between Jordy's utterance and her own utterance toward a female student in the classroom. "He's [Jordy] saying it, as noted by the way it's written, like she's going girls sh:" Mr. Michelson's statement gets nods from the teachers, particularly when he states how he could "totally" see himself missing out on a similar opportunity.

These statements were particularly interesting, since we had already documented, ethnographically, how both Mr. Alcordo and Mr. Michelson consistently drew on youth contributions that were not uttered in so-called "academic" or "standard" varieties of English. An example is when Mr. Alcordo asked a student in his class to predict what Romeo and Juliet might be about, an opening prompt that garnered various predictions. A Black female student in his class simply stated, "they beefin'" to which Mr. Alcordo replied, "Yup, there's beef of some sort." Mr. Michelson in another observation uttered language closely aligned to youth when after hearing the word "slap" by a student several times, he took up this word during classroom instructions, letting students know, "you may also slap" while working on assignments. Here "slap" meant to listen to music and hang out. The initial disappointment we witnessed by both teachers seemed to signal their commitments to supporting and elevating youth language, but there was also a sense of tension when Mr. Michelson realized how teachers could not be accountable for leveraging, or building on, every youth utterance.

The remainder of the conversation was devoted to the final stretch of the interaction. Both Mr. Alcordo and Mr. Michelson immediately predicted that Ms. Luz would reject Henry's response to her question in line 19: "But when his best friend (Brutus) stabbed him (Caesar), what does he say to him?" When the clip was played, their assumptions were correct. Henry's response "I'm from the projects" was met with: "He does not say I'm from the projects Henry." Mr. Alcordo and Mr. Michelson expressed disappointment, again, about another missed opportunity for leveraging youth talk, or ideas, within this interaction. There was uncomfortable laughter and hand rubbing on foreheads when they heard Ms. Luz's response to Henry. Mr. Alcordo stated that perhaps Henry was attempting to relate this interaction to his life noting that some youth have close experiences having witnessed or having been a victim of violence. There were some nods here, however, Mr. Michelson interjected as soon as there was an opportunity to enter the discussion ready to think about what he would do if he were the teacher.

Mr. Michelson was the only person to acknowledge Henry's contribution could have been a joke. He stated:

I really can see myself honestly reacting, thinking that he's answering my question "what does he say to him" by joking and saying "I'm from the projects" … and I can imagine myself saying, "He says I'm from the projects?" (rising intonation at the end). And, I can just see myself reacting in that way.

Here, Mr. Michelson again is imagining himself within the discursive interaction, playing out the possibilities. This comment captures how youth do joke, and that Henry could have been joking around. His peers definitely had a laugh after his statement. And perhaps, given the research on youths' verbal dexterity, Henry could have been exercising his skills. It's interesting, however, that in Mr. Michelson's performance of what he would do, he never rejected the notion that Caesar would say "I'm from the projects" as proposed by Henry. Mr. Michelson stated: "I can imagine myself saying, 'He says I'm from the projects?'" The rising intonation at the end of his utterance here left room for a response.

Mr. Michelson elaborated on his contribution with the following:

I kind of think that this, plus an addendum, might work really well. He doesn't say, "I'm from the projects," but what are we saying here? What do we mean by that? This is not answering my question but what is this entering into the conversation? The addendum allows that voice to still be heard.

Again, Mr. Michelson is performing his response out loud with his contribution. He articulated that he would still leave room for Henry to have an opportunity to make meaning about his statement, "I'm from the projects." Ultimately, Henry, who was a quick-witted youth, could have been doing many things with his comment: attempting to get a laugh from his peers, working to frustrate Ms. Luz, and/or make an honest contribution. While we cannot know exactly what Henry's purpose was, Mr. Michelson and Mr. Alcordo argued that there was, in fact, a missed opportunity to build on youth ideas.

At the conclusion of this first LLWG meeting, there was a buzz of excitement from teachers who participated. Mr. Michelson and Mr. Alcordo noted that watching videos and hearing audio from real teachers was a new experience for them. Mr. Michelson commented that after having recently completed the Performance Assessment for California Teachers (PACT), which requires teachers to film their instruction, he missed the opportunity to use video for reflection. Both teachers also shared that while being videorecorded seemed intimidating, they could see the potential for collegial reflection through conversation mediated by videos of instruction. As a research team, we were excited and motivated by teacher responses to our first LLWG and particularly honored to have both Mr. Michelson and Mr. Alcordo agree to more documentation of their teaching via audio- and videorecording.

Days after our focus group Mr. Michelson referenced a specific part of the WHS clip and made connections to interactions he experienced within his own classroom. He also shared that he thought about how he used language more closely since reviewing the youth cultural data sets presented. At the beginning of one of our follow-up observations, Mr. Michelson told Danny: "I think about language all the time!" He noted that he was a bit more careful about how he was responding to students, particularly when youth communicative practices did not mirror standard varieties of English. Both teachers would often tell the research team how they wish we could have documented an interaction because of the language used by youth, and how they took up the contribution in the service of learning. Both teachers were also a bit hard on themselves when they said that they believed they did not leverage youth communication in the most meaningful ways. For example, Mr. Michelson would quickly reflect with a research team member after observations saying things such as: "I should have said ..." or "I did not react well to ..." Mr. Alcordo continued to reflect on how he did not allow youth in his own class to talk enough in authentic ways.

We took these moments of reflection as powerful experiences for both teachers. We also concluded that both teachers were ready to have their own practices on display for their own colleagues. This is where our future work is headed, capturing youth cultural data sets from Mr. Michelson and Mr. Alcordo's classroom to then display short video clips to colleagues.

Researcher Reflections and Future Research

After concluding our first LLWG meeting, we believed that we were on to something with teachers. Teachers were excited about talking about youth communicative practices within real classroom instruction. They were noticing moments that were potentially rich, yet disappointedly ignored within classroom interactions. Our researcher and teacher partnerships were growing in ways that seemed to facilitate teacher learning in new ways. While we cannot claim that teachers made dramatic changes in their classroom talk after a single LLWG meeting, we can say that teachers showed a clear commitment to taking up and leveraging youth language. Over time, we saw them choose more texts that reflected youth communicative practices, such as YouTube videos produced by local poets and musicians. Even when canonical texts were used, supplemental texts were included to attend to the diverse languages of youth. Both teachers spoke more about hearing different languages, and about responding to these varying languages instructionally. One of the most interesting shifts became visible in both teachers' classrooms and we observed both engaging in style and codes-witching themselves during instruction.

Subsequent Observations

After the LLWG meeting, we noted a few shifts in Mr. Alcordo's and Mr. Michelson's practices. We observed, and Mr. also Alcordo noticed, his own closer attention to youth communicative practices in his classroom. There was also an increase in his use youth communicative practices within his own communicative practices and in the selection of texts, which included voices not aligned traditional standard varieties of English. After our meeting, we continued observing and began video recorded Mr. Michelson's teaching. We documented him using a range of texts, a variety of culminating tasks, and multiple modes of presenting instruction. We also observed him "constraining" himself as a way to not interrupt youth meaning making practices. In subsequent interviews, he noted that, participating in LLWG meetings, he realized teachers always seem to want the last word. Therefore, he became conscious of how in the ELA learning, youth must learn to engage in conversations with one another without seeking approval from the teacher. He noted that traditionally, he wanted students to get that approval from him. He later realized that his approval process simply stumped the "somewhat" natural conversations that were happening in his classroom.

Conclusion

Lee's (2007) notion of cultural data sets makes clear that non-dominant youths' everyday practices are rich, dynamic, and meaningful. To this end, we were cognizant that teachers, even those who share racial and/or ethnic, and linguistic backgrounds with youth, may not fully understand the cultural and communicative repertoires that youth are engaged with at a specific time and space. Youth cultural data sets offered one way that classroom practices could be reflected on by teachers, particularly as they showcased actual teaching interactions. While there was no personal connection to Jordy, Henry, or Ms. Luz from WHS, the teachers at NCHS, Mr. Alcordo and Mr. Michelson specifically, shared the collective experience of "doing" school. Mr. Michelson and Mr. Alcordo knew of the participation frameworks displayed in the clips, and understood how youth and teacher discourse practices could collide into awkward teaching moments. Yet, within our short LLWG meeting, teachers were able to grapple with tension-filled interactions (*He was shanked* and *I'm from the projects*), and imagine what they might have done. The LLWG was the first step toward preparing teachers to watch youth in classrooms engage in interactions that might not always be sanctioned in the ELA classroom because of communicative or meaning-making differences that do not align with literacy learning ideals of traditional classrooms.

As former teachers, our research team understood the complexity of classroom discourse, the dynamic nature of youth language, and the challenge teachers face when held accountable for the uptake of each youth's utterance. The classroom data set presented in this chapter offer a few examples of many that were used with teachers. What we offer here is acknowledgement that ELA classrooms must be interrogated using various methods that move us away from the constraining experiences of schooling, where youth are expected to check their communicative practices at the door. Rather, we believe providing teachers with opportunities to reflect on and explore "what they would do" allows for a future oriented approach to their development.

References

Alim, H. S. (2004). *You know my steez: An ethnographic and sociolinguistic study of styleshifting in a Black American speech community.* Durham, NC: Duke University Press.

Alim, H. S. & Smitherman, G. (2012). *Articulate while Black: Barack Obama, language, and race in the US.* New York: Oxford University Press.

Borko, H. (2004). Professional development and teacher learning: Mapping the terrain. *Educational Researcher, 33*(8), 3–15.

Cole, M. (1996). *Cultural psychology: A once and future discipline.* Cambridge, MA: Harvard University Press.

Franquiz, M. E. & de la Luz Reyes, M. (1998). Creating inclusive learning communities through English language arts: From chanclas to canicas. *Language Arts, 75*(4), 211–220.

Goodwin, M. H. (1990). *He-said-she-said: Talk as social organization among black children.* Bloomington, IN: Indiana University Press.

Gutiérrez, K. D. (2008). Developing a sociocritical literacy in the third space. *Reading Research Quarterly, 43*(2), 148–164.

Gutiérrez, K. D., Morales, P. Z., & Martinez, D. C. (2009). Re-mediating literacy: Culture, difference, and learning for students from nondominant communities. *Review of Research in Education, 33*(1), 212–245.

Kennedy, M. M. (2016). How does professional development improve teaching? *Review of Educational Research, 86*(4), 945–980.

Lee, C. D. (2007). *Culture, literacy, & learning: Taking bloom in the midst of the whirlwind.* New York: Teachers College Press

Martinez, D. C. (2017). Emerging critical meta-awareness among Black and Latina/o youth during corrective feedback practices in urban English language arts classrooms. *Urban Education, 52*(5), 637–666.

Martinez, D. C. & Montaño, E. (2016). Toward expanding what counts as language for Latina and Latino youth in an urban middle school classroom. *Literacy Research: Theory, Method, and Practice, 65*(1), 200–216.

Martinez, D. C., Morales, P. Z., & Aldana, U. S. (2017). Leveraging students' communicative repertoires as a tool for equitable learning. *Review of Research in Education, 41*(1), 477–499.

Martínez, R. A. (2010). "Spanglish" as literacy tool: Toward an understanding of the potential role of Spanish–English code-switching in the development of academic literacy. *Research in the Teaching of English, 45*(2), 124–149.

McCarty, T. L., Romero-Little, M. E., & Zepeda, O. (2006). Native American youth discourses on language shift and retention: Ideological cross-currents and their implications for language planning. *International Journal of Bilingual Education and Bilingualism, 9*(5), 659–677.

Moll, L. C. (2000). Inspired by Vygotsky: Ethnographic experiments in Education. In C. D. Lee & P. Smagorinsky (Eds.) *Vygotskian perspectives on literacy research: Constructing meaning through collaborative inquiry*. Cambridge: Cambridge University Press.

Moll, L. C., Amanti, C., Neff, D., & Gonzalez, N. (1992). Funds of knowledge for teaching: Using a qualitative approach to connect homes and classrooms. *Theory Into Practice, 31*(2), 132–141.

Orellana, M. F. (2009). *Translating childhoods: Immigrant youth, language, and culture*. New Brunswick, NJ: Rutgers University Press.

Orellana, M. F., Martinez, D. C., Lee, C. H., & Montaño, E. (2012). Language as a tool in diverse forms of learning. *Linguistics and Education, 23*(4), 373–387.

Orellana, M. F. & Reynolds, J. (2008). Cultural modeling: Leveraging bilingual skills for school paraphrasing tasks. *Reading Research Quarterly, 43*(1), 48–65.

Paris, D. (2011). *Language across difference: Ethnicity, communication, and youth identities in changing urban schools*: Cambridge: Cambridge University Press.

Reyes, A. & Lo, A. (Eds.) (2009). *Beyond yellow English: Toward a linguistic anthropology of Asian Pacific America*. Cambridge: Oxford University Press.

Rogoff, B. (2003). *The cultural nature of human development*. Oxford: Oxford University Press.

Rymes, B. (2015). *Classroom discourse analysis: A tool for critical reflection*. New York: Routledge.

Rymes, B. (2010). Classroom discourse analysis: A focus on communicative repertoires. In N. Hornberger & S. McKay (Eds.) *Sociolinguistics and language education* (528–548). London, England: Multilingual Matters.

Shannon, S. (1995). The hegemony of English: A case study of one bilingual classroom as a site of resistance. *Linguistics and Education, 7*, 177–200.

Sherin, M. G. & Han, S. Y. (2004). Teacher learning in the context of a video club. *Teaching and Teacher Education, 20*(2), 163–183.

Smitherman, G. (2000). *Talkin that talk: Language, culture, and education in African America*. New York: Routledge.

Zentella, A. C. (1997). *Growing up bilingual: Puerto Rican children in New York*. Malden, MA: Blackwell Publishers.

Zisselsberger, M. (2016). Toward a humanizing pedagogy: Leveling the cultural and linguistic capital in a fifth-grade writing classroom. *Bilingual Research Journal, 39*(2), 121–137.

DON'T BELIEVE THE HYPE: REALITY RULES

Carol D. Lee

Language and Cultural Practices in Communities and School: Bridging Learning for Students from Non-Dominant Groups is a powerful volume in its breadth: the range of contexts examined, of cultural communities explored, of disciplinary learning and policy contexts interrogated. The chapters build generatively on frameworks that individually and collectively have pushed our thinking about relations between knowledge constructed in everyday contexts and knowledge examined in the contexts of schooling: culturally responsive pedagogy (Ladson-Billings, 1995), funds of knowledge (Gonzalez, Moll, & Amanti, 2004), translanguaging (García & Wei, 2014; Orellana, 2009), learning through observation and pitching in (Rogoff et al., 2003), culturally sustaining pedagogy (Paris & Alim, 2014), and Cultural Modeling (Lee, 1995a, 2007). Prior research and studies reported in this volume built on these frameworks have empirically demonstrated the affordances of understanding and building on everyday knowledge. At the same time, there are several persistent challenges that these research paradigms have faced. Typically, the work is not conducted at scale; there are not systemic supports in terms of assessments, commercially available curricula, accountability standards, or teacher preparation and professional development that would facilitate uptake at scale; and there remain persistent metanarratives and hegemonic ideologies that warrant claims about hierarchies of knowledge and hierarchies of language uses. In this afterword, I want to tackle this last set of challenges because I believe these ideologies sustain the other challenges around scale, practice, and policy. Thus the chapter's title: "Don't Believe the Hype."

I want to start by interrogating our use of the term "non-dominant groups." This term typically is used to classify groups of people, often within nation states, who are disproportionately discriminated against based on attributions having to do with ascribed statuses – race, ethnicity, first- or second-generation immigrant, economic class status, competence with a version of a national language, religious minority, gender and/or sexual identity and orientation, or presumptions around conceptions of ability (Lee, 2009). There is no question that across nation states you will find explicit discrimination based on some version of these social categories, although recognizing the differences in their manifestations and differences in the structures that either support or resist them is useful in our thinking (Darling-Hammond, 2010; OECD, 2010). At the same time, I think it is safe to say there are no periods in human history in which persons in any of these disenfranchised communities have not engaged in active resistance; and over time that active resistance has shifted relations of power. Certainly, in the United States, virtually all of our advances around political rights for all of these groups have been deeply and directly influenced by the organized resistance in these communities. So to influence and counter warrants underlying these hegemonic ideologies, it might be useful for us to rethink our own language around difference.

A second conundrum that persists is our debates around everyday knowledge and its implications for learning in disciplines. Everyday knowledge is situated in practice and language. Hegemonic ideologies typically construct deficit ascriptions to both these practices and ways of using language when situated in minority communities. One fascinating fact about languages is how they travel across space and time, and the diverse ways in which through historical and cultural interactions among peoples, languages shift, including the ways in which so many communities across the world are indeed multilingual across many dimensions (Collins, Slembrouck, & Baynham, 2009; Pinker, 2007; Stavans, 2004; Wolfram, 1981). Let's take the U.S. for example. How many cities, towns, and waterways have been or are derived from indigenous languages? In how many cities will you find a Chinatown? In Chicago, where I'm from, we have neighborhoods in which you'd think you were in India, Greece, Italy, Poland, Mexico based on public signs, commercial ventures, languages seen, heard, and spoken. The advantages of multilingualism and bi-dialectism are the access they provide to participate in a diverse array of cultural communities. We have research in the neurosciences documenting the intellective affordances of learning and becoming competent in speaking more than one language, especially from birth or early childhood (Kuhl & Rivera-Gaxiola, 2008; Meltzoff et al., 2009).

There is then the question of language variation and its relation to learning in academic domains. This is one question that I have explored in my own work in Cultural Modeling (Lee, 2005a, 2005b). In formal narratives—whether literature, film, other narrative programming in digital media—creative uses of multiple languages abound. In everyday linguistic repertoires, speakers deploy rhetorical tools to communicate point of view, figuration, satire, irony, rhetorical tools employed in text communication across disciplines, especially in the study of literature and history. In mathematics, there is interesting research documenting the affordances of different national languages for representing number concepts and other research examining how the recruitment of multiple languages in classroom discourse around mathematical reasoning serve as resources for generative thinking (Fuson, Smith, & LoCicero, 1997; Moschkovich, 2007; Moschkovich & Zahner, 2018).

A third issue has to do with the affordances of diverse patterns of social organization that support learning and development and the implications of such organizations for learning in the contexts of schooling. Chapters across this volume document ways of organizing learning that look quite different from traditional schooling. Some occur in out of school settings and some are innovations in schools. A major challenge here has been the assumption that kids need to adjust to schools rather than schools need to adjust to kids' needs and resources. This assumption is what undergirds the metanarrative that schools need to "fix" some kids. This assumption is non-scientific because it does not take into account what we have learned across many disciplines about the nature of human learning (Lee, 2017); and certainly what we know from navigating our own learning in families and our own social networks. One basic and well established tenet is the role of prior knowledge in learning (Bransford, Brown, & Cocking, 1999). The debates arise over what prior knowledge counts for what learning goals.

However, one of the most interesting findings from across this related body of research, including the chapters in this volume, is a revisiting of what constitutes generative disciplinary knowledge. For example, research in indigenous epistemologies and routine cultural practices for studying the natural world (Bang, Medin, & Altran, 2007) align with evolving epistemologies in a number of domains of western science around relations among humans and other members of the natural world (e.g., *The revolutionary genius of plants: A new understanding of plant intelligence and behavior*, by Stefano Mancuso (2017)). The opportunity to examine conceptual, epistemological, and linguistic relationships between problem solving in academic disciplines and the uptake of analogous problems in everyday contexts is an extraordinarily fruitful and intellectually compelling endeavor—for teachers, developers of curriculum and assessments, for theoretical research around learning in content areas—an endeavor that pushes the boundaries of knowledge development forward in ways that restrictive notions and deficit assumptions around such relationships forestall.

Questions often arise around what recruiting everyday knowledge to support learning in schools entails when classrooms have students from across different cultural backgrounds. There is, however, research that suggests that diversity in experiences, knowledge and points of view actually open up unanticipated and generative opportunities for creative problem solving (Page, 2007). This work has been taken up in corporate communities, with the belief that in order to facilitate creativity in a competitive environment, having diverse experiences, knowledge, and point of view are an asset. There are pedagogical practices with histories of success that highlight navigating difference. For example, in Japan, mathematics classrooms invite multiple and competing points of view as a stimulus for new learning (Stevenson & Stigler, 1992; Stigler & Perry, 1988).

We know that robust learning environments seek to foster the following (Lee, 2017):

- position the learner as competent
- anticipate sources of vulnerability
  - race, ethnicity, poverty, gender, state of existing knowledge, perceptions of self, task or setting
- examine and scaffold resources the learner brings
  - knowledge, dispositions, relationships, interests and goals of learners, experiences
- make public the social and/or personal good and utility
- make problem solving around generative knowledge explicit, conceptual, procedural and public; within the learners' ZPD
- provide supports and feedback as learners are engaged in complex problem solving
- provide expansive opportunities to apply knowledge
- remain adaptive and dynamic.

The argument for the robustness of these features derive from research findings across disciplines: cognitive psychology, social psychology, cultural psychology, human development, the learning sciences, and the neurosciences (cognitive, social, cultural). The most recent update of *How people learn II: Learners, contexts and cultures* by the National Academies of Science (National Academies of Sciences, 2018) highlights the centrality of participation in cultural practices as a central element in the dynamics influencing human learning and development (e.g., biological affordances from our evolutionary history; participation in routine cultural practices; intertwining of influences of multiple levels of ecological systems; dynamic relationships among cognition, perceptions, relationships, affect, and the mediational role of artifacts). In synthesizing across the chapters in this volume, we find illustrations of the diverse pathways through which such goals can be achieved: positioning the learner as competent by scaffolding knowledge and dispositions that learners from diverse backgrounds bring to acts of learning; examining problems that are generative both because of their disciplinary relevance, but also because of their relevance to personal and community challenges and using knowledge to do good in the world; being adaptive in the social organization of learning settings; and by virtue of careful analyses of relations between everyday and disciplinary domains, enabling the ability to make what is often tacit problem solving explicit for all key stakeholders.

At the same time, it is important that we not oversimplify the program of linking everyday and disciplinary knowledge and productive dispositions toward complex learning. The connections are not always a clear fit. There are discontinuities. For example, Dowling (2003, 1990) has argued that there are limitations to teaching mathematics rooted in applications to everyday problems when it comes to theoretical mathematical constructs and has argued that such everyday framing may, in fact, limit learning opportunities. We know people can hold on to everyday or what are sometimes called naïve concepts derived from observations in the natural world that are inconsistent with formal scientific explanations (e.g., study of college engineering students who hold on to both naïve as well as formal constructs around gravity) (DiSessa, 1982). In my own research, I have documented the use of nuanced rhetorical moves in everyday narrative genres such as signifying in African American English akin along many dimensions to the uptake of such rhetorical tools in formal literary genres (Lee, 1993, 1995b), but, at the same time, there are qualitative differences in how such tools are deployed in literature. At the same time, there are bridging relations among such oral genres, music lyrics, and literary genres in texts, film, and other digital storytelling (Lee, 2011). From my perspective, the point is that opportunities for multiple stakeholders (teachers, researchers, students, families, policymakers) to wrestle with such continuities and discontinuities open up interesting and generative possibilities for learning; and for the students and communities engaged in these chapters, examining the breadth of knowledge across contexts can only open up new opportunities for navigating across life spaces.

And then there is the complex issue of deliberations around what cultural knowledge is to be sustained, to be engaged, to be built on. The emerging paradigm of culturally sustaining pedagogies raises very interesting and ambitious questions (Paris, 2012; Paris & Winn, 2013). As we wrestle in this space around what cultural practices are to be sustained, by whom, for what purposes, and where, we must start by interrogating the very notion of cultural membership. Too often cultural membership is conceptualized in terms of what Gutierrez and Rogoff (2003) call the box problem, the assumption that people belong to single cultural communities and that such communities are stable and constant. The work in culturally sustaining pedagogy raises important attention to the diversity within what we can think of as youth culture, youth culture that interestingly in this day and age crosses national boundaries. For example, we have hip-hop communities across the globe, including Afrikaner hip-hop community in South Africa or language minority hip-hop communities in China, who share many practices with African American youth culture (Alim, Ibrahim, & Pennycook, 2008; Morgan & Bennett, 2011). But there are also important differences. And the hip-hop community is not limited to young people. In indigenous communities in North America, the U.S. in particular, communities wrestle with the idea of membership in a particular ethnic or tribal community versus a pan indigenous or Native American identity, what are relations between traditional knowledge and practices and the challenges of navigating the U.S. nation state. Communities do not necessarily have unanimous agreement in these deliberations. Thus it is also crucial that we do not homogenize cultural communities and that work in such communities must be adaptive to local contexts, and sufficiently pliable to navigate through differences in such communities.

The scope and focus of this volume captures a Kuhnian revolution (Kuhn, 2012), a substantive and deeply conceptual shift in how we as a community of researchers and practitioners think about the design of learning environments that take as a foundational opportunity scaffolding repertoires of knowledge that students develop from their lived experiences within and across formal and informal settings. Diversity of cultural practices, of language repertoires, of epistemological orientations have always been the norm within and across nation states, but are especially evident in the 21st century. Hegemonic ideologies among sectors that assume contested positions of power seek to make people believe that such diversity is not a resource, that patterns of practice that do not reflect hegemonic norms are somehow deficits and bear no meaningful relations to disciplinary knowledge, that diverse repertoires of knowledge and practice are not deeply intertwined into fabric of society.

Don't believe the hype.

References

Alim, H. S., Ibrahim, A., & Pennycook, A. (2008). *Global linguistic flows: Hip hop cultures, youth identities, and the politics of language.* New York: Routledge.

Bang, M., Medin, D. L., & Altran, S. (2007). Cultural mosaics and mental models of nature. *Proceedings of the National Academy of Sciences, 104,* 13868–13874.

Bransford, J., Brown, A., & Cocking, R. (1999). *How people learn: Brain, mind, experience and school.* Washington, DC: National Academy Press.

Collins, J., Slembrouck, S., & Baynham, M. (2009). *Globalization and language in contact: Scale, migration, and communicative practices.* New York: Continuum.

Darling-Hammond, L. (2010). *The flat world and education: How America's commitment to equity will determine our future.* New York: Teachers College Press.

DiSessa, A. (1982). Unlearning Aristotelian physics: A study of knowledge-based learning. *Cognitive Science, 6,* 37–75.

Dowling, P. (2003). *The sociology of mathematics education: Mathematical myths/pedagogic texts.* Washington, DC: Falmer Press.

Dowling, P. (Ed.) (1990). *Mathematics versus the national curriculum.* Bristol, PA: Falmer Press.

Fuson, K., Smith, S., & LoCicero, A. (1997). Supporting Latino first graders' ten-structured thinking in urban classrooms. *Journal for Research in Mathematics Education, 28,* 738–760.

García, O. & Wei, L. (2014). *Translanguaging: Language, bilingualism, and education.* New York: Palgrave-Macmillan

Gonzalez, N., Moll, L., & Amanti, C. (Eds.) (2004). *Funds of knowledge: Theorizing practices in households, communities, and classrooms.* Mahwah, NJ: Lawrence Erlbaum Associates, Inc.

Gutierrez, K. & Rogoff, B. (2003). Cultural ways of learning: Individual traits or repertoires of practice. *Educational Researcher, 32*(5), 19–25.

Kuhl, P. K. & Rivera-Gaxiola, M. (2008). Neural substrates of early language acquisition. *Annual Review of Neuroscience, 31,* 511–534.

Kuhn, T. S. (2012). *The structure of scientific revolutions.* Chicago, IL: University of Chicago Press.

Ladson-Billings, G. (1995). Toward a theory of culturally relevant pedagogy. *American Educational Research Journal, 32*(3), 465–491.

Lee, C. D. (1993). *Signifying as a scaffold for literary interpretation: The pedagogical implications of an African American discourse genre.* Urbana, IL: National Council of Teachers of English.

Lee, C. D. (2017). Integrating research on how people learn and learning across settings as a window of opportunity to address inequality in educational processes and outcomes. *Review of Research in Education, 41*(1), 88–111.

Lee, C. D. (2011). Education and the study of literature. *Scientific Study of Literature, 1*(1), 49–58.

Lee, C. D. (2009). Historical evolution of risk and equity: Interdisciplinary issues and critiques *Review of Research in Education, 33,* 63–100.

Lee, C. D. (2007). *Culture, literacy and learning: Taking bloom in the midst of the whirlwind.* New York: Teachers College Press.

Lee, C. D. (2005a). Culture and language: Bi-dialectical issues in literacy. In P. L. Anders & J. Flood (Eds.) *Culture and language: Bi-dialectical issues in literacy.* Newark, DE: International Reading Association.

Lee, C. D. (2005b). Double voiced discourse: African American vernacular English as resource in cultural modeling classrooms. In A. F. Ball & S. W. Freedman (Eds.) *New literacies for new times: Bakhtinian perspectives on language, literacy, and learning for the 21st century.* New York: Cambridge University Press.

Lee, C. D. (1995a). A culturally based cognitive apprenticeship: Teaching African American high school students' skills in literary interpretation. *Reading Research Quarterly, 30* (4), 608–631.

Lee, C. D. (1995b). Signifying as a scaffold for literary interpretation. *Journal of Black Psychology, 21*(4), 357–381.

Mancuso, S. (2017). *The revolutionary genius of plants: A new understanding of plant intelligence and behavior.* New York: Atria Books.

Meltzoff, A. N., Kuhl, P. K., Movellan, J., & Sejnowski, T. J. (2009). Foundations for a new science of learning. *Science, 325*(5938), 284–288.

Morgan, M. & Bennett, D. (2011). Hip-hop & the global imprint of a black cultural form. *Daedalus, 140*(2), 176–196.

Moschkovich, J. (2007). Using two languages when learning mathematics. *Educational Studies in Mathematics, 64*(2), 121–144.

Moschkovich, J. & Zahner, W. (2018). Using the academic literacy in mathematics framework to uncover multiple aspects of activity during peer mathematical discussions. *ZDM, 50*(6), 999–1011.

National Academies of Sciences. (2018). *How people learn ii: Learners, contexts, and cultures.* Washington, DC: National Academies Press.

OECD. (2010). *Pisa 2009 results: Overcoming social background. Equity in learning opportunities and outcomes, Vol.* 2. Paris: OECD Publishing.

Orellana, M. (2009). *Translating immigrant childhoods: Children's work as culture and language brokers.* New Brunswick, NJ: Rutgers University Press.

Page, S. E. (2007). *The difference: How the power of diversity creates better groups, firms, schools and societies.* Princeton, NJ: Princeton University Press.

Paris, D. (2012). Culturally sustaining pedagogy: A needed change in stance, terminology, and practice. *Educational Researcher, 41,* 3.

Paris, D. & Alim, H. S. (2014). What are we seeking to sustain through culturally sustaining pedagogy? A loving critique forward. *Harvard Educational Review, 84*(1), 85–100.

Paris, D. & Winn, M. T. (2013). *Humanizing research: Decolonizing qualitative inquiry with youth and communities.* Thousand Oaks, CA: Sage.

Pinker, S. (2007). *The stuff of thought: Language as a window into human nature.* New York: Penguin.

Rogoff, B., Paradise, R., Arauz, R. M., Correa-Chávez, M., & Angelillo, C. (2003). Firsthand learning through intent participation. *Annual Review of Psychology, 54*(1), 175–203.

Stavans, I. (2004). *Spanglish: The making of a new American language.* New York: Penguin.

Stevenson, H. W. & Stigler, J. W. (1992). *The learning gap: Why our schools are failing and what we can learn from Japanese and Chinese education.* New York: Simon & Schuster.

Stigler, J. W. & Perry, M. (1988). Mathematics learning in Japanese, Chinese, and American classrooms. *New Directions for Child and Adolescent Development, 19*(41), 27–54.

Wolfram, W. (1981). Varieties of American English. In C. Ferguson & S. B. Heath (Eds.) *Language in the USA* (44–68). New York: Cambridge University Press.

INDEX

Please note that page references to Tables will be in **bold**, while references to Figures are in *italics*. Footnotes will be denoted by the letter 'n' and Note number following the page number.

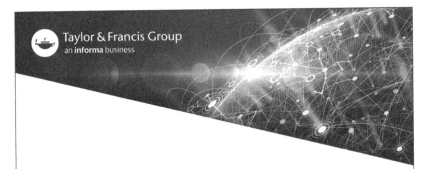